Seasons of Life

Seasons of Life

LIFE DECISIONS AND CONSEQUENCES

An Autobiography

Dr. Burrell David Dinkins

ISBN: 151199116X

ISBN 13: 9781511991162

Introduction

There is a time for everything,
and a season for every activity under heaven.

—Ecclesiastes 3:1

Though I knew it was time to retire from my teaching career, I dreaded the loss of a significant aspect of my identity. I loved what I was doing and the opportunity to make a difference in the lives of students. I carefully planned my exit and helped choose my successor. My wife, Phyllis, and I bought a house next door to our oldest daughter, Ruth, and her family in Atlanta, Georgia, had it remodeled, and moved to start a new season of life. The first months were like a vacation, with no external obligations and deadlines to meet. Then reality came crashing in. I was loved for who I am, but I no longer felt needed. My role as a professor had given me meaning, purpose, and a deep sense of satisfaction. Now that it was gone, I started feeling an existential sense of loss deeper than any previous loss when I simply moved to another job. For the first time in my life I had no future job to look forward to a new season in life.

In the months following retirement I experienced the loss of attachments to my profession, students, and colleagues. In a dark night of the soul, I struggled with relinquishing people and activities once so important to my identity. A new sense of freedom and joy emerged as I dug in the dirt in the spring to create an organic garden. A new interior season of life was emerging in my soul, along with the physical plants growing in the garden.

As I struggled to keep from flunking retirement, it was time to take advantage of this new creativity. I decided to write. But what would I write? Writing about professional subjects seemed too much like work, so I chose to write about what I knew best: my life story. Or rather, the interwoven stories of the lives of two ordinary people deeply in love and dedicated to serve God the best we knew how in communities where we lived and worked.

You will not discover outstanding achievements or descriptions of great events on the following pages. Instead, you will read stories of struggles, doubts, changing circumstances, and starting over again and again as we describe the seasons of our lives and ministry.

We use the word *season* to indicate an undetermined number of years where we lived and served in a variety of ministries. This word has taken on a special significance to us as we took a retrospective view of the many stages of our life journey. As one season ended, a new one was developing, often without our awareness.

Phyllis and I are grateful to the people who made these stories possible and others who will keep the stories alive by reading about them on the following pages. Our hope is that they will help you consider your own seasons of life stored in the banks of your me

CHAPTER 1

Florida Crackers to Georgia Peaches

> If you want to know me, then you must learn my personal story—not a finished story, but one I continue to create, revise, and tell myself and others who want to know me.
>
> —Burrell David Dinkins, *Narrative Pastoral Counseling*

Gists of stories past come to mind like clusters of potatoes waiting to be unearthed in the summer as I recall memories of my early life. Little did I realize until now just how many memories were hidden in that soil, not exactly as they were put there, but as they grew and matured to be recalled in my early eighties. I know where these stories came from, but I do not know where they will take me. They reveal more about who I have become than who I was. My inspiration for writing what the reader will see on these pages is from the words of Graham Swift, in his book *Waterland.*

> Man—let me offer you a definition—is the storytelling animal. Wherever he goes he wants to leave behind not a chaotic wake, not an empty space, but the comforting marker buoys and trail signs of stories. He has to keep on making them up. As long as there's a story, it's all right. Even in his last moments, it's said, in the split

second of a fatal fall—or when he's about to drown—he sees, passing rapidly before him, the story of his life.

The reader might call this an autobiography or a memoir because it is about my life; however, it's intended to be read as a series of multiple stories within a life story of one soul. My purpose in writing is to bring coherence to events in my life that helps me make sense of who I am today. It is more than history. I write it to complete my healing. It will help me understand, not only how I have lived my life, but also how I should live the remainder of my years. Should the reader find the stories interesting will add to the significance of my life.

These stories are a continuation of a family history that started long before I was born. It is not intended to be a history of my family of origin. A genealogist could trace both my father's and my mother's families back to their arrival in the mid-1700s. I have little interest in genealogy, so I will not attempt to go beyond my immediate family. My siblings contributed to my understanding of our family history. I'm especially indebted to my sister Ruth and my brother Ed for their written accounts of our family history.

All families have secrets, some of which are discovered, if at all, later in life. Mine is no exception. I choose to wait until later to tell the story of the best kept secret in my family of origin.

I was born April 30, 1933, in a small wood-frame house in the little town of Pinetta in Madison County, Florida. This was the year of the lowest annual birthrate of the twentieth century as the country struggled with the consequences of the Great Depression. Most likely my birth was not planned, rather it was caused by the limited knowledge of a country doctor who knew how to deliver babies but little about ovulation and conception. He told my mother exactly the opposite of what she needed to know to keep her from getting pregnant using the rhythm method of birth control. Without realizing it, he became one of many people who contributed to my life. I guess he should be included, along with my parents, in the long list of persons to whom I owe a debt of gratitude.

The Great Depression found my family barely surviving as sharecroppers on worn-out farms in North Florida and South Georgia. To say that we were poor would be an understatement. The price of farm commodities seldom paid back the money borrowed to buy seeds and fertilizer. In the fall of each year sharecroppers usually owed more to the landowner than the price of crops sold on a depressed market. Without money to repay their debts to the landowners, grocers, and doctors, sharecroppers packed up, sometimes in the middle of the night, and moved to another farm to start the cycle over again with nothing but hope and a high possibility of the same results.

For my family, it was often across the Florida-Georgia state line, where the arm of the law was too short to reach the other side. As a young child I knew little of these troubled times, though the experience of rootlessness had a powerful impact upon my life. We did not feel inferior to other families, because the majority of other families were as poor as ours. Had we lived in Oklahoma we might have joined the Okie migration to California.

A new baby was born into our family every other year for twenty-two years. For sharecroppers this was both a blessing and a curse. The curse was a new mouth to feed and clothe; the blessing had to wait until the child was old enough to become a productive field hand to contribute to the income of the family.

On the other hand, another child meant an additional playmate for the siblings and the assurance to parents of being blessed with a large family. Sharecropper mothers and fathers often took pride in the number of children they could have, and my parents had no trouble having children. I was the seventh of eleven children and took my turn as a male in the alternation between males and females, except for the next to last one: a total of seven boys and four girls

Whether I was wanted or not was not an issue to me because I felt accepted and cared for by a loving family. Edna, born two years later, pushed me out of my mother's lap. Lonnie pushed her out. Then Del and lastly Horace pushed the others out.

As my mother shifted her primary attention to each new baby, the major responsibility for looking after me passed to my older sisters. My sisters were the first of many women who nurtured me into adulthood. Unlike an only child or the oldest child, I have been blessed with both older and younger siblings. They had an enormous influence on how I relate to women.

My earliest stories from memory start with my oldest sister, Norma Jan. She was ten years old when I was born. She became a mother figure to me, not that my mother neglected me, rather she was overwhelmed by the responsibilities of nursing babies, feeding a family from a wood cookstove, washing, drying, ironing clothes, plus making clothes from the remnants of hand-me-downs and trying to keep us warm in the wintertime with cold winds blowing through the cracks in the walls and floors of sharecropper farmhouses. This was no easy task. Neither did my other older siblings neglect me; rather they were my playmates and my first teachers during the many moves we made.

What confused me the most as my mind tried to make sense out of each new experience was the way that Norma Jan could be so caring yet sometimes totally out of control while writhing on the ground and foaming at the mouth. I knew that she loved me and that she was a good person, but why would she act so strange? I wasn't told until much later in life that when she was a young child she had a high temperature that left her with epileptic-type seizures. At that time, no one understood her convulsions, neither had a medication been discovered to control them. Epilepsy was a mystery to the medical community and a source of embarrassment to a family.

The one creature that did understand her was our dog Nellie, who could sense the approaching brainstorms and would stay close to her and lick her face to calm her when the storm of electrical impulses in her brain took control of her body. The only thing anyone else could do to help was try to control her body as much as possible and keep her from swallowing her tongue. I was frightened by these episodes of strange behavior but drawn to her companionship. Perhaps her illness sowed the first seeds of my interest in psychology, the study of the inner workings of the mind. The one thing that brings me the most joy, in my earliest memories of her, was walking with her in the woods and watching her fascination at the beauty of wildflowers and bugs. As a toddler I spent a lot of time outdoors with her.

Another bewildering thing happened when I was between four and five years old: I developed a dislike for my father. I wanted to be close to him, and yet I was afraid of him because he was so unpredictable, especially when he was drinking. He was incomprehensible to me, and I never felt close to him. I knew that he loved his family and that he was doing the best he could after his injuries as a soldier during World War I, not overseas but not far from his military base, where he lay on the ground in a driving rain for two days after a motorcycle accident. Pneumonia and pleurisy left his lungs in permanently weakened. He could work no more than two or three hours a day before he was exhausted, but he could command his children to work.

He tried to run the household like an army sergeant, which only drove me further away from him. As a strict disciplinarian he tried to control my older brothers with physical punishment that included the use of a wide army belt. The marks the belt left on the body would today be considered child abuse. I feared him more than I loved him and tried to keep my distance from him as much as possible to escape his punishment. Sometimes I failed and had my turn with the belt.

He began to change when I was five years old. He was converted by an itinerate group of lay evangelists of the Holy Sanctified Church of Jesus Christ. This group had its beginnings at a holiness camp meeting on the Chesapeake Bay in Maryland in 1895 when an evangelist challenged the members of the church to do what Francis Asbury had called the North American Methodists to do by putting into practice the purpose of the Methodist Church: to "spread scriptural holiness across the land." They accepted this challenge by selling their farms, businesses, and houses so they would be free to travel throughout the East Coast and the southwest and central parts of the United States They supported themselves as carpenters by day and held evangelistic services at night and on weekends.

One of the many towns they choose to evangelize was Valdosta, Georgia, about thirty miles from where we lived in Madison County, Florida. When they were contracted to do some building in our community, they started holding worship services within walking distance of our house. My father was hired by them to work on this construction project. As they worked together they also talked to my father about his relationship with God.

My mother was raised in a strong Methodist home. She desperately wanted her husband to become a Christian so her family could go to church on Sundays. She became aware of his spiritual struggle from the conversations at work and their attending the evangelistic services at night. One day she told my sister Pauline to take care of the family so she could be free to spend all day locked in the bedroom, praying that he would be converted. When the invitation to accept Christ was extended that night, he walked down the aisle to kneel at the altar and give his heart to Christ. This led to a major change in his personal life and his relationship with his family. He quit drinking, smoking his pipe, and cursing. He tempered his strict disciplinary approach to his children, though he still used his belt to discipline us, but not as much as before his conversion. Gradually his behavior changed, and he took his place among the male leaders of the church.

As a preschool-aged child I was too young to understand the highly emotional worship services of singing with only voices and no other musical instruments and stomping one foot on the ground to keep time for the music. There was plenty of loud praying, usually by the women. One of their favorite prayer petitions was, "Lord, save us from isms and schisms."

The preaching was done by the male leaders. Worship started with a time of joyous singing and praying. Then silence fell over the group as the leader of the day picked up the Bible, walked down the aisle, and placed the Bible in the hand of one of the male leaders who was expected to walk to the pulpit and preach an extemporaneous sermon. As my father's behavior started to match his Christian faith, he was one of the men chosen to preach. This fascinated me. I waited to hear what he would say. We had no paid pastor, musical instruments, or hymn books. This practice freed the itinerants to travel light and move from town to town without the burden of a salary and packing things.

Another important part of the worship service was the long invitation at the end of the service to come to the front to be saved and/or sanctified. They believed every human being needed to be saved with a witness to a specific time and place. They also believed in sanctification as a second work of grace with a specific time and place. Another important part of the culture of this group was that they had the custom of calling each one another brother and sister. This greatly expanded my sense of family to include those who went to our church.

These Christians were a significant influence upon my life. I felt saturated with a sense of the divine from the highly emotional worship services and caring Christian community. From them I learned the importance of shared leadership and pastoral care as the ministry of all members of the church, not just a paid pastor.

The only snapshot picture I have of my mother before she was married shows her standing in a rose garden. She was a beautiful young woman. She loved plants and treated them almost like her children. From her I learned the joy of seeing things grow. When I was a preschool-aged child I asked her to teach me how to plant something. Though she was very busy she took the time to show me how to prepare the soil and helped me plant some zinnia seeds she had saved at our previous house. She taught me how to water them, which I did every day that it wasn't raining. Then she taught me the importance of not overwatering plants.

Zinnias, unlike most other plants, form flower buds out at the very top of the plant, where they sit for many days before they open into a flower. I waited only as patiently as a small boy could wait. Then I had the bright idea of helping the flowers open. Without my mother's knowing it, I borrowed her tweezers and tried to help the blossoms open. The result was a disaster. She was puzzled as to the cause of these deformed zinnia flowers. I confessed my role in playing plant scientist to get the flowers to open before they were ready. From this experience I learned patience and how to trust in the wisdom of the inner timing of plants. After I became a professional counselor I often remembered those zinnias when I became impatient with the progress of counselees.

Another time, I wanted to build some birdhouses but could not get anyone to help me with the tools. My mother said we could make birdhouses from gourds. She said we would have to plant the seeds and wait for them to grow and develop blossoms and small green gourds that would mature before turning yellow and hard in the fall. Then we could pick them and make birdhouses for the birds that wintered in our area of Florida.

Days are like weeks or months for small children. It seemed to take forever for the little green gourds to grow large enough to make birdhouses. One day a neighbor boy came to play with me. He suggested that we pick the little green gourds and play with them and when we finished playing we could put them back on the vines. I raised objections to this plan but was soon overwhelmed by his belief in the magic of restoring the picked gourds to the vines.

Late in the afternoon his mother called him home. We kept on playing until she used his full name, as mothers tend to do when they want to get the attention of their children. As he got up to leave I insisted that he could not go until he helped me put the gourds back on the vines. After several attempts we discovered that his magic of reattachment would not work. Neither would my prayers help them reattach to the vines.

I ignored my mother's call to come home, even when she called my full name. I was determined not to go until I reconnected the gourds to the vines. She found me crying in the garden because I could not help the little gourds continue their development toward maturity. This was the sad ending of my project of growing birdhouses, but it was the beginning of an awareness of the importance of skepticism, of not believing everything I was told and learning to trust my own understanding of reality.

Though we were living in the depth of the Great Depression there were times of family fun. The thing I enjoyed most was going to Blue Springs, near Madison, Florida. Today it is a major source of bottled drinking water, but in those days it was just a community swimming hole on the edge of the Chattahoochee River. Around this huge spring were tall trees with steel cables and ropes tied as high as possible to swing over the spring. Wood boards were nailed on the trunks for steps to climb up and grab the cables.

I had not learned to swim by age four or five, but this did not stop me from enjoying the thrill of swinging from the trees over the center of the spring and dropping down several feet into the power of the surging spring water. My older brothers let me climb on their backs and wrap my arms tightly around their necks. When we reached the apex of the swing over the spring, I held my breath as we dropped into the cold spring water. My heart beat with excitement. As soon as we broke the surface of the water I would yell, "Let's do it again!"

I was in a hurry to grow up so I could do the things my three older brothers did, even if this meant working in the field with them. There was a four-year gap in our ages because sisters were born in between each of us. In the spring and summer the boys were given the responsibility of planting the garden. I wanted to help, though I was too small to use a hoe. They let me carry small bags of seeds for them to drop in the furrows.

One day they decided to complete the chore of planting bean seeds by digging a deep hole at the end of a row and poured the remainder of the seeds into it. We made our way back to the house, looking as tired as we could, and reported we had finished; however, we underestimated the power of wet, swelling bean seeds. Several days later they pushed the carefully packed soil above them into a mound that let the young sprouting bean plants find the sunlight. Our father soon solved the mystery of the bean sprouts and administered punishment, starting from the oldest to the youngest. My loud crying before he got to me helped me escape the worst of the punishment with his army belt.

While I stayed home to play, my older siblings went to school. As soon as they got home, they had their chores to do around the house, such as working in the fields, chopping wood for the kitchen stove or fireplace, helping to cook meals, wash clothes, and clean house. My oldest brother, Randy, dropped out of high school to work at part-time jobs to help bring in some cash for the family. There was a great deal of tension between him and my father. By age fifteen he was pushed to drop out of school to become the primary family breadwinner.

When Randy was sixteen, he got a job cutting pulpwood with a crosscut saw (this was before there were chainsaws). The black man on the other end of the saw felt pity on him because he was so young and weak from inadequate nutrition. He told Randy that he heard that the army was recruiting again after a radical reduction following the Great War. No one told me that Randy enlisted. Neither did they tell me that our parents had signed a waiver for their underage son to get into the army at age seventeen. To my knowledge he just disappeared. It was not until he came home in uniform that I was aware of where he had gone. He sent home to our mother as much of his salary as possible to help her buy groceries. He was greatly offended when our father convinced the local congressman to have the army deduct part of Randy's salary and send it to him for family support. Randy trusted our mother to use the money wisely, but not our father.

My brother Gene also worked at odd jobs outside the home to make money to buy the basic food necessities, and he dropped out of high school to work in construction. Everyone pitched in to help raise and preserve as much food as we could. We also looked for opportunities to make money, such as selling boiled peanuts and vegetables. This helped buy food that we could not raise.

A few weeks after Delma (Del) was born on May 2, 1939, a serious illness struck the family. My memory about this is vague, because most of the time I was struggling for life in a coma in a hospital. It started with my oldest sister with what seemed to be a bad cold or the flu, but later it was called double pneumonia. Today it's called viral pneumonia.

My brother Gene walked to town to get the doctor. When he arrived at the hospital, he was sick with the same symptoms. When the doctor arrived at our house, he went from bed to bed, examining each child. When he thought he had checked all of us, someone told him he had not checked the baby. The doctor's reply was, "Oh my God, not a baby." Our Uncle Tommy, my mother's only sibling, drove from Gainesville, Florida, as soon as he got the telegram that described the seriousness of our situation. He loaded Norma Jan, Gene, Ruth, Edna, Lonnie, and me into his automobile and rushed us to the hospital in Madison.

The doctor worked day and night to keep us from dying. Finally he administered an experimental drug to treat pneumonia—sulfur. This drug probably saved our lives, with the exception Norma Jan. She had another seizure and died at age seventeen. I was too sick to know about her death or go to her funeral. Neither can I remember anyone explaining to me what had happened to her. She just disappeared, just as my oldest brother had disappeared when he joined the army. If someone told me that she had died, I probably was too young to understand what death meant.

I remember awakening two weeks after falling into the coma in a very clean environment. A woman who looked like an angel dressed in a clean white dress approached my bed. I asked who she was and where was I. My first thought was that I had arrived in heaven. In my weakened condition someone told me how close to death I had been. We were discharged from the hospital one by one. My brother Gene had the narrowest escape from death. Norma Jan was the only one who did not survive.

My brother Ed did not get sick. He remembers our father standing at the train depot, where the train seldom stopped, holding a pole with a large ring on the other end so that the conductor could stick his arm through the ring to grab a tethered note without having to stop. Written on the note was a request that when he reached Valdosta to call the telephone number on the paper and tell Mr. Hagan, the primary leader of the Holy Sanctified Church of Jesus Christ, about the sick children in our family. During our illness and weeks of recuperation, the people from the Holy Sanctified Church of Christ made many trips from Valdosta to Hanson to help with the housekeeping and nursed us back to health. They encouraged my parents to move across the state line to Valdosta, Georgia, where they lived, because Valdosta had better medical services, schools, and opportunities for the older children to work outside the home. These people demonstrated with their lives the essence of both personal and social holiness. They were my first living examples of pastoral care for families.

When we were well enough to travel, our furniture was loaded on a truck. I joined my siblings on top of the furniture for the migration to Valdosta. When someone said we were crossing the state line, I asked what that meant. The answer given was, "We are no longer Florida crackers. We have just become Georgia peaches."

> The end precedes the beginning,
> And the end and the beginning were always there
> Before the beginning and after the end.
>
> —T. S. Eliot, *Four Quartets*

CHAPTER 2

Growing Up in Valdosta

A person's spiritual life is always dwarfed
when cut apart from history.

—Rufus Mosley, "The Double Search"

Almost City Slickers

When the truck arrived in Valdosta, we unloaded our belongings into an old house on the northeastern edge of the city. The house had a tin roof but no ceilings. When it rained, the full sound of water hitting tin echoed throughout the house. The floors and walls had cracks that let in the cool air in the summer and the cold wind in the winter. There was no electricity or plumbing. We had progressed from a one-seater to a two-seater outhouse. Water came from the bucket of a well, and Saturday-night bathwater was heated in an iron washpot for pouring into a galvanized tub that was screened off for privacy.

We were still in the country but close enough to walk to town. The primary advantage of the new house was that it was in the middle of a small pecan grove, with plenty of room to roam and gather firewood for cooking, heating the water in the washpot for the washing clothes, Saturday baths, and for heating the house with the fireplace in the wintertime. Gathering pecans on a fifty-fifty share with the owner provided extra income toward the end of the year.

I remember this house as being the coldest place we ever lived. Though we were only twenty-five miles from Florida, I though the northern state of Georgia was too cold for me. Looking back, I realize we did not have adequate clothes to keep us warm, and none of us had gloves. I recall helping my brother Ed chop wood. At age six I was too small to use the ax, so my job was limited to holding the limbs while he chopped them on a stump or log. I held them loosely because I knew the vibration from the ax hitting the limb would sting my cold hands. This only increased the vibrations and made my hands hurt even more. Ed would get mad with me because the limbs would jump when they were not held tightly against the stump. Quitting was not an option, because we all had our jobs to do and no excuses were allowed.

I started first grade by walking over a mile with my siblings to the Leila Ellis Primary School in Valdosta. It was a beautiful brick building where all the white children in Valdosta went to school. Vallotton's Dairy was situated between our house and the school. The cows often slept on the dirt road at night and used the road as much as cars and pedestrians did as they crossed from the pasture to the barn for milking. This made it difficult to find a clean place to step as we passed the dairy on the way to school.

My first traumatic experience at school happened when I needed to use the bathroom. The teacher told me to go down the hall to the first room on the left. I went to the room but soon returned and sat down because I could not find a toilet. I asked her again and she told me the same thing. I looked again and still could not see a toilet. I was too embarrassed to ask her again, so I did not go to the bathroom that day. On my way home I lost in my pants all that should have been left at the school bathroom. When my mother asked me why I didn't go to the bathroom, I explained that I had asked the teacher and she told me to go into a room, but all that I saw there looked like water in a spring. I said, "I know I'm not supposed to mess up a spring, because that's where people get their drinking water, so I didn't use it to go to the toilet." My mother was surprised that I had never seen a commode before this, and no one had ever told me about an indoor toilet with water in the clean bottom. I was probably too sick to remember the one in the hospital.

Other than this traumatic start, I enjoyed going to school, especially getting all the free books. I especially liked not having to work when I was in school. I was a good student from first through the third grades.

I had plenty of chores after school and on weekends, except for Sunday, but still found time for play with my siblings. Sundays were reserved for church. It was about a mile on the same road as the way to town. Sometimes we went in Daddy's old car, but most of the time we walked. The church was only a shell of a building. It had no ceiling. The walls were a simple wood construction with solid-wood sliding windows and sawdust for a floor. The seats were made of one-by-ten-inch bench seats with two one-by-four boards for backs. The sawdust floor was a perfect hiding place for my mother's peach switch. Our family usually occupied two of the benches on the right side of church. She sat in the middle of the second bench where she could reach any one of us. If we misbehaved, she would first tap us on the shoulder with her switch to warn us not to misbehave in church. If we persisted, the second time the switch came down lightly on the ear, with a sting that would last for quite some time. The third time meant a trip outside, where the whole switch was put to more effective use.

By this time my father had grown in his faith and changed his behavior enough to be one of the male leaders in the church. They took turns leading the worship services. The leader of the night chose the songs and stomped with one foot on the floor to keep time for the passionate singing. He called on someone to pray, usually a woman, while everyone knelt on the floor. The leader then picked up the Bible on the pulpit and prayed silently before walking down the center aisle to place the Bible in the hand of another man. This was the signal for him to open the Bible to a text and go up front to preach a spontaneous sermon, after which he gave an invitation to come to the altar to be saved or sanctified. I often responded to the altar call, especially when no other person responded to the invitation, because I felt sorry for the preacher whose effectiveness as a preacher would be questioned if he failed to get at least one person to the altar. I do not remember how long the leaders prayed for me one night, but I do remember my father shaking me awake. I had gone to sleep during the prayer for my salvation. He was very angry with me, but his anger was constrained by the presence and laughter of the other men. I was not upset by their reaction, because I thought God accepted me whether I was asleep or awake during their prayers for my salvation. I must have been the most frequently saved person in that church.

Not long after we moved to Valdosta, and before I completely recovered from the near-death experience with viral pneumonia, I had another medical problem. My throat became swollen and I had a persistent fever. My parents finally took me to a doctor. He sent me straight to the hospital for a tonsillectomy. My overnight stay in the hospital must have been too short. Soon after arriving at home the next day, I started hemorrhaging blood and might have bled to death had my mother not insisted on getting me back to the hospital.

My brother Gene dropped out of school to go to work to help provide food for the family and to avoid conflict with our father who insisted on getting his money. My mother said many times it was one of the saddest days of her life when he went to work instead of school because she considered him to be her smartest child. To get out of conflict with our father he went to St. Augustine, Florida, where the holy sanctified people had moved to continue their evangelist ministry. Before long he married one of the girls in the Parker family.

The move of most of the families in the Holy Sanctified Church of Jesus Christ to Florida meant closing the church that had become so important to us. My father talked about moving with them, but my mother insisted that we remain in Valdosta because it had better schools with free textbooks, which Florida did not provide. The city also had better medical care and more opportunities for jobs for the children.

After the Holy Sanctified people moved to Florida, we started going to church at the First Methodist Church in Valdosta. Our mother had grown up in a strong Methodist family in Melrose, Florida. Many of the town leaders were members of this church. We did not have adequate clothes to attend a big-city church, but our clothes were clean and our mother had taught us to sit quietly in church. The sanctuary was the biggest room I had ever been in, and the pews were very comfortable to sit on.

I usually went all the way to the front seat so I could get a good view of the preacher. What impressed me most about Rev. Leonard Cochran was that he could speak so distinctly and forcefully. He preached with an over-supply of saliva in his mouth. This caused his eloquent words to include a spray of spit. I tried to immolate him during the week, making sure I was outdoors to spit while I spoke. (Years later I told this story to the congregation of the large First Methodist Church in Albany, Georgia, before I preached for missions Sunday. I had trouble stopping the laughter caused by years of observing their pastor do the same thing when he preached.)

In 1940 we moved from the small farmhouse closer to the center of Valdosta. This was the first time I lived on a paved street, only four blocks from the county courthouse, the post office, the Methodist church, and a supermarket. This house had running water instead of a well or spring. We now had electricity for the first time. It was a large house with three bedrooms, a living room, dining room, kitchen, and a wraparound porch. The porch provided a wonderful place to play when it was raining and to sit in rocking chairs on hot nights. A vine that had recently been imported from Southeast Asia to help control roadside erosion grew on the front of the house. This was my first experience with the wonders of kudzu. It had small blue flowers in the springtime, provided shade and screen in warm weather, and allowed an open space for the sun to shine through during wintertime. Kudzu also provided many opportunities for us to entertain ourselves. One of our favorite games was to catch a grass snake and tie a very thin copper wire around its neck and hide it in the grass across the street, ready to be pulled out in front of someone walking by. We hid behind the vines, laughing so hard we had to keep our hands over our mouths to keep from giving away our hiding place.

The pasteurizing and bottling plant of Vallotton's Dairy was directly across the street from our house. A lot next to it had stacks and stacks of crates of empty milk bottles. They provided a wonderful place for hiding, building forts, and playing war games.

The bathroom in this house was small and unheated, but we had a commode and a claw-foot bathtub for the first time.

Instead of going to the woods to collect firewood, we now had to buy wood in bulk to be chopped into smaller pieces for use in the home. The house sat on a foundation of concrete blocks about three feet tall. This open space under the house created a wonderful place for kids to play, especially when it was raining. There were some large and very productive pecan trees on the double-lot property. I climbed as high as possible in them many times. We also had an open space for a garden in the back. A large yard meant plenty of space for running and playing games with other children in the neighborhood in the evenings. We thought we were now city folks, but we were just country hicks living in the city for the first time.

Up to this move our mother had always used a cast-iron woodstove to cook our meals. Although the house had a connection for natural gas, she was not about to risk using it. With no hot-water heater, we still heated water for washing clothes and for baths in an old cast-iron washpot in the back of the house.

Two illnesses hit me close together and me in a weakened state. I was skinny and not developing as some people at church thought I should. The primary leaders in the church, Mr. and Mrs. Hagan, asked my parents to let me live with them for a while so they could feed me better and make sure I got plenty of rest. That was another example of church families looking after each other. I enjoyed the food and the conversations with adults, especially the Hagans' two beautiful teenage daughters. Neither did I have to compete with my siblings for food and attention. A few weeks later my father said I would have to come home. He claimed that the Hagan family spoiled me and I was making my siblings jealous when I talked too much about the different things

I had to eat. I made the mistake of acting like Joseph with his brothers by bragging about having things they didn't have.

I well remember Sunday, December 7, 1941, when our father called us inside to listen to the news on our small table radio to hear the announcement that Pearl Harbor had been bombed by the Japanese navy. We knew about Pearl Harbor because our brother Randy had been stationed at Hickman Field four years before this infamous day and had written many letters to us about it. He was discharged only a few months before the attack on Pearl Harbor and was now living as a civilian in St. Augustine with our brother Gene. After hearing the news, our father said, "This means war, and that means Randy will be going back into military service." Two days later President Roosevelt spoke to Congress and proposed that war be declared on Japan. Germany declared war on the United States the day after Pearl Harbor, and the United States declared war against that country too.

After a few months of our attendance at the big Methodist church downtown, I was disappointed to learn that a new pastor had been assigned by the bishop. My parents told Rev. Harold about our former church being closed and how there were people in the community without a shepherd. The land and building were available to rent. He led First Methodist in starting a new church mission, which later was named Forrest Street Methodist Church. A part-time lay pastor, D. R. Dixon, was appointed to be the pastor of the church. He worked forty hours a week at the cotton mill and served the church mostly in the evenings and on weekends. Brother Dixon, as we called him, became the most influential person in my life outside my own family. He became my mentor and model for ministry during the nine years he was our pastor.

First Methodist also sent a team of laypersons to help plant the church. Mr. Bullock, a businessman, served as treasurer and frequently prayed at our Sunday evening services, usually the same prayer. Miss Whitaker was the pianist, and Mrs. Mary Love Tucker was the youth Sunday school teacher. Several families who had attended the Holy Sanctified church came back to form the nucleus of the new congregation. The church became the center of our spiritual and social life. It occupied five acres of level land that we soon turned into an outdoor basketball court and baseball field.

I was considered a smart student during my first three years in school. Then, in 1942, at age nine, my motivation changed after my father died and did not return until my senior year in high school. My father's health had always been precarious since his motorcycle accident during World War I. Over a period of several weeks he became very sick, but he was refused treatment by the doctors in Valdosta, probably because they knew he did not have any money. In desperation he sought treatment in the veterans hospital in Lake City, Florida, about fifty miles south of Valdosta. My mother went with him. The doctors diagnosed him with a serious case of appendicitis. Mother notified my brother Gene in St. Augustine by telegram that his father was very ill in the hospital. When Gene arrived, the receptionist told him my mother was in a boarding room across the street from the hospital and he should get her back to the hospital as soon as possible because the doctor wanted to see her. When they returned to the hospital, the doctor told them that my father was dying from peritonitis after the appendix ruptured. They sat with him while he died, and then they caught a bus in the middle of the night to go back to Valdosta. When they arrived at daybreak I was awakened by the loud crying of my older siblings and was told that my father had died. For some strange reason this did not bother me like it did my siblings. I do not remember shedding a tear.

The next morning my next-door friend, who had heard about my father's death, came over to see how I was doing. When he found me in the back whistling while chopping wood as if nothing had happened, he said he did not understand me because I did not appear to be sad about my father's death. For some reason I felt more relieved than sad. I was sad for my mother, but not for myself. I felt free.

My brother Randy received a leave from military training to come home for the funeral. Though we did not talk about it, I think he felt like I did. When he got back to his base he initiated the process of having us declared to be his dependents.

I remember the funeral at the church and traveling to the cemetery in Melrose, Florida, where the burial took place. Dad was buried next to my sister Norma Jan. When I saw her small tombstone, I fully realized for the first time what had happened to her. While there I was also introduced to some of my mother's relatives and her family history by looking at the many Price family tombstones dating back to the mid-1800s.

On the way back home I sat in the backseat with my mother on one side and my brother Gene and his new bride on the other side. They constantly hugged and kissed each other on the way back to Valdosta, which I though most inappropriate for what was supposed to be a sad occasion. I asked my mother after we got home why they acted this way. She said, "This is just what young married people do. They hug and kiss lots." I had experienced what I later learned from studying Freudian theory: where there is *thanatos* (death) there will be *eros* (life).

The days that followed were clouded with sadness, but not for me. My mother continued her housework during the day but sat and rocked in her chair on the porch until late at night to cry. Though I did not cry because I was not grieving, I would sit with her even when she insisted that I go to bed. I did not want her to be alone. I had no way of comprehending the depth of her loss, but I knew she needed someone who loved her to be there in her grief. She was now a widow with ten children, eight of us were between the ages of sixteen and one. This was my first experience in grief ministry, something I later specialized in as a counselor.

My ambivalence over the loss of my father and relief from his burdensome presence created a good bit of spiritual turmoil and mental confusion. My school grades suffered and my attention turned more toward activities at the church. One Sunday night when I was nine years old, I responded to the altar call to receive Christ and join the church. After Brother Dixon questioned me, he was satisfied with my sincerity. My spiritual awakening was probably an attempted solution for my guilt over the lack of emotional response and confusion over my father's death.

Ed, the third boy in the family, now age thirteen, dropped out of school to work full time by delivering papers in the morning and afternoon and working at a radio repair shop in between paper routes. When Moody Air Force base opened in 1942, about twelve miles north of Valdosta, he had an opportunity of selling newspapers there. The income from this provided most of the food for the family during the war.

Ed became a successful entrepreneur on the base by the way he distributed papers for sale at the airmen's barracks. He also gave a free newspaper to the commanding officer of the base, the provost marshal, guards at the gate, and the chief cook in the mess hall. This kept other newspaper boys off the base. The chief cook let us eat breakfast in the mess hall without paying.

When Ed's business grew to be more than he could handle, I was asked to help him distribute the papers. This meant getting up at two thirty or three in the morning, when he did, and riding my bike downtown to catch the first bus after the newspapers from Atlanta and Jacksonville arrived well before daybreak. The papers often filled one side of the bus. After unloading them at the base bus stop, Ed would get the delivery bicycles that were chained inside the bus stop. The bicycles had a small front wheel and a large basket in front of the handlebars and a large back wheel. Ed would stack papers so high in the basket that my only way to see where I was going was by looking around the pile of papers as I distributed the papers around the base. I stacked the papers at a strategic place at the entrance and placed some change on top to be collected later. The papers cost a nickel apiece. Later I returned to count the remaining newspapers and the change to make sure all the newspapers were paid for. These were the days before newspaper dispensing machines and when people could be trusted to be honest.

My sister Pauline continued going to school and worked at a downtown department store as much as she could. The store stayed open until nine o'clock on Saturday's. I often met her so she would have someone with her as she stopped at the supermarket to buy groceries. The five-pound sacks of flour and sugar and various cans got very heavy before we arrived home. Sometimes the paper sacks would split open along the way. Realizing that we would have something to eat made them feel lighter than they were.

All of this was taking place during World War II with its many blackout nights to practice what to do should an air raid happen. Scrap metal drives and community activities helped raise money to buy war bonds. Food was rationed because so much food was being shipped overseas to feed the troops. Each family received books of stamps according to the number of people in the family to purchase necessities. Our victory garden provided extra vegetables for the family and often enough to sell to the neighbors. Mother told me that I was responsible for the garden, but the three younger brothers had to help me do the work. I was ten years old and they were six, four, and two. I tied some rope on the front of the push garden plow for them to pull while I pushed the plow. If they refused to work, I would call Mama, and she would make sure they did their job of helping me in the garden. She told me what to do, and I drove them like three mules. It would be called child cruelty today, but then it was considered family teamwork to grow food for the family. (Years later I asked Del, the next to youngest brother, if he wanted to grow a garden with me. He immediately responded, "You are not getting my rear end in front of a plow again.")

I remember most of the major events of the war because I was selling so many newspapers. I read the headlines as soon as possible so I could sell more papers by yelling the headlines out about the major battles. In Valdosta I sold newspapers to the troops guarding the rails from Washington to Warm Springs, Georgia, for President Roosevelt's last trip to his favorite retreat and encounter with his secret lover. A few days later the nation was in mourning over his death from a cerebral hemorrhage. My brother Randy says he served as one of the army guards on the train that returned the president's body to Washington.

The war movies at the theater made me wish I were old enough to fight for my country. Instead, I could only play war games with my friends. We could have had a great time with the modern game of paintball, though I doubt paint could have been purchased when everything was in short supply.

It was disappointing to be on my cousin's farm in Florida the day Germany surrendered. I could have sold a lot of newspapers. Everyone was happy that the war in Europe was over. There were major celebrations in every city. The end of the war in Europe meant that the troops there would either be coming home or would be redirected to the war in the Pacific. So many families had lost husbands, brothers, sons, and sweethearts. It was a sad time even though we were celebrating the victory in Europe.

Randy was in the Philippines, training for the invasion of Japan. My brother Ed was old enough to be drafted. He joined the navy in 1945, shortly before Japan surrendered after the United States dropped the two atomic bombs. Ed's stint in the navy was shortened when Japan surrendered, but he got to circle the globe in his new ship before being discharged, along with millions of other soldiers and sailors.

Our sister Pauline began dating Aaron, a marine who had been wounded in action in the Pacific. He hired Pauline as his administrative assistant when he came to Valdosta as an Olan Mills photographer. Soon they were dating. One night my mother opened the front door to the porch and surprised them as they were hugging and kissing. Pauline was very upset with mother for sneaking up on them. My mother said, "You were backed against the doorbell. What else would you expect me to do when the doorbell rings but answer the door?" Pauline also had to put up with her younger siblings for naming a frog that seemed to get into the bathroom of the house through cracks in the floor Aaron, the same name as her boyfriend. A few months later they were engaged. Pauline had the first wedding in our church. Brother Dixon didn't let the lack of money to pay for flowers keep him from decorating the church. He invited me to ride in the car with him to pick wildflowers and blooming vines in the woods to use for decorating the church. It was a simple but beautiful wedding.

My brother Randy and his friend, John Shellnut, decided that my mother needed a gas stove, because heating and cooking on the woodstove was so difficult and time consuming. She refused to accept it. She said she had been cooking on a woodstove since she was a young girl, and she didn't need to start using gas to cook our meals. She wouldn't admit that she was afraid of the gas stove. They finally got her to agree to try it for three months, and if she didn't like it, they would put the old cast-iron woodstove back in the kitchen. I was thrilled when we no longer had to chop wood to cook our food. After the three months were over, Randy and John asked mother if she wanted her woodstove back. She responded, "Well, I guess I'll just try this gas stove a little longer." The old iron stove sat in the back of the garage that we never used for parking a car because we didn't have one. It collected dust and was left behind the next time we moved.

Christmas was always a special occasion for the family. We worked hard at whatever part-time jobs we could find to make money to buy presents for one another. We often cracked and shelled pecans to sell in order to have enough money for gifts.

One year, the day before Christmas, Horace, the youngest child in the family, managed to make some money by doing chores and went downtown to buy a present for mother. While looking in a shop window, he saw a flower vase that he liked and went inside to ask the owner how much it cost. The owner asked, "How much money do you have?" So Horace pulled out all the coins he had. It was less than a dollar. The owner said, "That's exactly how much it costs." Horace's joy at purchasing a gift for mother was short lived, however.

On the way home on his bike, the bottom of the paper bag split open while it was swinging back and forth from the handlebar. The vase broke into several pieces when it hit the asphalt. He picked up the pieces and came home crying about his misfortune. When he told Mother what had happened, she took the pieces and carefully glued them back together. She said, "It probably won't hold water, but it's just what I have been looking for." After wrapping it in Christmas paper, she asked him to put it under the Christmas tree.

When she opened it Christmas morning, she excitedly said: "Oh look. This is just what I have been wanting: a beautiful pencil holder." As long as my mother lived, that flower vase was her favorite pencil holder.

Christmas mornings everyone had gifts, though they were inexpensive ones. We didn't make a big deal about Santa Claus because we knew it was all about the birth of Jesus and showing our love for one another. We always had Christmas plays at church to help retell the story.

We liked living at the rented house on Jones Street because the large yard provided plenty of room to play with the other children in the neighborhood. In the evenings our favorite game was kick the can. It was especially fun to hide with the girls and try to steal a kiss.

When I was fourteen, my brother Randy managed to scrape together enough money to make a down payment on a house on Forrest Street, three blocks away from where we were living and three blocks farther from the center of town. It was only two hundred yards from our church. This meant that we were now homeowners for the first time. Our mother lived there the last thirty years of her life.

Forrest Street served as a shortcut from one major highway to another on the east side of Valdosta, though it was not paved. Our house was only a few feet from the road. There was a garage next to the house, which we used for storage. Behind the garage was a small room that once was a shortwave radio room. I claimed it as my bedroom. Since it was not connected to the house, I had the freedom to come and go as I wanted. It was unheated and often very cold in the winter and hot in the summer, but this did not bother me since I had never slept in a heated or air-conditioned room. I can still feel the weight of many quilts and covers on the bed to keep me warm in wintertime.

The house had a living room, dining room, kitchen, and three bedrooms, with one bath and a sink in the hallway. We often stood in line to get our turn to use the bathroom. If one person took too long inside, they would hear the shout, "Hurry up and get out of there!"

One of the best things about living at the new house was Frederick and Anne Carlo who lived across the street and owned a small grocery store next door. Since they did not have children they claimed all the children in the neighborhood as their own. They didn't make much money because they gave away popsicles and candy to so many of us.

Living farther away from the center of town made grocery shopping more difficult for our mother. She was one of the greatest shoppers I have ever known. She would go from one grocery store to another to check on the price of a can of food to see where she could get one a penny cheaper. If she saw a can with a dent in it, she would take it to the manager and say she would buy it if he would give her a discount on it.

My mother taught me valuable lessons about money management. The first 10 percent of what I earned went to the church, 40 percent was for savings, and the rest of the money was for family expenses. She taught me to keep very little money in my pocket so I wouldn't be tempted to spend it. I still owe her a debt of gratitude for teaching me the value of wise money management. She despised owing anyone money. She never bought groceries on credit, because she said the most difficult bill to pay is for food already eaten. We went to the dentist only when we had a toothache. If the dentist sent a bill to her, she would go into his office and lecture him on wasting a good three cents stamp because she would pay him when she had money and not before.

Much of my teen years were centered on church activities. The Valdosta First Methodist Church raised money to buy a wood tabernacle situated on five acres of land. Then they helped finance the building of a new sanctuary and three Sunday school rooms. Consecration and moving day was a joyous occasion. I still have the handful of sawdust and wood shavings my mother scooped up from the floor in the old building as it was being torn down. She kept it in a small fruit jar as a memory of how God had blessed our family in the old church building.

Brother Dixon's pastoral leadership style was to teach us how to be leaders too. Before long we had one of the most active Boy Scouts troops in the region and one of the largest Methodist Youth Fellowship (MYF) groups. I remember one year when Ruth was the president of the South Georgia Annual Conference. I was president of the Valdosta District MYF, and Edna was president of our local church MYF.

Though I did not play on the Valdosta High School football team, I taught my friend Robert Burgess how to kick extra points by holding the football for him to kick over our church building. He dared not miss less he smash a window with the football. Then I encouraged him to show Coach Bazemore how far he could kick the ball. The next week he was the first-string kicker for the team. A few weeks later Robert saved me from suffocation by quickly digging me out when I was buried under several feet of dirt while digging a cave along the edge of a ravine that led to the Withlacoochee River.

By the time I reached puberty I started growing much taller. I grew twelve inches between age fifteen and sixteen. I tried to play basketball for the high school team but was too uncoordinated. The coach couldn't keep my body going in only one direction at a time. I was good at pickup basketball and often scored the most points, but games involved too much pressure. I was also good at playing football and calling the plays, but I only weighed 120 pounds. This meant I was easily run over by the bigger players. In spite of this, I wanted so much to play team sports but had to work after school.

Girls became a fascination for me when I turned fourteen years old. A girl at church, Virginia Wood, became my steady sweetheart. I don't remember if she chose me or I chose her, but before long I walked her home after church or rode her home on my bike to sit with her on the front porch in all kinds of weather. Her younger sister and younger brother (he had Down syndrome) often pestered us. I do not remember ever going inside her house. Her mother was not a happy person and was considerably overweight. Her father was rarely there. When he came home late in the evening and found us sitting on the porch, I knew it was time for me to leave. He never spoke to me but would say to Virginia, "It's time you went inside and got to bed." It was a strange sort of family.

Virginia and I liked each other very much. She taught me how to kiss, which we did every chance we got. She set firm limits on where my hands went, because her older sister had a baby out of wedlock. Virginia remembered how much shame, sadness, and turmoil this created for her family. To my disappointment but good fortune, she was determined not to have sex until she got married. My buddies often pressured me by asking if I had "done it" yet. I told the truth because I never considered lying about something that important. They wanted to know what was wrong with me. They often claimed to have done far more with girls than I had, though most of the things they said were lies.

I dated Virginia for three years, until I was a senior in high school. I decided I did not want to marry her because I did not want to be a part of her family. My best friends challenged me to have sex with her, marry her, or break up with her so she could find somebody who would marry her. I chose the later.

My buddy Jimmy Wetherington awakened me early one morning to tell me about the exciting time he had the night before when his older brother, home on leave from the navy, had taken him to a prostitute to teach him about having sex. He wanted me to go too. This idea was completely against my values, of sex being related to love. I'm grateful I had sense enough not to buy sex, and my girlfriend helped us keep our clothes on. Had she gotten pregnant I would have done the honorable thing by marrying her, and that would have completely changed the trajectory of my life.

The last night Virginia and I saw each other as a couple, I told her this was my last time to see her and gently slipped my class ring off her finger. She did not act surprised, because I had been seeing her less and less. She asked that I kiss her good-bye. That kiss was a caring closure for our first love relationship. I felt amazingly free, as if a huge burden had been lifted from my shoulders. When my mother found out that we were no longer dating, she said she was relieved because she worried about my relationship with Virginia. I was now free to date other girls, which I had never done. By this time I was a senior in high school, and it was not easy getting a date when most of the pretty girls I was interested in had been claimed before their senior year. I had better luck with girls from out of town. I was the president of the Valdosta District MYF and often traveled to other towns and churches to lead meetings, which provided many opportunities to date.

I was not a good student in high school until the last semester, because school did not interest me as much as my activities in church, work, dating, Boy Scouts, pickup sports, and hanging out with my friends. I was not a leader in school like my sister Ruth, though I was often chosen as a leader at church.

By my junior and senior years in high school, my work had shifted from delivering newspapers to working in a supermarket. The manager seemed to like me because I was so customer friendly. First, I was a package boy, then a cashier. When I was not in school, I worked as much as I could. The manager assigned me to separate departments of the supermarket as pretraining to become a manager. In my junior year of high school, I told my mother I was going to drop out of school as my older brothers had done and work full time in order to help with the family finances. Since the death of my father, I had expected to drop out of school when I got old enough to get a full-time job like my three older brothers had done. My mother told me that I did not have her permission and I was to get myself back to school and stay there until I graduated. Little did she know I was facing a spiritual crisis.

For some time I felt that God was calling me to become a pastor. Dropping out of school was my way of running from that call.

In my senior year of high school I took a class on the Bible as literature. In this class I saw the full range of the Bible for the first time. Though I had been going to church since I was five years old, I had learned bits and pieces of the Bible, but never a historical sequence. One Sunday night after church I wanted to find the highest place I could to pray, because in the Bible God seemed to speak to people on mountaintops. In the dark of the night I walked through the woods and along the railroad tracks to a place where the railroad company had piled some dirt when the rail line was constructed. Though it was only ten to fifteen feet high, that was higher than most places around Valdosta. There I prayed and felt God confirming what I had felt for some time: he called me to the vocation of ordained ministry.

Two years earlier my brother Ed had been called to the ordained ministry. I provoked him several times to see if he would lose his temper. I thought that preachers did not get angry. My mother caught me one day taking advantage of his newfound ability to control his temper. He now had a higher purpose in life than to be upset with his brother. She told me I had better be careful about provoking him, because God might call me to be a preacher too. She was right. He did. And I also had to learn a new way to handle my anger and other emotions. I do not know why a controlled temper goes with ministry, but they seem to go hand in hand.

Socially, I had been well prepared for ministry by Brother Dixon and the many opportunities I'd had to show leadership in the church; however, I was completely unprepared academically. I finished high school with a D- average, and that was only because my grades improved during the last half of my senior year after I was called to preach. I once took an algebra class with my sister Edna and was determined not to let her make a better grade than me. Edna had little time to study, because most of the housework that our mother couldn't do was her responsibility after our oldest sister, Pauline, was married. Our other sister, Ruth, seemed to be too busy in college to spend her time on housework. In those days most clothes had to be ironed. Edna spent many hours with that ironing board and cooking. She was also a good athlete and a starter on the girl's basketball team.

By this time I was the oldest boy at home, because the other three had left and the three other brothers were too young. Some called them the Three Musketeers because they frequently got into trouble together. This caused them to suffer the same punishment when they would not tell our mother who was guilty for things that caused the trouble.

One day the mother of a neighbor boy angrily confronted our mother to tell her that Lonnie, Delma, and Horace had taken off her son's pants. She said two brothers held him down while the third climbed a tree and hung the pants in the top of the tree. He went home crying with nothing on his bottom. When his woman left, our mother got her trusty switch and started working on all three. When Lonnie objected and said, "But Mama, we did that because he called you a bad name when he cursed us." She stopped the switching and said, "Why didn't you tell me that in the first place?" She apologized and told them they did the right thing to teach him a lesson.

Another very influential person in my life was Mrs. Mary Love Tucker. She was part of the original team that helped start Forrest Street Methodist Church. She was the most joyful, loving Christian I have ever known. Every Sunday she taught our youth Sunday school class as if it were the most exciting thing she had ever done. Her joy made me want to be a Christian. She worked very hard to prepare lessons appropriate for our age. She also arranged opportunities for us to broaden our vision of the world beyond what we had been exposed to. Her husband died soon after their marriage, during the flu pandemic in 1917–18, and she had never remarried. She was the private secretary of Mr. Langdale, the largest timber landowner in South Georgia. Through working for him, she knew the wealthy and the most influential people in Valdosta. She got some of them to open their large homes for our Sunday school class to have social parties. She wanted to expand our vision by seeing more of life than we were accustomed to seeing from where we lived.

She encouraged us to go to college and often found financial resources to help us do that. My sister Ruth, a straight-A student, graduated two years ahead of me and was the first in our family to go to college because Mrs. Tucker found the money to pay her tuition.

After I graduated from high school in 1951, I enrolled at what is now Valdosta State University. It had been a woman's college where my sister went until the year before I enrolled. There were fourteen girls to every one boy the year I started. My high school D average grades didn't seem to matter to the admissions office, because they were looking for as many males as they could find.

I befriended a guy named Buck, a big handsome fellow who owned a big automobile. My family did not own a car. This did not stop me from going wherever I wanted to go on my bicycle as my main mode of transportation. Every week Buck said, "Burrell, I have a date this Friday, and she has a friend. Will you double date with us?" How could I refuse? I was put on probation at school when my lack of study was reflected in my grades. When I was at the point of flunking out, I made the decision to drop out of college at the end of the semester and work full time at the supermarket. I realized this meant the end of a response to a call to the ordained ministry. If I was not a good student, perhaps I could work my way up to become a supermarket manager.

That decision changed when I met my Sunday school teacher, Mrs. Mary Love Tucker, at the post office, where most people picked up their mail. She asked how school was going, and I told her that it was not going well and that I was thinking about dropping out. She laughed and said, "Burrell, you can't be a preacher without finishing college and seminary.

You are failing in school because you are having too much fun dating girls. You've got to get out of Valdosta to go to college or you will never answer the call to ministry." I told her that that was impossible, because my family did not have the money to pay for me to live away from home and go to college, and I could not make enough money to pay for it myself and study at the same time. She asked me where I would go to college if I had the money to go. I immediately responded that I would go to Asbury College in Kentucky, because the best pastors I ever heard preach had gone to school there.

Mrs. Tucker told me not to drop out of school and that she would get back in touch with me in a few days to talk some more about college. Later, she told me she had found the money for my tuition if I were willing to work to pay for my room and board. She explained that a friend, Mrs. Dewberry, a member of a Sunday school class she used to teach, had planned to send her son to college, but he had been killed during World War II. Instead, she paid for other mothers' sons to go to college. I became one of the many lucky boys she sent to college over a period of forty years.

I applied to Asbury College and was accepted on probation. I asked for a job where I could make the most money possible to pay for my room and board. They told me the best place to work would be the school farm, where the room was free and I would get paid to help raise the meat and milk for the school cafeteria. The letter said I should get there in early June to take the place of a graduating senior.

As soon as classes ended in May 1952 at Valdosta, I left home to work full time during the summer and part time during the school year on the Asbury farm. I had saved twenty dollars. This would either pay for a bus trip to Kentucky or pay for food for a week. So I decided to hitchhike from Valdosta to Wilmore, Kentucky, so that I could eat until I earned enough to pay for food. I packed the few clothes I owned in a small suitcase and attached a sign with large letters on the outside: WILMORE, KY.

A friend agreed to take me in his car to the city limits on Highway 41 where I would try my luck at hitchhiking. I planned to slip out of the house before daylight in order to avoid saying good-bye. To my surprise, my mother had gotten up some time before me and prepared a big breakfast in order to send me off with a full stomach.

As I waited on the side of the road for someone to pick me up for the first leg of my trip by faith into the unknown, I was sad to be leaving behind a wonderful family, friends, and supportive church. I was incredibly fortunate to have lived in Valdosta during all my public school years. My calling was stronger than ever. I was determined not to let a poor start in my first year in college hold me back. I vowed I would concentrate on my studies and not get into a serious dating relationship until I graduated from college.

> There is a tide in the affairs of men.
> Which, taken at the flood, leads on to fortune;
> Omitted, all the voyage of their life
> Is bound in shallows and in miseries.
>
> —Shakespeare, *Julius Caesar*, 4.3.218–221

CHAPTER 3

College and Early Marriage

Seeing yourself as you want to be is the key to personal growth.

—Anonymous

Before the interstate highway system was constructed, it took most of a day to travel on US 41 from Valdosta to Atlanta. With good luck hitchhiking, I made it to Atlanta before dark and spent the night at the YMCA. Early the next morning I took a city bus as far north as it went on US 41. Several hours passed before I got a ride to Chattanooga, and it took even longer to make my way through that city. I was about to give up hitchhiking by late afternoon when a truck and a car pulling a trailer stopped to pick me up. I soon found out that the truck driver was a professor moving from a college in Alabama to another one in West Virginia. He and his wife planned to travel through the night. They picked me up to help with the driving, which I did when his wife got sleepy about midnight.

On the way down a mountain in Tennessee the brakes on the car began to smoke and give out from being pushed downhill by the heavy load in the trailer. We stopped long enough for the professor to chain the car to the truck, thus making a three-piece vehicle going up and down the mountains. I was afraid the smoking brakes on the truck would give out on the way down a mountain and not stop until we ended in one big pile at the bottom. At daybreak he stopped to tell me I should get out, because he was crossing the highway that I needed to travel to get to Lexington. I was not disappointed to be put out on the side of the road in the middle of nowhere.

A short time later a couple saw the Wilmore sign on my suitcase, guessed that I was a college student, and picked me up. They asked if I'd had anything to eat. When I told them I had not slept or eaten for twenty-four hours, they bought me breakfast and then told me to lie down on the backseat to get some sleep. They drove several miles out of their way to take me to my destination on the Asbury school farm in Wilmore.

I soon discovered I was one of only two student summer workers. My roommate and coworker was Marcus Barbano from the Philippines. Living with him was the first of many cross-cultural experiences. Marcus was energetic, impatient, and volatile. Once he showed me how to do something he didn't want to show me again. We lived in a side part to the house of Mr. Witt and his family. He was the primary farmer and supervisor of student helpers.

Summer was harvesting and hay-baling time. Before I had the money and time to buy gloves, my hands were cut and blistered by the wire on the hay bales. It was hard work to throw bales of hay from the ground onto the rising stacks on the trailer. Once we pulled into the big barn, I had to throw them up to the loft, where Marcus caught and stacked them. I soon developed lots of muscles. I learned to drive the tractor and got to a place where I could back up three trailers of hay into the barn for unloading. This required a great many calculations on which way to turn the steering wheel.

I also had to help feed the hogs, shovel out the barn where the cows were milked, mend fences, and paint barns and fence posts. When we were not baling hay, we built stone fences from the piles of rock that were dumped on the land during the construction of the college swimming pool. Marcus and I enjoyed taking the big cans of milk and butchered meat to the dining hall kitchen at noontime. We often had a table to ourselves because other students did not like the way we smelled.

One reason I worked on the farm in the summer was to save money for the fall. I was burning so much energy doing the hard work that I had to eat extra food in the dining hall, which meant spending more money. Sometimes in the evening I would go to the barn, lift the lid on the cooler, and drink a glass of cream off the top of the milk in order to get extra calories.

One day Marcus got a package of homemade chocolate-chip cookies in the mail. His classmate and friend, Phyllis Diehl, had sent the cookies to him because she knew he missed seeing his family back home. My mouth watered from the smell of those cookies. He gave me only one and ate the rest of them. That was the best cookie I had ever eaten in my life. In my envy I told Marcus he was fortunate to have a friend like that.

By the end of the summer I was as healthy as I had ever been, with lots of muscles on my thin body. In September the students started returning to campus. The students who worked in the dining hall arrived first. As Marcus and I went through the line to pay for our meal, he introduced me to Phyllis, the cute cashier who had sent the cookies to him.

My intention was to continue living and working on the farm through the school year; however, in the fall Mr. Witt saw me working in a cold wind and asked why I was not wearing a jacket. When he discovered I didn't have sufficient winter clothes for farm work, he suggested I ask the dean if the college had some indoor work and a room for me in one of the dorms. Another student who had dropped out of college after only one week left a place for me in the dorm.

I was fortunate to be assigned a room with Bob Neimiller. He was something of a mystic and a very smart student. He had a strong influence on my life because he introduced me to the Brother Lawrence and other authors, such as Glenn Clark, Starr Daily, and Rufus Mosley, and the movement called the Camp Farthest Out. When I visited his home in Fort Thomas, Kentucky, his father introduced me to classical music, which he loudly played on a record player.

Since I had to work to pay for my room and board, I asked for a job that paid the most money. I was given the task of washing pots and pans in the dining hall kitchen for fifty-five cents an hour. It was a hot, greasy job that hardly anyone wanted to do, but it paid 10 percent more than any other jobs on campus. This job became a blessing to me once I got over my frustration from the never-ending task of scrubbing the huge greasy pots and pans that were used and sent back for washing as fast as I could wash them. The cooks kept an eye on me, thinking I would get frustrated and quit as so many other students had done.

But after reading Brother Lawrence's little book *The Practice of the Presence of God*, which my roommate had given me, taught me that I could do any task as long as I practiced an awareness of the presence of God in what I was doing, even to picking up a piece of straw from the ground. After reading this book I discovered the joy of God's presence while doing my job.

Sometimes I would take a short break from work. Still wearing my wet, greasy apron, and with the encouragement of the cooks, I walked to the front of the cafeteria to talk with the girl practicing her piano lessons. She claimed there were not enough practice rooms for all the students, so she had asked permission to practice on this one. This was the same girl who had sent the cookies to Marcus and the same one who worked as a cashier in the cafeteria.

Phyllis and I developed a friendship, but I never thought about dating her until she asked me to be her escort for the Sadie Hawkins annual girl's football game and banquet on Thanksgiving Day. I accepted but regretted my decision when I almost froze to death in my thin-lined jacket in the cold November wind. We enjoyed the banquet and started seeing each other more regularly after that. I had planned to have only casual dates while in college and had promised myself not to get serious about any one girl, because I could not afford the expenses of serious dating. I also was afraid of getting distracted from my studies and fail to graduate from college.

Phyllis was also a friend with Mario Vagara from Chile and many of the international students. He became my dorm mate and friend when Bob Neimiller transferred to another college after his sophomore year.

Mario was tall, handsome, and popular with the students, especially the girls. He kept asking me if I had kissed Phyllis and got frustrated with me when I responded that I had not because I did not want to get too serious with any one girl. Finally he threatened to kiss her himself if I didn't. Even with that pressure I kept delaying that first kiss, though I knew Phyllis was waiting for that to happen when we said good night with her head uplifted and her eyes closed. I kissed her for the first time when we were saying good-bye the night before we left college for Christmas break. I left quickly and ran all the way back to my dorm room. Cupid had shot his arrow into my heart. My vow not to get serious about a girl before completing college ended on that last day of the first quarter at Asbury.

(Note: I'm including here Phyllis's account of her life before meeting me in order to give the reader some background to her life before marriage.)

I was born in a log house in Pennsylvania on February 2, Groundhog Day, 1932. Because it was February and a heavy snow had fallen, the doctor couldn't get there in time for my birth. A neighbor, who was also a midwife, came to help my mother deliver the fifth of her six children.

My parents inherited the pre–Revolutionary War log house, situated in the lea of a hill on a forty-acre farm, after caring for mother's parents until their deaths. Grandpa Weston took early retirement from working as a railroad brakeman after a terrible accident caused a friend to loose both legs. He purchased the farm and invited my parents to live with them to help farm the land after Papa returned from fighting in France during World War I. As a returning veteran, my father, known as Papa Diehl, had the right to take the test for the position of rural mail carrier. He passed the test and supplemented the family income as a mail carrier for thirty-seven years. He was fortunate to have a job with a steady income, especially during the Depression when many neighbors did not.

The parlor, dinning room, kitchen, and living room were on the first floor of the house, and our four bedrooms were on the second floor. Siding had been installed over the outside of the fifteen-inch-wide walnut and oak logs and paneling on the inside by the time I was born. An indoor bathroom was installed when I was very young. Before this, a path led to the cold outside toilet.

The original owner must have built the house here to take advantage of an all-season natural spring. The steep hillside was not easy to farm, but the house was protected from the cold winter winds and had the best water in the county.

I grew up a happy farm girl in a strong Christian family. Grandpa Weston died when I was too young to remember him. I have a photograph of him balancing me as a toddler on a horse. I slept in my parents' bedroom until my younger brother, Dicky, was born four years later. Later, I slept with Grandma Weston until she died when I was age twelve. I will always be grateful for her patience in teaching me how to sew. She and I were right-handed, but my mother was left-handed. I still have a full wardrobe of clothes that we made for my favorite doll.

I learned from my parents the importance of doing a good job whether I felt like it or not. The 150-yard lane had to be cleared when it snowed so that my father could get out to deliver the mail. The farm animals had to be fed, eggs gathered, the garden weeded, the corn and hay harvested, firewood brought in, and other chores done around the farm. There was no arguing or excuses about doing our chores.

My mother was a full-time housewife with great cooking and baking skills. My parents were high school graduates. This was unusual in the early twentieth century when most teenagers dropped out of school to help on the farms.

Our social activities evolved around the United Brethren Church, situated a mile up a steep hill in the community of Middletown, Westmoreland County. Our family had daily devotions and faithfully attended all Sunday services and Wednesday evening prayer services. On holidays and other special occasions we celebrated together with our friends and neighbors.

The community pulled together to help neighbors in times of need. I was blessed to have healthy Christian neighbors who believed in me and supported me by being people I could admire.

With three older brothers and an older sister, I was protected from most of the more strenuous jobs around the farm, though I loved working with them according to my ability. Dicky, my younger brother, followed in the footsteps of my father whenever he was home.

Tragedy struck the family when Dicky was eight years old. He complained about pain in his side but tried not to worry my parents too much. By the time my father took him to see a doctor, his appendix had burst. He died from peritonitis a few days later. I was twelve years old at the time of his death. I lost not only my little brother and playmate, but in some ways I lost my father. He went into a deep, prolonged depression from the death of his son and guilt over not taking him to the doctor sooner than he did. Male neighbors and friends at church gave him as much support as they could, but nothing seemed to console him. Though he had been one of the strongest men in the community and a war veteran, his depression was so severe that he stayed in bed for weeks. Mother delivered the mail to keep him from losing his job, and the older boys did his farm chores.

The tragedy of Dicky's death may have saved my life. A year later I complained about pain in my side and was taken immediately to a doctor, who sent me to the hospital to have surgery for appendicitis.

School consolidation began before I started school. The small elementary school in Middletown closed, and the children were transported by bus to larger schools. The county constructed a small covered bus stop for children in our neighborhood across the road from the long driveway leading to our house.

In front of our house was a big old barn made from the same kind of ax-cut logs that were used to build the house. I loved to play in the barn. I knew every nook and cranny of it, especially the best hiding places. Papa hung a swing inside that we use to compete to see how high we could swing. My brothers sometimes played corncob battle games with other boys, but they wouldn't let me play because they were afraid I would cry if I got hit with one.

When I was old enough to walk by myself up the path to the top of the hill, I would go there to look at the distant hills. In one valley I could see vehicles speeding along on the Pennsylvania Turnpike.

I liked to visit the families of my cousins in Pittsburg, about forty miles away. We could go out to eat and see movies in the big city, which I could never do where I lived. When my cousins came to visit me on the farm, they wanted to walk with me up the hill behind the house, pick berries, and play in the barn.

Clarence, my oldest brother, graduated from Asbury College in Wilmore, and on the urging of a classmate, he took the necessary exams for aspiring doctors. To his surprise, his scores were in the top ten in the country. Carnegie Mellon gave him a full scholarship. My sister Ruth completed her freshman year at Asbury, but fell in love with a boy from Georgia. When he was drafted into the army during World War II, she quit college to marry him and moved to be close to him until he was shipped overseas. She lived in Atlanta with his relatives awhile, then returned to the farm in Pennsylvania until he was discharged after the war.

When I decided to go to Asbury College, Ruth knew I had no dating experience because there were very few boys my age close to where I grew up. I had lots of girl friends, but no boyfriends. She warned, "Watch out for those Georgia boys." I must have considered this a dare, and so I looked for them. Two out of the three boys I dated my freshman year were from Georgia.

The summer after my first year at college, I sent some cookies to Marcos, a classmate who worked on the college farm during the summer. He was from the Philippines and couldn't go home until he finished college. When he wrote a thank-you note, he told me he had shared the cookies with a boy recently arrived from Georgia who worked with him on the farm.

When I went back to college at the end of summer, Marcos introduced Burrell to me as they came through the dining hall line, where I was working as cashier. I liked his looks and the way he told me how much he liked the cookie. I learned later that Marcos had given him only one of the cookies. I still use the same chocolate oatmeal recipe. It has become a sensory symbol in our home.

I saw Burrell date other girls, but he seemed to be interested in me only as a friend. I got tired of waiting for him to ask me out, so I took advantage of the opportunity to invite him to be my escort for the Sadie Hawkins Day football game and dinner party. I played end on the football team on a very cold windy day in late November. I stayed warm by running up and down the field, but Burrell nearly froze while watching from the sidelines.

When he finally asked me for a date, I happily accepted and enjoyed being with him. A few days later I saw him dating another girl who was very nice. I said to myself, "Okay, he returned the favor, but that's probably the last time he will ask me for a date. He likes that girl more than me." To my surprise he asked me out again a few days later.

By the end of the fall quarter term we were dating regularly. I thought he liked me, but I couldn't understand why he never tried to kiss me. The last night before we went home for Christmas, I finally got my kiss. It was a short and sweet good-night kiss, but I knew then that it was a sincere message that he loved me.

In 1953 we dated as much as the school would allow. Dating couples were not permitted to be together after 7 p.m. on weeknights from Monday to Thursday, after 11 p.m. on Fridays and Saturdays, and after 2 p.m. on Sundays. I had always been a good student and accustomed to getting good grades, but Burrell was just learning how to study. I did not want to interfere with that, but I did help him as much as he would ask for my help.

Burrell went home to Valdosta to work as a carpenter's helper during the summer months after my junior year, and I went to Brownsville, Texas, to work with a missionary couple serving in Mexico. I couldn't understand their Spanish, but I helped as much as I could and got a taste of missionary life.

I returned home to Pennsylvania in time to pick wild berries that my father sold to his mail route customers. This money paid for a bus ticket to Hendersonville, North Carolina. Bob Neimiller, Burrell's college roommate, was dating my friend Mary. He arranged with the leadership of the Camp Furthers Out (a precursor to the charismatic movement) to give the four of us student-worker scholarships to attend the two-week meetings at the Lake Kanuga Conference Center. Burrell and I fell more deeply in love in the environment of joyous Christians in love for Jesus. After completing our work responsibilities one night, Burrell and I went with the other couple to the Kanuga rapids. As couples, we chose different spots to have some privacy. It was there that he asked me to marry him. He promised to give me an engagement ring when he could save enough money to buy one.

During most of my senior year in college, I had to be off campus a lot to do student teaching as a requirement for my English and elementary education degree. This made it more difficult to have time with Burrell. We got around that by getting up early so we could see each other in the classroom in the basement of my dorm. I graduated a year before Burrell and was offered a teaching job in the county where I did my student teaching. I was concerned that we would want to get married before Burrell graduated, and this would complicate his completing his degree program. I told Burrell that the Corbetts, two of our college professors who had been missionaries in Cuba, said they could arrange a one-year teaching residency for me to teach English at Colegio Buena Vista in Havana, Cuba. This would give me additional teaching and missionary experience before we got married. The distance would keep us from getting married before Burrell finished college.

(Back to Burrell's story)

I made friends with other students from South Georgia. One of them was an older student from Adel, a few miles north of my home in Valdosta.

He owned an automobile, and his car became our transportation back and forth to college until we graduated. At the end of the fall quarter and the end of the school year we took our exams in the morning and left school soon after lunch for the eighteen-hour drive to South Georgia. We dropped off classmates the next morning along the way. Tom Barrett, the owner of the vehicle, was an experienced song leader. He knew the words of many hymns and gospel songs. We sang a lot, told stories and jokes, teased each other, and took turns driving over the two-lane highways before the construction of the interstate.

During Christmas breaks I worked in the post office, managing the shipment of packages. I always visited my former Sunday school teacher and longtime friend, Mrs. Tucker. We went to see Mrs. Dewberry so I could thank her for paying my college tuition. After the first quarter she asked me if I needed anything. When I told her I didn't have a winter overcoat, she went to a closet and pulled out a dark camel hair overcoat that had belonged to her son and gave it to me. I did not realize at the time that this was a very expensive camel-hair coat from Egypt. It was very warm, but I was embarrassed to wear it at college because it really stood out as something strange and different.

My friend Buck, who had invited me to go on many double dates with him at Valdosta State University, came to welcome me back home and said he had two girls lined up for dates. When I told him I didn't want to go on a date, he said, "Burrell, are you in love?" To keep from lying, I had to say something I had not admitted to myself. I was in love with Phyllis. So I wasn't interested in dating other girls. I had broken my vow not to fall in love until after college.

College was hard for me because I had never learned how to take exams and structure my study time. I gradually learned to apply myself to my studies because I wanted so much to become a pastor. I also had a new motivation with Phyllis as my girlfriend. She was an A student, and I wanted her to be proud of me. She helped me by correcting and typing my term papers. Her encouragement and love were a great inspiration for my academic career. My grades improved each year.

The three weekly chapel services enriched my spiritual life during the first two years at Asbury. I enjoyed the many special music events in the chapel on Friday or Saturday nights, and they also were opportunities for cheap dates with Phyllis.

We did not have classes on Mondays. Phyllis and I often went for walks in the countryside on Monday afternoons. While we were walking one afternoon, it started raining. Phyllis said, "Let's run to that farmer's barn before we get wet." Once there she quickly climbed to the top of the hayloft. She had grown up on a farm with a barn and was familiar with how they were constructed. She invited me to follow her and taught me that a hayloft is a wonderful place for hugging and kissing.

Since couples weren't allowed to be together after set times at Asbury, the rest of the time was devoted to study. There were strict rules about dating, and no one dared get caught kissing. Young people, however, are known for circumventing rules, and we were no exception.

By my junior year and Phyllis's senior year, we were engaged. In order to have time together, we got up at 5:30 a.m. to meet at her dorm door as soon as the night watchman went off duty at 6:00. We then went to the basement classroom, turned on the lights, and turned two right-arm desks side-by-side to eliminate the barrier to hugging and kissing. Mario, my roommate, thought I was crazy for getting up so early in the morning. In his sleepiness he would say, "*Tu estas loco*." He was the one who encouraged me to kiss Phyllis. Now I was disturbing his sleep to go kiss her a lot.

The summer before Phyllis's senior year, we had gone to Camp Kanuga near Hendersonville to participate in a two-week Camp Farthest Out retreat. They were the most joyous people I had ever been with. I really fell in love with Jesus while we were there. We sang some wonderful new songs and had opportunities to hear Glenn Clark, Starr Daily, Rufus Mosley, and other leaders of this new charismatic spiritual life movement.

It also helped that I was deeply in love with Phyllis and had planned to ask her to marry me while we were there.

One night after we finished our programs, we walked with two other friends to a waterfall about a mile from Camp Kanuga. About halfway down the side of the shoals, Phyllis and I found a smooth place to sit beside the rushing water. There, I asked her the question of my life: "Will you marry me?" She did not hesitate a second to accept my proposal.

In our excitement and affection, we had not noticed a storm gathering on the other side of the mountain and were suddenly faced with getting soaking wet unless we ran back to the camp dorms. The rain, lightning, and thunder overtook us. We were frightened by the storm and totally drenched but joyous as we quickly said goodnight and went to our rooms in separate buildings. That was a quick ending to one of the most exciting nights of our lives.

My junior and her senior year were an enjoyable time for us because we knew we were going to get married. Phyllis graduated in June 1954 with a degree in elementary education and was offered a teaching job in a nearby Kentucky town. Rather than accept this offer, she volunteered to go to Cuba on a one-year contract as an English teacher at the Buena Vista Methodist School. She wanted to get some missionary experience before we married. She also thought it would be best for her to be some distance away from me to keep us from getting too intimate before I finished college.

Instead of going home to work the next summer, I enrolled in summer classes to make up for the courses I had failed at Valdosta State. It was very lonely for me in the fall without Phyllis being there. It was also very tempting with other girls desperate to get married when they finished college. I stopped playing tennis with a female classmate when I found myself paying more attention to her agile body than to the tennis game.

I had a serious spiritual crisis my senior year. I could not integrate the joy of the charismatic Camp Farthest Out retreats at Camp Kanuga, plus reading the inspiring books written by the speakers, with the legalism and seriousness of the Asbury Holiness ethos. I was getting tired of going to three weekly chapel services and managed to quit going by scheduling my pot-and-pan washing when chapel services were scheduled. The dietician caught me doing this. She had been around too long to be fooled by a student trying to escape chapel attendance. She knew what I was doing because this often happened to students in their senior year. She said I had to go to at least one of the three chapel services a week.

I attended worship at the small Presbyterian church across the street from the college. Dr. Vandermeter, the pastor, must have flunked retirement. He had served very large churches and was well known among Presbyterian leaders. He chose to serve this church to influence young lives going into Christian ministries. His short, pithy, challenging sermons attracted so many students until we almost crowded out the church members. He became my intellectual mentor. Upon hearing a professor criticize theologians like Karl Barth, Rudolf Bultmann, Paul Tillich, the Niebuhr brothers, and others for their liberal views, I went to the library to read their books—only to be told that the library could not order such liberal books. Dr. Vandermeter would not let me borrow his books, but he would let me read them in his personal library while he did his pastoral visiting. Professors did not appreciate me challenging their criticisms of writers they had not read.

My spiritual crisis, combined with missing Phyllis, deepened into a depression to the point that I couldn't or didn't want to eat. The cooks in the dining room probably noticed the loss of weight on my skinny body. They often place sandwiches with thick slices of meat in the storage room where I changed clothes after work. I became concerned about my physical health and mental stability. I knew I needed help, but I didn't want to go to a psychology professor, because I was a psychology major. So I went to the home of Melvin Himes, a married student who had been a field cook during the war. His wife, Vera, was a cook in the dining hall and most likely had told him about the concern for me among her co-workers. Melvin was a man of deep and joyful spirituality. He had attended a Camp

Furthest Out retreat. I participated in a prayer group that met in his home. He understood my spiritual, physical, and emotional needs. After talking with me, he prepared extra-toasted sandwiches so I could eat without throwing up afterward. I learned a lot about what was later named the theopsychsomatic spiritual direction from him.

Mario, my Chilean friend and roommate, had no trouble eating, but he was lonelier than me. He had not been home in four years. We often walked to the top of the hill behind the college to watch the sun go down. He had grown up in Iquique, a coastal city in Chile. Sunsets reminded him of home and brought tears to his eyes as we sat in silence until almost dark.

Mrs. Dewberry paid my tuition, but the room and board expenses were my responsibility. They increased to the point that I had to take on extra work responsibilities besides washing pots and pans. I was assigned to mop the floors of the library in the evening after it closed. This meant I often got to bed rather late, but I could sleep later now that I was not getting up early to see Phyllis.

My mother wrote that two men, dressed in suits, came to the house to ask if I lived there. At first she thought they might be FBI agents, but she soon found out that they were Methodist laymen from Albany, Georgia, and members of a group, after giving their tithe to their churches, contributed extra money to help young men and women going into full-time ministry to get their education. These were the days before loans and government assistance to pay for post-secondary education. They called their group My Brother's Helper. The two men asked my mother if I needed help to pay for college. She urged me to write them as soon as possible. So I wrote that I needed some financial help to pay for my room and board so I would not have to work so many hours, which took away previous time that I needed for study. They sent the money and later arranged a loan for me to buy my first automobile so I could get a pastoral appointment after graduation.

During my senior year, Phyllis was in Cuba. We corresponded a great deal. Sometimes it would take two to four weeks to get an answer to a question. We still have her letters in a notebook. I regret throwing away my letters to her when we were packing things for one of our moves.

Phyllis traveled to Valdosta for Christmas in 1954 to meet my family. I do not know how she survived getting to know the names and putting up with the antics of such a large family. On Christmas Day I asked her to see my home church, which was seldom locked. We made our way to the back Sunday school room to have some privacy. I put the engagement ring that my brother had made for me in a town in Germany close to where he was stationed. He brought it home for me to give to her at Christmas. I had saved money for a long time to buy the ring. It was my Christmas present and a big surprise for her. I wanted her to go back to Cuba with an engagement ring on her finger.

When I returned to college after Christmas break, instead of riding with my friends, I went to Atlanta to see Bishop Moore to ask for an appointment in the South Georgia Annual Conference after I graduated in June. He required an eye-to-eye visit before he would appoint a new pastor. He was delayed getting home from a trip overseas. So I had to spend another night in Atlanta to see him. This meant I would be one day late returning to college.

The rule at Asbury for not being there on the first day of classes was the reduction of a grade in one subject. I got enough coins to call Dean Kenyon's office to explain why I would be one day late for my classes and asked to be excused. I thought he had excused me, but when I got my grades on the morning of graduation I saw that my chemistry grade, which I had worked so hard to earn a B had a C. I went to the professor's office and found that he had submitted a B grade to the dean's office. I immediately went to see the dean. He said, "The rule is the rule, and there are no exceptions." Though I pleaded for justice, he refused to change my grade to a B. I had done my best to live with the many restrictive rules of Asbury College, but this legalistic approach to school administration left me with a bitter feeling about the college that lasted many years. It also took away much of the joy of graduation. My mother had made a special sacrifice to travel by bus from Valdosta to Wilmore to be with me on graduation day, because she was so proud that one of her boys was a college graduate. I was angry but kept it to myself in order not to spoil her excitement.

Looking back fifty-four years later, I realized that my three years at Asbury influenced my life more than any place I ever lived. I fell in love with a beautiful woman. I fell in love with learning and discovered that I could be a good student. I was introduced to classical music and joyous Christianity through the influence of my first roommate. My faith was deepened and my vision was expanded to include world missions as a vocation. I learned to think for myself and developed the courage to challenge classmates, professors, and administrators when I thought their views were wrong or too limited.

> It took me a long time to realize that the way one leaves a place and people is like dye. It colors the whole experience of being there until forgiveness and gratitude changes that color.
>
> —BDD

CHAPTER 4

Marriage, Seminary, and Ministry

All my life I have been haunted by God.

—Dostoevsky, *The Possessed*

Mrs. Dewberry offered to pay my tuition to go to Asbury Theological Seminary, which was across the street from Asbury College. The seminary had recently lost its accreditation because the faculty voted to fire a popular tenured theology professor for an insignificant theological difference. He and the professor of Methodist studies moved to Atlanta to teach in the Candler School of Theology at Emory University. The chairman of the South Georgia Annual Conference Board of Ordained Ministry informed me that if I graduated from a nonaccredited seminary, I would have to go to an accredited seminary an additional year. This would mean four years instead of three. I also wanted to leave Wilmore to broaden my theological education and loosen the restraints of the holiness movement. I thought it would be easier to get an appointment as a pastor in South Georgia and for Phyllis to get a teaching job in Atlanta after we were married in August. So I moved to Atlanta in June to live in a boardinghouse close to where I got a job at a supermarket to make as much money as possible before getting married in August.

Another reason I wanted to move to Atlanta was that my brother Ed and his wife, Patsy, lived in Mudville, the married student military surplus student housing apartments. Ed had finished his first year in seminary at Emory and was a pastor in Riverdale, a town south of the Atlanta airport.

I soon discovered that no matter how many hours I worked in the supermarket, it was not enough to pay the boardinghouse expenses and automobile upkeep. I also had a weird roommate who seemed to think that taking girls to bed was his main purpose in life.

As August approached, I realized I had very little money for the wedding and honeymoon expenses. My brother Ed rescued me by lending me his credit card so I could charge the gasoline and motel expenses and pay for them later.

My mother came by bus to Atlanta to travel with me to Phyllis's home in Pennsylvania for the wedding at her home church. I planned to travel from Atlanta to Roanoke, Virginia, to spend the night and take the Blue Ridge Parkway and Skyline Drive on our way to Pennsylvania. Mama was so excited to see the mountains and views. She kept asking me to stop at the overlooks so she could admire the beauty of the mountains. I thought they were beautiful too, but I was in a hurry to see my beautiful fiancée and not as interested in mountains as my mother.

Phyllis and I were married on August 5, 1955. We had a simple, low-cost wedding. My mother stayed with Phyllis's family in their home. Orlo, my college buddy from Ohio, came to be my best man, and Phyllis's brother-in-law Olin was both the officiating minister and photographer.

I memorized my wedding vows so I could say them without being prompted, but as I looked at Phyllis and the beautiful wedding gown she had made, my mind went blank and I couldn't remember what I was supposed to say. Fortunately, Olin prompted me by saying each phrase for me to repeat.

The custom in her home church was to bring presents to be opened at the reception after the wedding. We had to open over a sixty gifts, hold them up for everyone to see, and express our appreciation. I was appreciative of the gifts, but I got frustrated with the delay of getting away from the church to start our honeymoon.

On the way to her home I took an exit on the Pennsylvania Turnpike at the town of Bradford to make motel reservations and order a dozen red roses for the room. The motel manager said, "Oh, a southern gentleman is going to stay here!" Phyllis and I were exhausted by the time we got to the motel after eleven o'clock that hot night. When I tried to put on my pajamas, I couldn't get my foot to go down the correct leg. Unwilling to turn loose, I was hopping around the room on one leg like a disoriented turkey, trying to force my foot down, when Phyllis came out of the bathroom. I discovered that my mother had sewn up my pajama leg with a needle and thread as a joke to pay me back for all the tricks I had played on my brothers and sisters when they got married.

We had a wonderful time on our honeymoon. We had planned to go to the Pocono Mountains, but before the wedding I wrote Phyllis to tell her I did not have enough money to pay for a motel in the mountains any longer than two nights. I apologized for the fact that she was marrying a poor man. And she responded: "About the poor man I'm marrying: as far as I'm concerned, I don't like too much money. So I'm happy that there seems to be little prospect of that problem for us. You can't ever tell me I'm simply marrying you for your money. I'm marrying you because I love you—for the person you are, for helping me to be a better person, for loving and longing to help others. I hope I can be a real helpmate for you. I want to give you the best that I am and have. And I am not afraid to marry a poor man who is so rich in friends, faith, and love."

Phyllis solved the problem of the motel expenses by contacting her aunt and uncle who had a mountain retreat near State College, Pennsylvania. We stopped to get the keys and directions from them and made our way along a gravel road and a dirt road, to go deep into the woods to a house by a mountain stream. I told Phyllis that if she had told me how far from civilization we were going, I would have brought my shotgun because I was sure there were bears in these mountains.

We were very much alone. We went for walks with no one in sight. On one walk Phyllis saw some Penny Royal herb plants and picked them to make me some Penny Royal tea. She claimed they were very special plants in Pennsylvania used for delicious tea. I asked her if she was trying to poison her rich husband. Forty years later it was discovered that Penny Royal is a carcinogenic plant. Fortunately, we were not there long enough to drink very much of it.

We had a wonderful honeymoon. I'm glad we stayed in the isolated mountain cabin, though the house had no running water. We heated cold spring water in the kettle on the stove for baths. We had plenty of time to enjoy each other. We returned to Phyllis's home in time to gather her belongings and wedding presents for our journey to Atlanta.

Before we arrived in Atlanta, my brother Ed had arranged housing for us with the Emory's housing department to get an apartment in Mudville, on Clifton Road and within walking distance of the seminary. It's the same land where the Emory University Motel and Conference Center is situated, across the street from the Centers for Disease Control (CDC) today.

We lived in a surplus military barrack that still had the tarpaper on the outside. They were moved there to provide housing for veterans going to college under the GI Bill and reserved for veterans with families. Since I was not a veteran and just married, the director of housing had said wasn't eligible to live there. Ed found three empty apartments and told the housing director that the university would lose money if they sat empty and didn't rent one to me. The rent was only a dollar a day, including utilities. Ed knew I couldn't afford to rent a commercial apartment. When we arrived in Atlanta I went to the housing office to sign the rental contract and pick up the keys, the housing secretary said, "I guess you know you have a very good brother."

Phyllis soon transformed the inside of this apartment into a beautiful home by making ceiling-to-floor curtains to cover all the walls, except for the windows. I encouraged ivy vines to grow up the wall outside to cover the tarpaper. Though we had to deal with mud in the Mudville complex, we were comfortable in our affordable apartment.

I had originally planned to serve a church or churches in South Georgia, but I realized in May that I didn't want my bride to teach school all week and have to travel several hundred miles on the weekends to help me serve in those area churches. I wrote to the district superintendent to let him know that I didn't want to take the appointment because I felt it was unfair for me to put so much stress on my wife. The district superintendant told me later that the bishop was so mad that he vowed to never give me another appointment in Georgia.

I was fortunate to inherit from a graduating senior a part-time job picking up dry cleaning on Monday and Tuesday evenings and returning the clothes on Thursday. I made 40 percent of the cost of the dry cleaning. To speed things up, Phyllis went with me to bundle up each customer's clothes and write the ticket to identify them. I also worked on Friday and Saturday as a cashier at a supermarket.

In January 1956, Mrs. Stowers, the beloved secretary and mother figure of the seminary who knew about my decision to turn down the appointment in South Georgia, introduced me to Gilbert Steadham, the pastor of the Duluth United Methodist Church. He was looking for a student to help him serve the Warsaw UMC, the smallest of his two churches. It was only twenty-five miles northeast of Atlanta. I would have to go there only for Sunday school and church, and I would not need the bishop's approval. This would give me an opportunity to gain practical experience by preaching each week. It also meant more income for us. I served the Warsaw church for two and a half years and learned a great deal from Reverend Steadham as my supervising pastor.

The people at the Warsaw church were very loving and tolerant of my youth and inexperience. The most embarrassing moment I had was the week I had prepared a communion sermon for World Wide Communion Sunday, but the communion steward forgot to bring the bread and wine for the service. It was too late for her to get it, so I tried to preach an extemporaneous sermon from another passage, but it went from bad to worse to terrible to awful. Finally, I quit and sat down in the chair behind the pulpit and cried from embarrassment. That was how I learned it was best to have a prepared sermon and a reserve outline just in case something unexpected happened.

In February 1956, just five months after our wedding, Phyllis said she wanted to talk with me about something important. She told me I was going to be a father. I was shocked, thrilled, and scared of the responsibility of being a father while still going to seminary.

Though I was from the South Georgia Conference, I was now serving a church in North Georgia and was ordained a deacon in the North Georgia Annual Conference when it met at Emory at Oxford College in June 1956 by the same Bishop Arthur J. Moore who said he would never appoint me to anything because I had turned down my first appointment. I don't think he remembered, but I did.

My grades improved each year through college and seminary. Much of this I owed to Phyllis for typing and correcting my papers before I submitted them. Her faith in me made me want to do my best so she would be proud of me.

One seminary professor was known as a tough grader. On the first exam of the semester, I got a D; the highest grade in the class was a C. After getting my grade, I was walking across campus, expressing my frustration at this professor's grading system, when I felt a hand on my shoulder. I looked behind me and came face to face with the professor I had been talking about— Dr. Claude Thompson, the professor who had caused Asbury Theological Seminary to lose its accreditation. He said, "Burrell, just keep working and you'll do better." Dr. Thompson later became my spiritual mentor and helped me integrate the Asbury holiness theology with the Emory liberal theology.

In his class on devotional classics, Dr. Thompson suggested I write my major term paper on George Washington Carver. This meant I had to use the libraries of Morehouse and Spellman Colleges to get the best research material. I was often the only white person on these campuses. This was at the height of the civil rights movement, but I was treated with great kindness in spite of the fact that no black students were allowed at Emory University at that time. Sometimes my seminary professors invited black civil rights leaders—Dr. Martin Luther King, Ralph Abernathy, Andrew Young, and Joseph —to our classes to expose us to their ideas about racial justice. Half the students would leave rather than listen to them. I found it very exciting to live in Atlanta at this time. This speeded up my healing from racism that was deep rooted from growing up in Valdosta.

At 2 a.m. on October 4, 1956, our son Randy was born at Emory University. I had to tell someone I was a father, so I awakened my brother Ed to tell him that we had a baby boy. Phyllis's mother flew to Atlanta for two weeks to help care for the baby. I felt like a fifth wheel because I was not needed except to pay bills and get groceries.

Phyllis was a natural mother. I had learned how to change diapers and care for the baby when my sister Pauline had her first child in Valdosta. I was glad Phyllis decided to nurse the baby, because this meant that I did not have to get up at night to feed him. Randy was born with long black hair. This soon became a problem for me because everyone said, "Oh, isn't she cute." When he was six weeks old, I took him to my barber and said, "Give him a crew cut like mine." The barber was very reluctant to cut Randy's hair, but with me holding him in my lap and keeping his head very still, the barber managed to give him a crew cut that looked like mine. That ended the talk about him looking like a girl.

Two months after Randy was born, Phyllis discovered a lump in her breast. This required exploratory surgery to find out if it was cancerous. The lab report said that it was a benign milk duct tumor and there was no reason to be concerned about it. After Phyllis's surgery, she was not allowed to hold the baby, except for nursing with the other breast, to keep from opening the site of the incision.

Two weeks before Christmas, I had an automobile accident while going around a downhill curve. Another car had stopped to make a left turn, and I couldn't stop before rear-ending it, because a construction crew had gravel on the roadway. Both vehicles had to be towed, but the policeman didn't give me a ticket when I showed him the gravel on the road. Phyllis and I had planned to travel from Atlanta to Valdosta to spend the holidays with my family. I very much wanted to go so my family could see our new baby. But now we had no automobile, and there were no rental cars in those days. I called a medical student from Valdosta to ask for his help. He offered to take Phyllis in his car but said he wouldn't have room for Randy and me or the suitcases. I bought a bus ticket and took ten-week-old Randy and his baby bag and two suitcases by bus to Peachtree Street in downtown Atlanta. Then I had to walk two blocks to the bus station. A black man, walking in my direction, saw me struggling with all I was carrying, stopped, and said, "Mister, you sure do need help." He took the two suitcases and walked with me to the bus station. I offered to pay him for his help, but he said: "I said you needed help. I didn't say I needed money." With that, he turned around and walked away as I yelled a thank-you in his direction.

I had no trouble caring for the Randy because the women on the bus wanted to hold him. They also helped change his diapers. When we got to Valdosta after midnight, my brothers and sisters were waiting to meet me. They were barefoot and dressed in rolled-up country hick clothes and speaking thick South Georgia slang. I was totally embarrassed. By this time the people on the bus were awake and laughing. I told the driver I'd rather stay on the bus and keep going with him to Jacksonville. But my family's way of kidding me was the best thing they could have done to cheer me up after the tough weeks we had been through.

Phyllis decided not to teach the year Randy was born so that she would not be stressed out during the last two months of her pregnancy, and then she'd be home to care for him. She took several seminary classes this year. We both made an A in a mission class we took together. The wife of Professor Floyd told her a few weeks later, in front of a group of student wives, that she was one of only a handful of students in her husband's long teaching career to made a perfect score on one of his final exams.

About the age when Randy was beginning to walk, I came home from school and immediately started to read the newspaper. Suddenly a toy hit the newspaper and didn't stop until it hit me on the chest. My first reaction was anger, because he had thrown something at me. Before I could punish him, Phyllis stopped me by saying: "He's been waiting all day for you to come home and play with him. After greeting us, the first thing you do is read the newspaper. He wants your attention more than you want to read a newspaper." That was a valuable lesson in parenting I never forgot. My wife and children needed to be my priority when I came home. In February 1958, my third and final year of seminary, Phyllis told me that our attempts to have another baby were successful. I was excited but concerned about supporting a growing family on a full-time pastor's salary.

We managed to get through seminary without going into debt. Phyllis taught school two years. I had three part-time jobs and loans from My Brother's Helper helped to pay my tuition. We did not spend money on movies or eating out. Our Friday night dates cost us only baby-sitting fees. We attended the Atlanta Symphony Orchestra and got in free by serving as volunteer ushers.

My brother served in the Florida Annual Conference a year before I graduated. Our mother was proud to see two sons, one daughter, and a son-in-law graduate from the Candler School of Theology at Emory University. I went to the South Georgia Annual Conference in Valdosta at the end of May 1958 to be ordained an elder by the new bishop and receive a full-time pastoral appointment. At that time pastors did not know where they would be serving the next year until the appointments were announced in May. My mother was present to see me ordained and to hear the bishop read the appointments. After going down the list to the Valdosta District, he continued to the Ray City Charge and said, "Burrell Dinkins." This meant I was appointed to serve the four churches on the Ray City Charge, about twenty miles north of Valdosta. After the conference was over, I found my district superintendant, Rev. Bernard Brown, at about the same time my mother found him. She wanted to thank him for appointing me so close to Valdosta. When he said, "Well, Mrs. Dinkins, are you satisfied?" I realized my mother had influenced him to appoint me close to her.

I knew Ray City well because I had dated a girl in this town. Brother Dixon, the pastor of my home church for nine years and my first mentor for ministry, was completing nine years of service on the Ray City charge. He was happy I would be his successor in these churches. While he was there, the church bought the house next door to the Ray City church. This was the same house in which my Ray City girlfriend had lived when I was dating her. By this time she was a married member of the church, and her husband owned the filling station on the street behind the parsonage.

I returned to Atlanta to inform Phyllis about our appointment and pack our belongings to move to Ray City on Thursday of the next week. This was the moving day for pastors appointed to new churches.

We were talking to some church members in the front yard a few minutes after arriving in Ray City when a fighter jet flew just a few hundred yards over the house on its final approach to Moody Air Force Base, the same base where I used to sell newspapers. Two-year-old Randy looked up when he heard the loud noise and didn't take his eyes off the plane until he fell over on his back.

The Ray City charge was composed of four churches: Community, King's Chapel, Bemis, and Ray City. The four churches had Sunday school every Sunday but worship services only once a month, both morning and evening. This custom had been in place years before I arrived here. I followed the same schedule during the summer but became very concerned that the churches were not growing as much as the Baptist churches that had worship services every Sunday, both morning and evening. This model was developed during the days when the roads were unpaved, but now they were, though they were rather narrow.

One day in August, I got in my car to see how long it would take to drive from one church to another. I discovered I could travel between two of them in fifteen to twenty minutes. I invited the lay leaders of each church to meet at Ray City church where I presented a strategic plan that would allow me to preach at each church every Sunday if they were willing to shift their Sunday school hours. They thought it was a good idea and agreed to present it to the members of their churches. With their approval, each Sunday I started a fifty-minute worship service at nine o'clock at the Community Church and left as soon as I shook hands with everyone. I drove to King's Chapel, where the lay leader had started the worship service. When I finished in this church at eleven o'clock, I drove fifteen minutes to Bemis. After preaching at Bemis, we ate lunch with a family or drove home to eat. We had evening services at Ray City. I was preaching in all four churches each Sunday.

Phyllis went with me to each of the church services. With much patience, she heard the same sermon four times when her attention was not focused on caring for Randy or Ruth. She was always very affirming with her comments about my preaching. She gave helpful feedback. To keep me from getting upset by something I may have not wanted to hear, we waited until Tuesday to talk about the week's sermon. With no secretary available, Phyllis typed the bulletins and newsletters on stencils for me to run off on a cranky mimeograph machine.

By the middle of October, Phyllis was eight months' pregnant with our second child. One day she was in the front yard where some neighborhood kids were playing with Hula-Hoops. One child threw hers in the air and it caught on a tree limb just out of Phyllis's reach. Without remembering that she was pregnant, she jumped for it so the children could continue their play. That night she started hemorrhaging. I immediately rushed her twelve miles to the small hospital in Nashville, Georgia. When the doctor examined her, he discovered that she had lost a lot of blood and needed transfusions as quickly as possible. The closest blood supply was thirty miles away in Valdosta. In the middle of the night I drove as fast as I could on the narrow back roads to Valdosta, where they had the blood ready to go. I got back to the hospital in Nashville in time for the transfusion to save the lives of my wife and baby.

The next month, in the middle of the night, Phyllis told me we needed to get to the Nashville hospital as soon as possible, because her water had broken. When we arrived, the sleepy doctor examined her and gave her an epidural, left the busy nurse in charge, and went to his office to sleep until she was ready to deliver. A short time later, Phyllis asked me to take a look to see if the baby was trying to be born. When I saw the baby's head coming out, I ran into the hall and yelled as loud as I could for the nurse to get the doctor. I went back into the treatment room, washed my hands, and prepared to catch the baby. I got angry when he arrived and told me to get out of the room, though I knew this was a common practice in the days when doctors were kings of the birth process.

We were pleased to find that our new baby was a girl with long blonde hair. We named her Ruth after my sister and Phyllis's sister. We were very proud to have her, but we soon realized she was not going to be as easy to deal with as our first child. She had a bad case of colic that caused her to cry most of the time. We got very little sleep during the first several months after she was born. Randy was thrilled to have a little sister, and he tried his best to get her to stop crying.

Randy gave us some frightening times. Once he pushed a chair into the bathroom to get a bottle of cough syrup out of the cabinet and drank all of it. He was too young to realize that it was full of codeine. When I saw the chair and the empty bottle, I rushed him to the hospital, where they pumped his stomach and kept him overnight for observation. A month later we bought some roach hives to help control an invasion of roaches in our house. Though we hid them as best we could, Randy found one and licked the tasty blue substance. When we saw it half eaten in his hand, we knew he had swallowed arsenic. We rushed him to the Nashville hospital to have his stomach pumped again.

Before the end of our first year in 1959, Phyllis and I realized that my $150 monthly salary wasn't enough money to support the family and pay for our automobile expenses, which had dramatically increased due to traveling hundreds of miles around a four-point church circuit. We were making 50 percent less than we had during my last year in seminary. I loved getting to know my people through systematic visitation, and I discovered that they had a custom of giving their pastor vegetables from their gardens and frozen meat from their freezer. I found myself visiting some families more often than others. I realized free food was not a proper motivation for pastoral visitation, but I also knew it helped provide for our growing family. I tried to grow a garden, but I was too busy to give it proper attention.

When we started going into debt, I called together the lay leaders of the four churches and explained to them our financial predicament. One of the laymen suggested that Phyllis get a teaching job to increase our income. I said: "My wife will not work to support your churches. If she gets a job, it will be to help us invest for the future, not to support your preacher." They finally realized I was making only $150 a month, a third of which was used for automobile expenses. One of the farmers confessed that he was embarrassed to learn that his pastor, who had gone to school for seven years to learn how to be a pastor, was making only $100 a month, which was less than his illiterate farm workers made. He said, "Boys, we got to do better for our preacher." They agreed to get their churches to increase my salary by a third.

The district superintendant said he would help us by taking King's Chapel, the smallest of the churches, off the district, and adding Unity Church, which for many years had been on the Lakeland charge. When some of the other pastors heard about the addition of Unity Church to my charge, they warned me there was a powerful layperson there who tried to control everyone, including the pastor.

When I drove up to the church the first Sunday, this laymen met me before I got out of my car and said: "Pastor we realize that the pastors usually pray the pastoral prayer, but in our church we like for my father-in-law, Mr. Pafford, to pray it before the pastor preaches the sermon. Could we do that today?" I thought my authority was being challenged before I could even walk into the church. I quickly decided not to pick a fight just before the worship service. I said, "Okay, let's try it for today and see how it goes." When I called on Brother Pafford to pray, I quickly realized he was a godly man. By this time I had heard thousands of prayers, but no one had ever prayed for me like he did. I felt anointed and preached a much better sermon than I had previously prepared. After that, he prayed every Sunday.

I continued the pattern of preaching at each church every Sunday. After another extensive visitation program with church members and guests, I proposed that we have a vacation Bible school at each church during the summer and a revival (preaching every evening for a week) during the month of August. Phyllis and I trained the vacation Bible school teachers in the afternoons and led the school at each church in the mornings One church didn't think they could do it, because it was summertime and everyone, including the children, usually worked on their farms during the summer months, but they agreed to try it. We had an average attendance of over seventy-five kids who had never been to a vacation Bible school. And several new families joined the church after this.

When I asked the leaders at each church who they wanted to invite to preach the revival meetings, all of them said they wanted me to do it. I preached every night for a month, except on Saturdays.

The last Friday was the most embarrassing sermon I had ever tried to preach. Members of the three churches where I had already preached the sermons decided they would come to support me on the last night. When I saw them, I realized they had already heard the sermon. I made the mistake of trying to preach an extemporaneous sermon. It was worse than the first time I tried to preach an extemporaneous sermon. It went from bad to worse to terrible to awful until I just sat down in the chair behind the pulpit, too embarrassed to go to the door and shake hands with the people as they left. When everyone was gone except the lay leader, he came to where I was sitting, leaned over, and said: "You got lost in the bulrushes tonight didn't you? But don't you worry. You'll get out. Because we've heard you preach some mighty good sermons." I loved his blunt assessment of his preacher. As I look back, I think it was probably a good thing for the people to see me at my worst when I had been working so hard to prove that I could be their pastor.

The second year the four churches on the Ray City charge were chosen as Churches of the Year for the Valdosta district. All four churches were growing, and I was happy to be their pastor. They responded with a willingness to make changes and try new forms of ministry.

In the fall of that year, Phyllis and I started talking about buying some timberland. I had developed a friendship with the county agent. He suggested I buy some timberland to grow pine trees to sell and build a fund for our children's college education. He found 120 acres of land with half-grown pine trees, but it would cost ten thousand dollars. Phyllis said she was willing to teach school again and use most of her salary to pay off the debt.

Only one thing held us back from doing this: in college we received a vocational call to be missionaries. We attempted to answer this call by applying to the Board of Missions during my senior year in seminary. A committee in Atlanta was chosen to examine us for an appointment. After receiving the packet of material from the personnel department, we were invited to meet with the committee for an interview. Phyllis was accepted, but I was turned down. The psychologists at Emory University must have sent a negative report about me. I made the mistake of using my limited knowledge of psychological testing to guess at the answers to his questions for psychological evaluation instead of stating how I honestly felt. The committee told me to get some full-time pastoral experience and reapply in two years. We were disappointed and angry about being turned down. I decided to follow my first calling to be a pastor and return to the South Georgia Conference. As I look back on the valuable lessons learned in the two years of pastoral service after seminary, I am grateful for the wisdom of the committee decision.

Now we were at a crossroads, because we knew that if we went into debt with the land purchase, we would not be able to be missionaries. I wrote to the Board of Missions to ask if they were still interested in our candidacy. Secretly, I hoped they would turn us down, because I was enjoying pastoral service in South Georgia. We learned that they still wanted us, but I would have to undergo another psychological exam. The personnel director referred me to a psychiatrist in Jacksonville, Florida. I made the appointment, and Phyllis and our two children went with me to Jacksonville so we could go to the beach after my meeting.

I found the building and the suite for the psychiatrist, but I was shocked to see his specialty under his name: Child Psychiatry. I was twenty-seven years old, married, with two children, and they had sent me to see a child psychiatrist. I thought about leaving, but since I had traveled eighty miles to see him, I might as well go through with it.

His introduction was the opposite of the cold, indifferent psychologist at Emory. His friendly demeanor helped me relax so I felt comfortable about talking with him. He asked many questions about my background.

Later he said, "You told me about everyone in your family except your father. I want to know about him." I gave a superficial answer, but he kept probing about my relationship with my father and my feelings about his death. I tried to be as objective and fair as possible by telling him the good and the bad. I don't remember exactly what he said, but I remember that I broke down and cried for a long time as I grieved the death of my father for the first time. The last thing he said to me was, "You don't realize how fortunate you were that your father died when he did." He explained, "Dying when he did freed your mother to help her children become who they are today."

I left his office with a great sense of relief from the burden of repressed feelings about my father. I was unable to conceptualize then what I later learned about encapsulated grief and ambivalent feelings that can be bottled up for years.

We went to the beach, where I saw the joy of my children's first experience with the ocean. The release of my own ancient grief freed me to experience this joy with them.

We postponed the option to buy the timberland until we heard from the Board of Missions. After sending another letter to the personnel director, we got a quick answer. He said that the board wanted to commission us to be missionaries, and we would get our assignment in a few weeks. Phyllis was very excited that we could finally fulfill our vision to be missionaries. I had mixed feelings, because I enjoyed being a town and country pastor in South Georgia. I wanted to become a missionary, but I didn't look forward to giving up what I loved. Neither did I want to give up the opportunity to invest in the land. I knew our calling to be missionaries was our first priority and had to be answered now that the door was open.

We had another problem to deal with. I had an outstanding balance of three thousand dollars in loans that I had signed for to pay for my seminary tuition, and repayment was scheduled to start two years after my graduation. That date was coming up in a few months. The Board of Missions required new missionaries to be free from debt or that their debts were manageable before they would make an overseas assignment. I sent a letter to Albany, Georgia, asking how we might stretch out our payments to keep them as low as possible. A few weeks later I received a thick envelope from the My Brother's Helper group. Upon opening it, I saw each of the nine IOUs that I had signed had been stamped "Paid in Full." A cover letter stated that since we were going to be missionaries, they had decided not to require repayment of our loan. In today's dollars that amount would probably be over twenty-five thousand dollars. Phyllis and I cried, hugged, and cried some more after we read the letter. We knew that our calling to be missionaries had been confirmed and we were doing the right thing.

A letter from the Board of Missions surprised us. We had assumed we were going to a Spanish-speaking country because both Phyllis and I had studied Spanish in college, and she had spoken Spanish during her year in Cuba. Instead, we were assigned to Brazil, a Portuguese-speaking country. We were told to report the first week in July to Scarritt College in Nashville, Tennessee, for six weeks of missionary orientation. This meant we would be saying good-bye to the people we had learned to love over the last couple of years. We decided to wait until a month before we left to tell the people in the churches.

When I met with the district superintendent, Bernard Brown, to inform him about our acceptance to become missionaries, he said that he was going to raise some money among the churches in the Valdosta District to support us as missionaries in Brazil. And he raised enough for our full support before the next Annual Conference.

Just when we thought everything was in place for us to become missionaries, we had to report a sudden complication to the Board of Missions.

Phyllis was pregnant again and was expecting the baby in August. This did not change their decision except to postpone the date for our departure until the end of the year.

I dreaded having to tell the four churches that I would be leaving at the end of June, because I knew I loved them and they loved me. The churches were thriving, and I really wanted to continue being their pastor, but I could not do that and fulfill the call to be a missionary. We cried together when I told each church at the end of a sermon.

Phyllis and I packed to leave for Nashville for six months of study and missionary orientation. We moved into an old house with high ceilings and no air conditioning on the campus of Scarritt College during that summer. There was plenty of room inside and out for the children to play with other future missionary kids.

Along with our missionary orientation, we had time to take a seminary classes. Phyllis signed up for a New Testament class and I took a theology class at Vanderbilt University. The evening of the day she took her final exam, Walter was born. I teased her by saying the reason she got an A in the class was for finishing the course before she gave birth. I enjoyed this time of study and was able to play a lot of tennis for the first time in my life. We traveled back to Valdosta in the fall to say good-bye to my mother and to have Walter baptized by Brother Dixon at a district preacher's meeting.

I was told that the best thing to use for packing things to send by ship was fifty-five gallon steel drums. I bought four of them at a bakery for a very cheap price. After cleaning them out, we packed dishes and most of our belongings in them. They were our major packing containers in Brazil and back to the States and are still with us today.

After completing our passports and other paperwork, we were told to arrive in New York City on December 22, 1960, and to sail two days later at 5 p.m. on an Argentine ship to the port of Santos in Brazil. We had to travel from New York to Brazil over the Christmas and New Year's holidays in order to arrive in Brazil to start Portuguese classes the second week in January. I will always be grateful to my brother Ed for flying to

New York on a cold Christmas week to bid us farewell. Without his help, we might not have gotten to the ship on time.

> There is a big difference between deciding to leave and knowing what I'm going to do.
>
> —BDD

CHAPTER 5

Becoming Missionaries

The universe is made of stories, not atoms.

—Muriel Rukeyser

As darkness fell, we sailed past the Statue of Liberty on our way to Brazil, the beginning of a fifteen-day journey. We had been told there would be maids aboard the ship to help care for our children: four-year-old Randy, two-year-old Ruth, and four-month-old Walter. The first evening they fed them and took care of them while we attended the required safety drill and the ship captain's reception, which was followed by a formal dinner.

While we waited for the late-arriving captain, I looked at Phyllis and noticed that her face was whiter than her dress. I thought she might be getting seasick before we were out of New York Harbor. I was afraid to ask how she was feeling until I got her back to our stateroom. I made up an excuse about needing to return to our room and barely got her inside before she started three days of miserable seasickness. Fortunately we had several cans of baby formula in a suitcase for Walter. She tried nursing him, but she was too sick to hold him.

We used most of Walter's diapers earlier, traveling from Nashville to New York and staying two days in New York City before boarding the ship. The morning after we boarded the ship, I sent a bundle of used diapers to the ship's laundry. I did not know that the Argentine crew had started celebrating Christmas at noon that day. I had a sick wife and a baby with only six clean diapers, which I soon used. (These were not disposable diapers.) All attempts to retrieve anything from the laundry failed. I threatened to wash them and hang them up on the ship's mast. Forced to get creative, I brought the children to the bed with their seasick mother while I washed the diapers by hand in the sink in the children's room, wedged them into the vent with a screwdriver, and turned on the ceiling fan to dry them as quickly as possible. Fortunately, it did not make the children sick. During the day, I took Randy, Ruth, and Walter on deck to allow Phyllis to rest as much as possible. Being small and having low centers of gravity, Randy and Ruth quickly became adept at walking on the rolling ship without having to hold on to anything—as I did. We enjoyed watching the fish fly out of the path of the ship.

The captain was too drunk to come to the Christmas Eve dinner. And most of the crew was drunk too. At all hours of the night they did a conga line dance down the halls, drunk as could be and still standing up. I was concerned that no one was sober enough to be in charge of the ship. After getting Phyllis and the children settled in bed one night, I made my way to the pilot's cabin to make sure somebody was steering the ship. I found the officer in charge very grumpy because he had pulled the duty on Christmas Eve. He wanted to be drinking with the rest of them. That reassured me enough to relax about the safety of the ship.

I went to an open space on the deck and looked up on a clear Christmas Eve night sky full of stars that seemed to be so close I could almost touch them. This was my first Christmas away from my family of origin. I experienced a deep sense of loss from leaving every security behind me for an adventure with no idea what would happen to me and my precious family. Anger welled inside as I started praying. I finally said, "Abraham, I do not like you. You started this missionary stuff when you became the first missionary to leave your country and go into a foreign land without knowing where you were going." I realized at that moment that I would need more faith and courage than I ever had if I were to fulfill the call to be a missionary.

As we were sailing past the Bahamas Islands on Christmas afternoon, I was convinced Phyllis to go up on deck into the warm sunshine. She recovered from her seasickness and enjoyed the rest of the trip. During a storm one evening, the ship rolled so much that we had to hold our plates steady on the table with one hand and eat with the other.

After fifteen days of seeing nothing but sky and water, we were told early one morning that the ship was approaching Rio de Janeiro. Even from a distance, the land of mountains, white sandy beaches, and buildings was beautiful. We did some sightseeing in Rio while the crew unloaded cargo and disembarked some passengers. Then we sailed overnight from Rio to Santos, where we disembarked. Two missionary couples were there to meet us. One of them was the treasurer who was responsible for getting us through customs. We were fortunate that we had packed most of our things in steel drums, because the custom agents had no intention of taking everything out to see how much he could charge us.

As we left Santos, we ascended the beautiful mountain highway cut through the tropical forest to the city of Rudge Ramos. Our first stop was the home of the treasurer, Mac and Jessie McCoy, on the campus of the Methodist seminary. After lunch they took us through the city of São Paulo on a two-hour trip to our house in Campinas, where we were to live for a year to study at the nearby Portuguese School of Language and Culture.

We anticipated some of the changes facing us, but we were soon overwhelmed by so many new things coming at us as soon as our new English-speaking friends left us alone. Fortunately, they had already purchased some basic necessities for us to start housekeeping. The language barrier was our major challenge. I arrived knowing only two expressions in Portuguese: hello and good-bye. We did not meet any Brazilians who spoke English. We had been told that we would live in Campinas for a year to study the language and get acclimated to the culture before receiving an appointment from one of the Brazilian bishops. I could hardly wait for school to start the next week so I could learn to communicate beyond hand signals. The men and a few single women went to classes in the morning. Most of the wives went to classes in the afternoon. This arrangement allowed one parent to be at home to care for the children and to study.

When the teacher in my first conversation class asked me in English to tell her my name, I said, "Burrell." She said, "Spell that." After spelling it, she tried to pronounce it in Portuguese, which sounded like "burro." She asked if I had a second or middle name, and I said, "David." She said, "You should not use your first name because it sounds too much like 'burro,' which is the Portuguese word for jackass. You may feel like one sometimes, but you don't want to be called 'Pastor Burro.' While you live in Brazil, you will be called 'Pastor Davi.'" And so I was.

Phyllis learned Portuguese much faster, as most women did. Her high school Latin classes and Spanish studies, plus college Spanish and English major, helped her understood the grammatical construction of the Romance language system. The year before we were married, she taught English in a Methodist girl's school in Cuba. Though this background helped her, she struggled to communicate in Portuguese.

Shopping was a major challenge for us. At that time there were no supermarkets in Brazil, but a lot of specialty stores. Bread in one, meat in another, dry goods in another, and so on. Shopping required a lot of time, patience, and communication. We waited until the clerk at the counter interpreted our hand signals or read the dictionary word we had previously looked up. Then he went to get each item we requested or pointed toward.

The language barrier was only part of the problem. Once we managed to get what we needed, we still had to pay for it in Brazilian money, called cruzeiros. This required mental translations of monetary values and a strange currency. The victory of shopping, or defeat from not being able to correctly communicate, was a strong motivator to learn the language as fast as possible.

Methodist missionaries in the language school usually had some help from other families that arrived a few months before them, who passed on a few tips they had learned. Bob and Pat Martin arrived nine months ahead of us and were very helpful. We were sad when they left for an appointment in Brasília, the new capital of Brazil.

After some initial adjustments, we settled down and began enjoying our life in Campinas. The tropical plants and multicolored flowering trees were beautiful. The children especially liked riding on the *bondi*, a brightly colored old-fashioned open-sided street car with a running board for entering and leaving. Bench seats allowed travelers to slide from one side to the other. Pull cords signaled the driver when to stop. Sometimes we rode a bus to town. The introduction of buses in Campinas a few years before we got there indicated the approaching end of the bondi era of public transportation.

We soon became familiar with the open-air farmers market, called the *feira*. We enjoyed doing most of our food shopping at the feira throughout the years we lived in Brazil. The fresh fruit, vegetables, grains, meat, and flowers were plentiful and cheap. We were not concerned about preparing them, because most families, including missionaries, had an *empregada*, or maid.

Before we arrived, we didn't know the missionaries had maids, but we soon realized why they were necessary. Shopping, cooking, housecleaning (with daily polishing of the wood and tile floors), and lack of electrical conveniences required a lot of work. The maid also helped care for the children, which freed up Phyllis and me to have time for study and attend language classes. Maids were at the bottom level of salaried workers, so we could easily afford one.

Our first maid took some getting use to, because we had trouble communicating with her. She had worked previously for a missionary family, which meant she understood some North Americans customs. She also knew how to take advantage of our ignorance by missing days from work to go to a funeral. I think her grandmother died at least a dozen times the year we lived in Campinas.

Randy was the first to learn Portuguese. We sent him across the city on a bus to attend kindergarten, accompanied by a teacher at the school. Church was a challenge. The pastor spoke very fast and clipped off the endings of his words. I had enough trouble conjugating verbs. Without the ending of the verbs, it was almost impossible to understand. We found out later that Brazilians laughed when we told them where we went to church, because they also had difficulty understanding him.

Before departing for Brazil, we had met the Goodwin family in the United States while they were on furlough. They told us about their work at the Methodist Rural Institute in the state of Minas Gerais and invited us to visit them after we learned some Portuguese. When the break at end of the first quarter came, I decided to take them up on the offer, though I could barely communicate. Leaving before daylight, I took a taxi to the bus station, the bus to São Paulo, a plane to Rio de Janiero, and another one to Vitória, Espírito Santo, a train to a small town on the Doce River. Jim Goodwin met me at the train station. We traveled across the river in a dugout canoe to where a student was waiting on a tractor with a trailer hitched to it. We traveled on a rough dirt road for more than an hour before we arrived at their home and school situated in a beautiful valley surrounded by green hills. The Goodwin family welcomed me graciously and seemed glad to hear someone speak English. The thing that inspired me most were the small lantern-lit groups of Christians walking the hillside trails after dark on the way to worship at the church. As they made their way on the winding paths, they sang gospel songs that echoed across the valley and from one group to another.

I returned home safely and was inspired to work harder to speak Portuguese as well as the Goodwins. I discovered after a few weeks that studying so much was tiring my mind. I needed to do something physical. I loved the beauty and the low cost of hardwood furniture. While looking through an English-language catalog of Christian Sunday school supplies we had brought with us, I saw a set of wooden kitchen furniture and some appliances. I asked my Portuguese conversation teacher to help me learn to ask for a handsaw, hammer, screwdriver, screws, square, and wood file so I could buy them in a hardware store. Then she taught me how to calculate English measurements into the metric system.

I visited a nearby lumber store. My nervousness grew as I waited my turn to place my order. I noticed the clerk signaling customers behind me to step to the counter ahead of me. Finally, a man saw my predicament and told the clerk to wait on me before him. The clerk said, "No! I'll not wait on him because he's an American and I don't like North Americans." The other customer responded, "If you do not wait on him, I will not buy from you." Begrudgingly, the clerk took my order and got the lumber while I talked the best I could with my advocate. He told me that he became a Christian because of an American missionary who lived in his town in the interior of another state.

While driving home with the lumber in a borrowed vehicle, I reflected on how my experience at the lumber store might compare to the treatment of blacks in the South who were denied service and treated as inferiors because of the color of their skin.

One day a kombi stopped in front of our house. Out stepped a missionary couple and their four children. We recognized them as the Renshaws. We had met them in 1957 when they lived in Atlanta while on furlough from Brazil. I invited them to speak at Warsaw, my student appointment church. We did not know they were coming to visit with us until they arrived at our front door. Neither did we know they would stay several days with us while looking for a house to rent. They had traveled a long way from Campo Grande, Mato Grosso do Sul, over dirt roads. We saw them covered with dust and knew they needed a bath, food, beds, and rest. This was our first introduction to the custom of Methodist missionaries in Brazil treating each other as family and assuming they would be welcomed guests, even without advance notice. The Renshaws were moving to Campinas because Parke had been appointed the new director of the language school. He was a good teacher and school administrator, and they were very helpful to us during our year in Campinas. He became my best friend after we returned to the United States.

As our year in Campinas was coming to an end, I decided it was time to buy a vehicle. Our treasurer, Mac McCoy, told me there was enough money for me to buy one. Usually, automobile dealers had only a demonstration vehicle for customers to see before they placed an order. Parke said a kombi was the most versatile vehicle for a missionary in Brazil, and he volunteered to help me make the purchase. He stopped me one day and told me to go immediately to the dealer to place an order and make a down payment on a vehicle, because the exchange rate on the American dollar to the Brazilian cruzeiro was going to change drastically the next day. The dealer was not happy when I picked up the vehicle and paid most of the cost with devalued cruzerios. I learned an important lesson about Brazilian inflation.

Before completing the year of language school, I was assigned by the coordinating counsel made up of bishops and missionaries to serve in the Fifth Ecclesiastical Region (Conference) of the Methodist Church of Brazil, which covered most of western São Paulo, the north of Paraná and the enormous state of Mato Grosso. Though I was considered to be ready to pastor a church after a year of language studies, I was far from speaking fluent Portuguese. I traveled to Lins, São Paulo, to attend my first Annual Conference. Bishop Sucasas very graciously introduced me. After hearing stories about the bishop's two- to three-hour sermons, I decided to slip out of the meeting and get some ice cream on the night the appointments were read. To my surprise, the bishop decided not to preach very long before reading the pastoral appointments. I never heard him say where I would serve because I had left the meeting on my ice-cream mission.

Fortunately, my new district superintendent found me and welcomed me to the Londrina, Paraná District. He invited me to stay at his house when we arrived in Londrina, and he would go with us to Arapongas. I had no idea where Londrina was, but I knew it would be where we would be living and serving the Arapongas and Apucarana churches. Park Renshaw found me and said his first appointment had been in Maringá, Paraná, about two hours farther west, toward Paraguay. He was a great help in getting us ready to move.

The first half of our journey in January 1962 was on a paved highway in São Paulo. When we crossed into the state of Paraná, we found ourselves traveling during the dry season on a dirt road with dark brown dust flying everywhere. January in Brazil is as hot as July in Florida. Without air conditioning, the option of closed windows was out of the question. Randy, Ruth, and Walter started accusing each other of having dirty faces as the dust mixed with sweat on their faces. Driving through the dust made it extremely difficult to see other vehicles trying to dodge the many potholes in the road. I wondered what it must be like to drive on this highway when it was raining.

After several hours of driving through the dust, we arrived in the city of Londrina, or New London, named by the English land company in charge of settling hundreds of square miles in the northern section of the state. We were happy to find paved streets in Londrina and to find the parsonage of the district superintendent, Rev. Angelo Brieneze. His family graciously welcomed us and provided a place for us to clean up and stay a couple of days.

The next day Reverend Angelo and I went to meet the lay leader of the church in Arapongas. Jose Morais was the delegate from Arapongas to the Annual Conference, and he had requested a missionary be appointed to be the pastor in Arapongas. When we found him, we discovered that nothing had been done to find a house for us to rent. This meant I would have to look for one. I made a reservation in the hotel on the main street of the city for the family to live in town while we looked for a place to live before our furniture arrived. Several people told me that people in Arapongas built houses to live in, not to rent.

Walter became very ill during the house hunting. The hotel manager told me where to find a pediatrician. I couldn't understand why the young doctor gave us five different prescriptions for Walter until a church member later explained that medical students usually went to parties and played politics while they were in medical school. They knew little about diagnosis, so they prescribed a variety of medicines in hope that one of them would cure the patient. I was glad the overdose did not kill my youngest. Walter was better after a few days.

After a week of looking, Jose Morais found a man who was willing to rent us his house. It was an unpainted frame house on a dirt street, only two blocks from the church. The owner said we could paint it if we paid the cost of both the paint and painter. Since we had no other options, we agreed. We moved into a brightly painted blue house a day before the truck arrived with our belongings.

We found the small, one-room, unpainted church in Arapongas without any trouble. It was at the back of the lot of land, leaving room for the construction of a future sanctuary. I soon discovered the Brazilian custom of each church having a *zelador* family living behind the church. They are the custodians of the church, responsible for cleaning, protecting the property, and providing information about the church.

Finding the church in Apucarana was a different story. I traveled about eighteen minutes from Arapongas on a paved highway and found the city of Apucarana atop a steep hill. Apucarana is an Indian word meaning "the laughing place." After driving around town for an hour, I had no clue where the church was. Neither did the people I asked for directions. When I introduced myself in my slowly developing Portuguese as a Methodist pastor, they often responded, "Methodist? What's that? Pastor? What does that mean?" Finally, my seminary class on the sociology of religion with Dr. Brewer at Emory came to mind. He had taught us how to access public information through government sources. So I went to the city hall to request help in finding the church, but no one at city hall knew about the church. They finally looked up "churches" in the city directory and found the address.

With the help of a hand-drawn map, I found the church on a paved side street, only a block from the main city square, fronted by a huge Catholic church with a twenty-foot statue of the black Madonna as its steeple. The little unpainted one-room church was in the middle of a double lot, with room to expand on either side. I understood why people knew nothing about the church; there were no identifying signs and no custodian on the property. I wanted to talk with a church member, but thought it would be too difficult to find one until the Sunday morning Sunday school or the evening worship service. I was glad that I did not wait until Sunday to find the church. Before long, I discovered another reason for the problem with finding the Methodist church: 95 percent of the population was Roman Catholic, and the remaining 5 percent was scattered over six Protestant denominations.

After eighteen months of transition from South Georgia, travel, study, and a lot of prayer, we were about to start the first Sunday of our missionary service—ready or not. I had only four sermons prepared in language school to use as a missionary pastor. My lack of preparation had to be overcome by my calling and passion to be a good missionary.

CHAPTER 6

People remember what they can live with
more often than how they lived.

—David Carr, *The Night of the Gun*

I was both fearful and excited about worshiping in the Portuguese language the first Sunday in my new churches. They were accustomed to having Sunday schools in the morning and worship in the evening. The pastors before me alternated Sundays between the two churches because they had to travel by bus between Arapongas and Apucarana. I continued to alternate between them for Sunday school in the mornings, because they met at the same time. When I suggested having worship every Sunday at each church, the church leaders gladly accepted my proposal by shifting the Arapongas church service to 6 p.m. and the Apucarana service at 7:30 p.m. It took only twenty minutes to travel by car from one to the other. I was thankful for my experience in Ray City, where I had traveled between three churches on Sunday mornings and preached at the other on Sunday nights.

My four sermons prepared while I was in language school helped to get me started, but they soon gave out and I was on my own, trying to preach in Portuguese. Brazilian pastors usually use rhetoric and formal Portuguese to demonstrate they are well educated. I could do neither.

I was still thinking in English and struggling to translate my thoughts into Portuguese. The people graciously listened to me without criticism or laughter. The Arapongas church had a piano but no one to play it, so Phyllis played and a layman led the singing. Women in the church looked after our three children.

The Apucarana church was as simple as a church could be; one room had to serve for both Sunday school and worship services. For the first few months we had no musical instruments, and instead of hymnals, each family brought their own pocket hymnal that had only the words of the hymns. I had to lead the singing and preach, and I depended on Phyllis's strong singing voice—and more proficient Portuguese—to help me lead the singing.

When we were in training to be missionaries, we learned about the problem of missionaries creating so-called rice Christians by providing most of the money for operating the church and using money from the States to pay for construction and social services, such as food for the poor. This practice often caused people to become dependent upon the missionaries. When the missionary moved on and national pastors took their place, the new pastors lacked the financial resources to support the churches and the people who depended upon them. This often created serious financial struggles for the new pastors. I was determined not to do this. Instead, I used a missionary philosophy of self-support through a strong stewardship program and a willingness to work within a budget the church itself could support. My salary, rent, and travel expenses were paid by the Board of Missions and mission specials from the South Georgia churches, but most of our operating expenses and construction had to be paid by the church members in Brazil. I also asked that they start paying the salary of a Brazilian pastor, beginning with 25 percent and increasing it that much each year until they would be paying the pastor's full salary in four years, after which we would be leaving for our first furlough. I wanted them to become self-supporting churches when they received their Brazilian pastor.

Phyllis had a much harder job at home, keeping three small children clean after playing in the red dirt. The water supply from the backyard well was limited during the annual dry seasons. As I mentioned before, shopping required a lot of time the small specialty shops.

When the weather turned cold from May to July, inside the house was often colder than outside. We soon learned what animals instinctively know: find the sun outside on the warm side of the house. Phyllis piled on the covers at night, and in the daytime she used our two-burner kerosene stove with a portable tin oven to bake bread cookies and other sweets. We bought wonderful, freshly baked soy bread the year we lived in Campinas, but we could not find it in Arapongas. The bread man came by each morning with a small horse-drawn cart to sell delicious French-style bread, but by evening the crust was almost too hard to eat. I remembered Phyllis's mother's delicious home-baked breads and rolls, so I asked Phyllis if she knew how to bake them. Her first try was perfect. The next day I fired the bread man, and Phyllis began a thirty-five-year career as our home bread baker. When cold weather limited the power of the yeast, she would put the dough in the baking pans and placed them in our silver VW bus (known as a kombi) to get heat from the sunshine on the roof. Several times I forgot about the dough in the kombi when I went visiting or shopping. Some overflowing dough and a very frustrated wife finally taught me to ask questions about her bread making—and to look in the back of the kombi before driving off.

Brother Dixon taught me by example that a good pastor was a visiting pastor, so I visited the people as much as possible. The more I visited and spoke Portuguese with them, the more I learned to speak Portuguese without first translating my words in my mind from English into Portuguese. I learned to speak the way the people spoke, which was not necessarily the way well-educated people spoke. My first attempt to pay someone to teach me Portuguese did not turn out very well. The young Catholic man I hired could speak some English, which made our communication easier, but I later found out that he taught me curse words without telling me what they really meant. We were told by church members to never go off overnight and leave a house unattended. We asked him to look after the house while we went on our first vacation. When we got back, a shy neighbor told us over the side fence that there had been some wild parties in the house while we were gone. We were learning who to trust and who not to trust.

We soon discovered how close we lived to our neighbors. This area of the city had electricity but no water and sewage utilities. We got our water from a well in the backyard, which was pumped to a tank on the top of the house. The toilet and household water flowed into a covered hole farther back in the yard. An indoor bathroom made us somewhat better off than our neighbors, who had no indoor bathroom. Before long we discovered that the proximity of wells and toilets created a breeding ground for intestinal parasites.

We started a routine of boiling drinking and cooking water before pouring it into a large filter pot. I took samples of the children's feces to a lab once a month to see if they had parasites that required medication. We tried to keep the children as healthy as possible. This did not protect them from the bicho-de-pé, the parasite that got in their feet and fingers between the epidermis and the dermis to lay its eggs. The eggs formed painful cysts on feet and fingers. Our children insisted on going barefoot, like their neighborhood playmates, so we had to periodically extract the egg sacks with a needle. This led me to think about getting a different place to live. We could not keep the children from playing with other children. They also got parasites while playing horse on a fallen tree trunk in the backyard.

One day we had an invasion of black ants. They covered everything and launched a deadly battle with the resident red ants. Insects were fleeing from them. Those unlucky to be grabbed were dissected and hauled off in pieces. Our neighbor saw us looking at them as they covered even the outside walls. She told us we were fortunate to have the army ants debug our house and suggested we keep our distance while they did their work.

The churches were very different from each other. Two generations of the Morais family controlled the Arapongas church. The older couple and the families of their two sons held most of the leadership positions, but they did not give much money to support the church. I gradually broke their control by putting new members into the leadership positions. It was not until the end of my four years as their pastor that I found out why I had so much conflict with them. They had lived in Maringá when our friend, Parke Renshaw, was the founding pastor of their church. He worked under the old "bring money from the States if they have too little to pay for it themselves" philosophy of missionary service. As I was packing to leave, José Morais told me he was disappointed with me because he had asked the district superintendant and the bishop specifically for a missionary pastor. His family had expected me to bring money from the States to buy or build a parsonage and pay for the building of their church. My missionary philosophy of working toward self-support clashed with their expectations. Without knowing this until the end, I decided in that first year to make the best of the situation, but to give most of my attention to developing the Apucarana church.

Most likely I would live and work in these two towns for four years before our first furlough to the States. This meant I needed a four-year development strategy to help them grow in membership and stewardship so they would be strong enough to support their own pastor. Since that pastor would need a place to live, without saying anything to the church leaders of either church, I started looking for a house to buy in Apucarana that would cost no more than the three remaining years of rent that we were paying in Arapongas.

I found a house only a block away from the Apucarana church. It would need remodeling and additional construction, but it would serve as a comfortable parsonage. I traveled by bus to São Paulo to talk with Mac McCoy, the Board of Missions treasurer, to see if he would advance me three years' housing rent allowance so I could buy the house. He was adamantly against it because he was concerned that the bishop would move me to another church. We argued until late at night without coming to an agreement. Finally, I asked him to telegraph headquarters in New York to see what they thought. They agreed with me and I got the check to take back and buy the house. The best thing was that the house was within easy walking distance to the church. Though it was on a dirt street, it had city water and sewage. The Apucarana church leaders agreed to pay for the building materials and do most of the remodeling construction themselves.

When the Arapongas church leaders learned that I was moving to Apucarana, the Morais families were very angry with me, but it no longer mattered. They were not paying my rent and they would not have paid for any remodeling. The decision to move freed me from their control. It also solved some serious health problems for my family.

The district superintendent, Reverend Angelo, threw me a curve when he said he needed to send a pastor to a nearby circuit of churches. He added three churches and some house congregations on the Jaguapitã charge to my appointment in Arapongas and Apucarana. This meant I had to travel several days a month to serve the people in this large rural area. He warned me to never pick up any hitchhikers because several robberies happened this way.

One Saturday I was on my way to preach and spend the night with a farm family when I saw a woman in the middle of the road with a bundle in her arms and another small child trying to pull her out of the road. She did not move when I blew the horn, so I stepped on the big air horn I installed to use when traveling through clouds of dust. She remained in the road no matter how I tried to drive around her. When I moved toward one side or the other, she moved in front of me. To keep from running over her, I had to stop. I spoke to her very angrily about blocking the road as I looked at the surrounding coffee trees for possible robbers. She begged me to take her to the next village to see the pharmacist because her baby was very sick. As she got in, I watched to see if anyone else was approaching from the sides of the road. We stopped in front of the pharmacy at the next village to get the pharmacist diagnosis and a prescription, which I assumed I would have to pay for. He said the baby was too sick and needed to have a doctor. She responded that she didn't have money to pay a doctor and the bus fare to get to the next town. I did not have time to take her farther, so I said I would give her enough money for the doctor and the bus fare there and back home if the pharmacist would give her the necessary medication. As I later drove toward the farm of a Methodist family, I remembered that I was going to preach a message that evening on the good Samaritan.

I did not like spending days and nights away from Phyllis and the children, but I enjoyed being a Methodist circuit rider. Fortunately, I was a generation older than the first missionaries who stated these churches by traveling on horseback.

I made a big cultural mistake at the home of one family. When I arrived, the man of the house asked if I wanted a basin of water to wash my feet. I told him I didn't need one because I had taken a bath before leaving home. His countenance told me I had offended him because I had refused his offer of biblical hospitality. He was courteous but never friendly toward me after that.

I loved spending the night with one family. The woman of the house had been a maid for a North American missionary family before she married. She not only cooked food I loved but also heated a kettle of water to knock off the chill of the cold water in the bucket used to provide water for a bath. She made sure after my bath that I took time to nap on her well-ironed sheets spread over the mattress and two extra chairs to accommodate my height.

The first night in another community, I stayed on a farm with a large family I soon discovered lacked some basic hygiene. I thought it strange that a teenage son had been given the same name as a deceased older brother, and the parents said he looked and acted exactly like his brother. I should have remembered that this custom was common in early Methodism. John Wesley was the third child named John. Earlier ones had died. The food was good, but the house was not clean. I had some stomach problems on this trip, so before going to bed, I asked this second-named boy where the outhouse was. He said, "We ain't got one." Then I asked where I should go if I needed to go to the toilet during the night. He responded, "Anywhere outside you want to go." I had seen several dogs around the house, so I asked him if they might bite me if I went out there during the night. "Yep! They sure will." Thank God, my prayers for bowel and bladder control were answered that night. I kept my promise to never again spend another night in that house. I spent other nights in that town in a cowboy motel with one narrow cot and a community bathroom at the end of the hall.

Though I had to spend a few nights away from Phyllis and the children, we were blessed by Neusa, who became our live-in maid. I met her during a visit with her farm family. She was the hardworking oldest daughter in her large family. When I heard her say that she wished she could live in town, I thought about Phyllis's needing someone to help in the home, because homeschooling our children, as well as doing all the shopping and housework, was getting to be more than she could do well. Usually, rural Brazilian girls were married by Neusa's age. When her father and I went outside, I asked him if he would let Neusa live in our home and work for us. He agreed to make a decision before my next visit. Phyllis liked the idea and reminded me that we could afford to pay her since the money exchange rate was favorable to anyone paid in US dollars. The next time I was in that area, I made their house my last stop on the way home. Neusa packed in a few minutes and was ready to go. Her father looked me in my eyes and said, "I'm lending her to you, and I expect you to take good care of her." As was the custom in Brazil, she sat in the seat behind me and every other time we traveled together. She was a wonderful cook and housekeeper and great with the children. She took a lot of responsibility off Phyllis's shoulders and was company for her whenever I was away from home.

Despite all the travel, I enjoyed being a circuit riding missionary pastor. The churches had suffered through some tough years while being served by some poorly trained Brazilian pastors.

Several weeks passed between the time a former pastor moved out of the small apartment in the back of the Jaguapitá church and my appointment to be the pastor. During that time, a family related to several other families in town moved into the pastor's apartment. The plan was for this family to serve as church custodians in exchange for a place to live. This was not a problem for me as long as one of the families would have a place for me to stay and food to eat on the few days a month I would be in town. Before long, I noticed the church building was not being cleaned, and I often had to do some quick cleaning before church services. People started complaining about the custodians. I talked with them about their responsibilities. When this did not help, I tried modeling by asking them to help me in cleaning the church property. My patience gave out when they went back to doing nothing. Traffic on the dirt roads left a thick layer of dust between Sundays. I told them that if they didn't do a better job of cleaning the church, they would have to move out so we could get someone who would. The threat did not seem to bother them. The man was accustomed to working just enough to buy the basic necessities and no more.

When I finally asked them to get out, they informed me that I could not make them move. After I told them I would get the police to move them off the church property, one of his relatives went to see the district superintendent to complain about me. Without contacting me, the district superintendent called a church conference to discuss the issue and make a decision. I was more than angry when the district superintendent called to tell me about the meeting. I went to the superintendent and begged him not air these problems at a church conference but to make a decision and I would abide by it. He refused to cancel the meeting. The church was packed on the night of the church conference, with a lawyer there to defend the custodian. The district superintendent was surprised by the spectacle of such a large crowd. I was chagrined that the problem had become town entertainment. When the district superintendent asked for a vote, I knew that no matter how the vote went, my effectiveness as a pastor in Jaguapitá was over. People who had not been to church during the time I had been pastor as well as others of whom I had no way of knowing if they were members voted. The vote was narrowly in favor of the custodian family to remain in the church apartment, because his relatives knew that if they had to move, one of them would be expected to let them live in their house.

The next morning I mailed a letter to Bishop Sucasas and made a copy to take to the district supervisor. I asked to be relieved of pastoral responsibilities for the Jaguapitá circuit. That afternoon I delivered the keys, records of the churches, and the letter to the district superintendent and told him I was sorry to do this because I loved being the pastor of these people, but when I needed his support, he did not give it. A few days later a letter came from the bishop supporting my decision.

One reason I was sad about leaving this church concerned a couple I usually stayed with in Jaguapitá. The woman was president of the women's society, and the husband was the church treasurer. Now in their midthirties, they had never been able to have a child, though she sometimes felt like she was pregnant. I arranged for a Methodist doctor, Alfredo Breninez, the brother of my district superintendent and owner of a hospital in Mandaqui, a town two hours west from Apucarana, to examine her to see if he could find out why they had not been able to conceive. He discovered a large lump in her uterus and recommended surgery to find out if it was cancerous.

When I took them for the operation a few days later, the doctor said, "Preacher, you brought her, now you are going to scrub up and help me operate on her." He cut open her abdomen while I watched and held back the skin with forceps and clips. I was fascinated by the surgical procedure and my opportunity to assist. I thought, *I bet I'm the first Methodist preacher to see the inside of a UMWS president.* As he extracted a five-pound benign tumor, he said, "Now we know why she could not have a baby, and she never will." They were sad to hear the news but relieved to know the cause. Leaving Jaguapitá meant I would be leaving them and also no longer able to visit Neusa's family.

A few days later the district superintendent came to apologize for not helping me solve the problem in Jaguapitá. He said he could not be the district superintendent, pastor of the large Londrina church, supervise the Jaguapitá churches, and serve the new area southeast from Apucarana where he was developing several preaching points on farms and new towns. I agreed to help him by taking on the area southeast of Apucarana. In doing so I knew the roads and living conditions would be more difficult than the circuit I gave up. My relief from no longer having to travel several days a month to serve distant churches was short-lived. I wanted to stay closer to home since Phyllis had told me she was pregnant, and the doctor had estimated that the baby would be born in June 1963.

With very little information to go on, I started looking for church members in the towns of Faxinal, Ivaiporã, and Borrazópolis. In these towns were several farm families that wanted their homes to become regular preaching points. Some stories from my two and a half years will give the reader an idea about my life of a missionary. I tried to develop a holistic approach to ministry in this area. Preaching and evangelism were my primary concerns. I also carried a footlocker of Bibles, gospel tracts, and books for both adults and children. I took garden seeds and some medical supplies, plus some educational videos on nutrition that I could project on the side of the kombi to show them at night. I had the excitement of showing the first projected films ever seen by some of the children. Their pure joy at seeing a movie the first time was worth all the effort to get there.

Forging streams created some tense moments, because I never knew if I would make it across. Ferry barges often meant long waits in good weather. In rainy weather, traffic would come to a standstill because of the problems created by trucks trying to get up or down a hill from the river. Tire chains helped, but they could not dislodge the trucks. The rule of the road was simple: you don't go until the driver ahead of you goes first. This meant that everyone pitched in to help the drivers in front of them.

I was preaching at a farm one night when a heavy downpour started. After the service, the neighbors started home under their umbrellas. My host family told me the roads would be impassable, and so they invited me to spend the night with them. I knew there was only one bed in the house, and that was for the parents. And the mattress was made of corn shucks. The children slept on the floor. I also knew that this area had a high infestation of chagas bugs, also called the kissing bug because they usually bit people's faces. These bugs transmit the chagas parasite, which targets heart muscle tissue and causes serious heart problems that may lead to death. So I was determined not to spend the night in that house. I told my host that it was important for me to be home by early the next morning. A few minutes later I was down in the mud to put on the rear tire chains. After prayer with the family, I got as fast a start as possible and did not slow down for the rain runoff humps (much larger than speed bumps) on the narrow coffee plantation road until I reached the main packed-rock road that led to the recently paved highway leading to Apucarana.

The churches in Arapongas and Apucarana were growing in number. We needed to build more space, but I did not want to spoil them by asking churches in the States to completely fund construction of the additional space for the churches. I proposed the people contribute as much as they could as well as do as much of the labor as they could to save money, and I would ask for help from our supporting churches in South Georgia. By this time inflation was running about 50 percent a year. As soon as we saved enough money to buy building materials—sand, rocks, and rebar—we would stockpile them. It was best to wait until construction started again to buy cement. I promised to raise in the States enough money to put a roof on the education building in Apucarana and the sanctuary in Arapongas. I designed the shape of the buildings and asked a civil engineer to volunteer to come up with the specifications for the construction work. It was slow going, but it inspired the people to see a better future from their own hard work.

I started youth programs in each church and led the first youth camps for the Methodist churches in the north Paraná. They camped out around a large farmhouse and did their own cooking. The owner was Dr. Breninez, the same doctor who had operated on the woman from Jaguapitá. His family lived in town so he would be close to the hospital. To get to the farmhouse required a drive on dirt roads and down a steep hill. When it rained, the road was almost impassable. Several times rain kept pastors I had counted on to speak to the youth from getting there. Either I spoke extemporaneously or I organized Bible study groups. When the youth camps grew too large for the farm, we moved them to the Rural Institute farm where the Strachans, our Canadian agricultural missionary friends, lived and worked. It was close to a major highway. Though it was not paved, access was much easier. Before our first furlough, Lloyd Strachan helped build some wood cabins for the youth to sleep in.

I was the unofficial leader of the youth camps. My scouting, MYF experience at the Valdosta Forrest Street UMC, and attendance at district and Annual Conference assemblies came in handy. Unlike at the camps in the States, I allowed no dating or couples to pair off. At that time, Brazilian dating was very controlled. Someone in the family had to be present when a girl was with a boy, even if they were engaged. Parents entrusted their young people to me. This meant I had to assume responsibility to make sure the couples were never alone or even holding hands. Anyone breaking these rules was given an additional explanation of why the rule was in place and a warning that they would be sent home if they broke the rule again.

This was an especially difficult time for older youth and university students in Brazil. After the military coup of the civilian government in 1964, repression of those who opposed government rule began in earnest. University students were imprisoned and some were tortured to get information about anyone working against the government. I tried to prepare the youth for the tough days ahead by strengthening their knowledge of the Bible and giving them theological reasons for supporting or resisting political power.

I temporarily suspended my travels in order to be at home when Susana was born in the Apucarana hospital. Dr. Faud told me, "You have a fine dark-haired baby girl." Her older siblings gladly welcomed her. Neusa was especially helpful in those days, and the women of the church demonstrated their support for Phyllis because they knew her mother could not be with us in Brazil. I was impressed with Phyllis's willingness to keep playing the Apucarana church organ almost to the end of her pregnancy. The people were glad when she returned to playing and singing again.

I was back on the road again but had to be cautious because the area was in a terrible drought. Farmers lost most of their crops, and food was getting scarce. President Kennedy's Alliance for Progress program shipped tons of food supplies to our area. I was asked to help coordinate distribution through the churches. I soon learned how easily free food could create serious morale problems in the churches when people started fighting over decisions about who should receive the food. This happened about the same time I learned from a Japanese family that President Kennedy had been killed.

The drought turned the unpaved roads into clouds of dark brown dust that reminded me of someone sneezing into a snuff container. I developed a serious case of bronchitis and was told to stop traveling until the roads were clear of the dust. This meant I was unable to serve as pastor to the people at the churches on my circuit. I decided to shift the burden to God. I prayed that he either heal me so I could serve or find someone to do the work in my place. No one came forward, but after that, I had no more problems with bronchitis.

Ivaiporã was growing very fast. The English land company was selling farmland at different stages of development and building lots in the city. I approached the director of the Ivaiporã office with a request for a donated lot on which to build a Methodist church. He offered a lot on a downhill side street, but building there would limit future development of the church. I declined his donation with the understanding that he would sell me a lot on the main road leading into town at a significantly discounted price.

While visiting with a farm family near the town, I told them about the lot, and they volunteered to donate some of peroba (Brazilian rosewood) trees still lying on their land from a few years earlier, when the trees were cut down for farming. I would have to pay for loggers to cut and haul the wood to a lumber mill for sawing and delivering the lumber to the church lot. I considered this a good deal. I also remembered the time, as a teenager at the Forrest Street Church in Valdosta, how we had gone to a church member's farm to cut down pine trees for lumber to build a new education building.

I think the sawmill cheated us out of some of the lumber, but we had enough to build an adequate sanctuary, two Sunday school rooms, and a small apartment in the back for the future pastor or caretaker. I stayed in this apartment when I was visiting until a young seminary graduate was appointed to be the pastor before I left for furlough in the States. I remember the look on his face when I drove away after bringing him to his first full-time appointment. It was an expression of dismay as if he were saying, Please don't leave me in this place. I made a down payment on a thirty-acre farm on the other side of town. The plan was to finish the payments with the 50/50 share of produce from the farm, then sell it for enough money to build a better parsonage. I found a good family to live on the farm and enjoyed supervising their farmwork. (Forty years later another young seminary graduate was appointed to the growing church in Ivaiporã. He baptized and received into church membership a beautiful young lady. A few weeks later he asked her to be his wife. I had the joy of welcoming them during the installation service when they came to be the first full-time pastors of Comunitas at the Roswell, Georgia, new Brazilian Methodist Church.)

A few miles from Ivaiporã is the village named Jardim Alegre (Happy Garden), where Plinio, a lay leader and worship leader when I was absent in Apucarana, owned a sixty-acre coffee and cattle farm. We visited it together when he met me on one of my preaching trips. I liked it so much that I said I would like to own a farm like that some day.

A few months later he showed up at the parsonage and offered to sell the farm to me at a very reasonable price. He told me the coffee crop that year would pay for the farm and the eighteen head of cattle would grow to produce additional income. I told him I would have to talk with Phyllis about spending that much money. She was not excited about buying it, but she did not veto the offer. After agreeing to buy it, I got a bad case of coffee farmers' anxiety (what if a heavy frost kills the coffee trees?). Then Plinio sent his daughter to the parsonage with a note that he resigned from all his positions in the church and wanted to withdraw from church membership. His daughter told me he was leaving his family to live with another woman. There was no divorce law in Brazil at that time, so he could not get a divorce, but he could leave and support both families. I asked to speak with him, but he avoided me for several days.

I was concerned that Plinio's decision to leave the church and his family would seriously damage the moral of the Apucarana church. I visited each family to inform them about his decision and asked them to remain faithful to the church. When I finally caught up with Plinio, he taught me a painful but valuable lesson. He said that all I talked about when I was with him was the church, never about him personally. He added that one reason he had been so active in the church was to avoid being at home with a very unhappy marriage. He said I never seemed to notice or care for his personal pain. He said it had taken him a long time to decide to leave his family and his church, and he was not going back to either. He asked that I no longer contact him and wished me well. I left him with tears, because I knew he was right about my failure in pastoral care. I decided to become the kind of pastor a lay leader needed. His penetrating words stayed with me a long time and influenced my decision to learn as much as I could about pastoral care and counseling. This eventually led me to get a doctorate in pastoral counseling.

I got the men of the church together to process what Plinio's decisions meant to them and their marriages. One of the men surprised me by asking, "Is anyone among us who has not had an affair?" I was shocked to see that I was the only one to raise my hand. Then the man said, "I suggest that we not judge Plinio too harshly. Perhaps, this is why Jesus said to the men who brought the woman caught in the act of adultery, 'Let him who is without sin cast the first stone.'" None of the church members left the church; rather, the church grew in numbers and spiritual strength after Plinio left.

I did not tell the men about the temptation I experienced with having another woman in my home. Neusa started flirting with me. In the midst of temptation I reflected on the trust and respect Phyllis and a multitude of others had given me. All this trust and respect could be lost in a few moments of sexual pleasure. Then I remembered that Neusa's father had entrusted her to my care. No matter how Neusa behaved, I would not allow myself to respond to her. To reinforce this decision, I put in place some firm boundaries about being alone with her in the house. I was relieved when a young man in the Arapongas church started paying attention to her. This led to their dating, an engagement, and my officiating at their wedding in the Arapongas church. She was a loss to Phyllis and the children, but her wedding was a blessing for me.

When I thought Neusa would soon get married, I started looking for another maid to help Phyllis with her many homemaking chores. Aparacida's mother and father agreed to let their oldest daughter work for us. She came from a large ebony-black rural African Brazilian farm family. She was accustomed to hard work and was glad to have a chance to get away from farm life and live in the city. Our family grew to love her, and we were sad to leave her behind to work for Da Bea, another church family, when we went to the States on furlough.

CHAPTER 7

More Paraná Stories

Dar um jeito ("find a way")
Quebra galho ("the one who helps break a limb
when you cannot break it by yourself")

Now that I was an absentee farmer, I had to find a sharecropper family to do the farmwork for me. A supervisor on a nearby coffee plantation recommended a hardworking three-generation Assembly of God family. At first I thought this family would not be suitable because the farmhouse had only two bedrooms. There simply was not enough room for the family, a married daughter, and the wife's parents to sleep. But they wanted the job so they could be close to their church. They told me they would build more rooms on the house and a larger coffee storage room on the side of the brick coffee drying floor if I would let them saw up the large peroba logs still lying on the ground among the coffee trees. Peroba is an extremely hard wood and resistant to insects. I agreed to let them try, but I said I didn't think they could move these four-foot high logs alone. My only expense was to buy heavy-duty nails and hardware for windows and doors.

When I returned to the farm a few weeks later, I was amazed that they had managed to cut the trees into eight-foot lengths. Then they rolled these sections downhill over four hundred feet to a makeshift sawing platform. The grandfather stood in a long hole beneath the log to saw, and his granddaughter stood on top of the log, holding the other end of the saw.

With only a chalk marker and a long crosscut saw, they had sawed a pile of perfectly straight four-foot–by-one-inch boards, which they planned to section into different size boards for construction of the extra rooms on the house. They finished most of the construction by the next time I came to the farm. I could not tell the difference between the lumber they had cut by hand and lumber cut by machinery at a sawmill.

The frost did not kill the beautiful coffee trees the first or second year I owned the farm. They produced a harvest large enough to pay me back for the purchase of the farm and other expenses. I took home my share of highland rice and bags of beans, avocados, oranges, and papayas, which I shared with a few poor families in the church. Another benefit of the farm was the two young steers that I helped butcher before hauling the meat in the kombi to Arapongas for a barbecue to help raise money for construction of the new sanctuary.

I was learning a great deal about the Brazilian farm economy from the perspective of both landowner and managing 50–50 shares with the extended farm family. I had no intention of dealing in real estate and was critical of other missionaries who were buying land they could buy so cheaply with US dollars for personal income. It was a good way to help pay the cost of building churches. I volunteered to use personal savings at a time of favorable exchange rates to buy some land that was available at a price I could afford. I was willing to accept certain risk. As a child of a sharecropper and a pastor of sharecroppers, I had seen enough of the risk they took when they had little power to determine their future.

Before returning to the States on furlough, I decided to sell the farm to the manager of a nearby coffee plantation. I did not want to suffer through the anxieties of a potential winter freeze while on furlough. I also was concerned about being able to manage the farm from wherever the bishop might appoint me after our furlough. I sold it for a good price with one-half upfront as the down payment and the remainder to be sent to me after the coffee harvest. The next winter, however, cold weather killed all the coffee trees. I had to wait three years for the buyer to finish paying me, but he kept his word the best he could.

The Methodist churches in northern Paraná were started as an extension of the Fifth Region, composed of churches in western São Paulo. The whole state of Moto Grosso was included in one big mission field. Together, they formed the Fifth Region (Annual Conference). Several pastors in my district told me that the bishop appointed pastors to serve in Paraná in Mata Grosso, but he had never visited with them or their churches. I told them that my bishop would visit us before the end of the year. They dismissed that as a joke, but I promised them he would be coming. I did not say I would be writing a letter to the bishop about my family being so far from our stateside families when our daughter Susana would be baptized. And I invited him to baptize her and offered to provide transportation for him to visit as many of the pastors and churches as he could during his visit to north Paraná. It worked. He came to baptize her in the Apucarana church, and we traveled together a week, visiting with as many pastors and church members as we could. This visit changed his impression of north Paraná. While he was there he said something about wanting to visit the pastors and churches in Motto Grosso. At that time Matto Grosso was two and a half times larger than Texas, but since then has been divided into two states. I noted his comment and often thought about how I could help make this happen.

A few months later I organized a mission team that included Bishop Sucasas, the conference secretary of missions, the secretary of evangelism, and me. My role was organizer, driver, and logistics. We met in Lins, São Paulo, and drove to the end of a paved road at the Paraná River and waited several hours in a long line for our turn to cross the river on a barge. We traveled in very hot summer weather on dust-clouded roads to the huge *fazenda* (ranch) of a wealthy Brazilian federal senator. When he heard the bishop was going to Motto Grosso, he invited him to spend some time at a private fishing house on the edge of a lagoon connected to the river.

When we got to the isolated house, we wanted to jump into the water to wash off the dust. While the other team members stripped to go swimming, I grabbed my fishing tackle and assembled my rod as fast as possible to get in a few casts before they scared off the fish. A fish grabbed my bait on the third cast and put up a fight. My butt-naked colleagues stood by me, waiting to see what kind of fish I had caught. When I lifted the large bream-sized fish out of the water they yelled, "Piranha! Piranha!" (Piranha are flesh-eating fish.) They soon had their clothes back on. I caught several more of them, but I was very careful not to let my hand get near their snapping teeth. I often wondered since that experience what would have happened if we had gone swimming.

We used some of the owner's boats to fish in the stream that ran to the river. When we reached a patch of lily pads in the middle of the river, I started catching dorados, which I later learned from *Field and Stream* magazine are the most fighting freshwater fish in the world. I lost most of them when they broke my twelve-pound-test fishing line. We cleaned some fish I caught to cook for supper. One of my colleagues thought the piranha he was scaling was completely dead because it had been lying in the bottom of the boat several hours, but he found out how long piranhas can live out of the water when the fish took a chunk of flesh out of his thumb.

The next day we traveled to Villa Gloria ("Glory town") for the bishop to preach in the church. The town reminded me of the movie version of Dodge City. While we were unloading at the first cowboy-style inn we saw, the pastor of the church came running to tell us he had made reservations for us at a *pensao* (inn) facing the town plaza. We re-packed the suitcases and followed him as he walked in the street. At first I was glad we had changed because this place looked much cleaner than the first place. The beds looked adequate. And a delicious dinner was waiting for us after we bathed. The waitresses were dressed rather sensuously (most restaurants in Brazil at that time had waiters).

After taking all this in, one of my colleagues leaned and whispered, "Do you know where we are staying tonight?" We were in a whorehouse. Our beautiful waitress asked us where we were from and what we did. She almost dropped a plate when she heard we were Methodist preachers. She responded that she used to be a *crente* (believer). Upon hearing this "used to be," the bishop called her over and put his arm around her and loving talked with her about becoming a believer again. She left the table with tears in her eyes.

We had to hurry to get the bishop to church on time. The rustic construction reminded me of the early days of sawdust floors and hard benches in the early days of the Forrest Street church back home. But I was too tired and anxious about spending my first night in a whorehouse to pay much attention to the sermon. The dim light from the lanterns hanging on the walls made the blankets on the floor in the back of the church, which were there for children, looked mighty inviting to me. As soon as we arrived at the church, the people started telling the bishop about the problems they had with their pastor and wanted him to send a replacement. Instead of dealing with the problem, the bishop preached until everyone was worn out and ready to go home. As we got out of the kombi to go to our rooms, I kidded two colleagues that I would be checking on them during the night to make sure they were behaving. Of course, they asked who would be checking on me.

As soon as breakfast was over the next morning, I wanted to get out of town as fast as possible. When I took my suitcase to the kombi, I was dismayed to see a crowd of men gathered in front of the bar on the other side of the plaza. They were there to witness a group of Methodist preachers leave Villa Gloria's whorehouse. Word had gotten out and they came by foot, horseback, wagons, and trucks to see for themselves. I was chagrined and angry with the pastor for putting us in this situation. Getting out of Dodge as fast as possible seemed to be the wisest thing to do, but the bishop was in no hurry. He insisted on stopping at the bar where the crowd stood so he could buy some bottled water. After he got the water, he said he needed to express his appreciation for the kind hospitality of the lady (madam) who owned the place where we stayed. I begged him to leave, but he insisted on walking back across the plaza to see her.

As I drove around to pick him up, the other men and I decided he was completely naive about the whorehouse and that we should inform him.

The others choose me to tell him, because they knew the bishop liked me. When I did, he said, "Jesus was right. Even the prostitutes shall enter the kingdom of heaven before the people who are only outwardly religious persons." I do not know if the pastor was ignorant about the main purpose of the motel where he reserved rooms for us, or if he wanted to embarrass the bishop for appointing him to Villa Gloria. I wondered why his people were so angry with him.

Several miles down the road, after breaking the news to the bishop about spending a night in a whorehouse, a huge hornet-like insect (about twice the size) bounced off my window vent and into my lap and stung me on the inside of my upper thigh. I stopped to get the insect out of the vehicle. My colleagues said the name of the insect and warned me that I would likely be unable to walk for several days. I quickly walked to the back of the kombi and pulled out my tackle box to get the snakebite kit. I dropped my pants, made an X cut with the razor, and extracted as much of the poison from the sting as I could. They were amazed I had only a little discomfort from the insect sting in the days that followed.

Our final stop, and the farthest west we traveled, was a town on the border with Paraguay. I asked the bishop not to preach too long Saturday night, because we had to travel over two hundred miles afterward to reach the larger town of Campo Grande for him to preach on Sunday morning. About forty miles down the road, I heard some noise coming from the motor in the back of microkombi. I turned around to try to get back to town before the motor quit. Suddenly, we heard a loud noise and the motor stopped. I coasted to the side of the road that ran parallel with the border of Paraguay. Illegal contraband trade made this a very dangerous place to be at night. People were known to shoot first and ask questions later. I had a rifle with me, but that was no match for high-caliber automatic weapons. The bishop said for me not to worry, because God had brought us here and would take care of us. We spread out on the seats to try to sleep, but I was too worried to sleep. And also the different pitches in the snoring of my colleagues made sleep impossible for me.

I became more anxious a couple of hours later when I saw lights in my rearview mirror. That meant either help or trouble. The truck driver stopped to tell us we shouldn't be out here at night. When we explained our predicament, he backed his truck in front of the kombi and connected some chains so he could pull us into town. The most harrowing miles I have ever traveled behind a steering wheel were those forty miles on high alert to keep the right tension on the chains as the truck driver dogged potholes and ensure our vehicle did not crash into the back of the truck or be jerked too hard.

The truck driver pulled us into town and unchained our vehicle outside a Volkswagen dealership. As daylight appeared, a policeman stopped to ask what we were doing there. He told us the owner of the dealership lived a couple of blocks away. Though it was Sunday morning, I awakened him. He said he would get his mechanic to take out my motor and install a new one if we could pay for the motor and the labor. By faith and with an idea I told him to do it.

While the new motor was being installed, we walked to the church parsonage. The pastor's wife prepared breakfast for us. I reminded the pastor about our conversation the day before when he said that an American couple lived in town, and the wife had told him that her brother was a Methodist preacher who had been a delegate to the General Conference. I asked him to take the bishop and me to meet them. After the acquaintance process was over, I told them about our predicament and asked if they would write a check, which we would consider a loan, to cover the cost of replacing my motor. The Volkswagen dealer was surprised that I had arranged to pay him on a Sunday morning. And he thought he would make some extra money by keeping my old motor, but I removed the backseat, rearranged the suitcases, and asked the mechanic to put the motor inside the kombi. I put the seat on top of it. We were on the road again before noon that day. We missed the Sunday morning Sunday school service, but we were back on schedule for the evening service.

When I returned to Apucarana, I sent a letter to Mac in São Paulo, asking him to send the money to the Campo Grande family that loaned us the money to buy the new motor. Then I took the damaged motor to an auto parts store and negotiated an agreement for us to have the motor repaired and exchanged to pay for the new motor.

The Mata Grosso trip was a huge success. The bishop expressed his appreciation, and after over two weeks away from home, I was happy to see Phyllis and the children again. The children were in awe of a sixteen-foot boa constrictor skin that a pastor's son gave me.

I always missed Phyllis and the children when I was away from home. Interestingly, the children no longer responded in English when we spoke to them. They had completely shifted to Portuguese, though the younger ones sometimes spoke some Japanese with the next-door Japanese children or Polish with the children across the street. Phyllis homeschooled Randy after lunch. In the mornings he went to a nearby Brazilian school. On our first visit to the school on parents night, we found that Randy had made a name for himself by putting the nun who taught the required religion class in her place. The nun told the children they had to go to a Catholic church and make their confession to a priest during Holy Week. If they did not go, they would go to hell. The teachers said Randy politely raised his hand and asked permission to say something. He told the nun there was something she needed to know. He said, "God loves children and he does not send them to hell." The other teachers were really proud of Randy. They had wanted to tell the nun what Randy told her, but they were afraid of losing their jobs if they did.

At the time we lived in Apucarana there were about twenty official religious holidays. Phyllis and I could never keep up with them. Randy often returned home a short time after leaving for school to tell us there was no school that day because it was some saint's day. After we returned to the States, Randy overheard us talking about the many religious holidays. He admitted that he had invented most of those saint's days to get out of school.

When Ruth turned five, we took her to the well-equipped city kindergarten. But we had to withdraw her after she came home crying several days because the teachers kept forcing her to do tiny cursive handwriting. Phyllis was only starting to teach her basic writing. Ruth wanted to learn and was always a good student, but the muscles in her fingers were not developed enough for small finger movements. As a result, Phyllis homeschooled Ruth until we returned to the States.

Walter enjoyed playing on our front porch with a neighbor boy. One hot day they took off their clothes and were surprised to hear applause at the front gate. (Instead of ringing a doorbell, Brazilians announced their presence by clapping at the front gate.) Realizing it was too late to run or put his clothes back on, Walter stood up, put his hands on his hips as he faced the visitors, and proudly said, "I'm butt naked and I'm not a bit ashamed." When my district superintendent and another pastor came to the parsonage, I thought they would never stop laughing about this. I was proud of Walter for defending his dignity the best way he knew how.

Susana first words were in Portuguese. Even when she understood what we said in English, she responded in Portuguese. We invited a wealthy coffee plantation owner and his wife to dinner one evening. He learned to speak English in Hungary, his home country. His father had been a minister of agriculture there. When the Soviets took over his country after World War II, he emigrated to Brazil. In fifteen years he went from washing pots and pans in a restaurant to owning a large coffee plantation near Apucarana. When Phyllis put a pumpkin pie on the table for desert, Susana pointed from her highchair and said, "Coco!" ("crap"). Phyllis and I were embarrassed, but the couple laughed and said she must be smart because she was learning the most important words first.

One of the most interesting things about being a missionary in Brazil was the practice of hospitality. When we traveled to major cities, we stayed at the homes of other missionary families. When they traveled our way, they stayed with us. Many times we did not know they were coming. Our children gave up their beds without complaining to accommodate guests. We also had US bishops and other dignitaries stay in our home. We called them "visiting firemen" because there are two kinds of firemen: one that puts out fires with their negativity and another that builds fires with their positive attitudes and encouraging words. Bishop Hendley and his wife from the Florida Annual Conference were the second kind. At that time he was the bishop of my brother Ed and brother-in-law Jim. Bishop and Mrs. Hendley commented about beautiful things that we hardly noticed.

Another VIP was Dr. Glen Burton, the famous grass geneticist from Tifton, Georgia. He was the creator of costal Bermuda grasses and dozens of other grasses for lawns and golf courses. Also he was a very active layman in our major supporting church. He was visiting Brazil to be a major speaker at an International Grasslands Conference and planned to spend three days with us so he could learn what we were doing and take pictures of our missionary work. We stopped at many farms where I held home worship services.

We stopped to see one family I had not seen for almost a year. The young couple greeted us, but I could clearly see that something was wrong. I asked about their child who had been miraculously healed by prayer. About a year earlier, when their baby was born, the doctor said the child had a rare and serious genetic defect and would not survive. He said it would be best to let the child die as soon as possible. Instead of watching their child die while doing nothing to help save him, they implored me to take them about ninety miles to his extended family farm. He firmly believed the prayers of his godly parents would cure the child. We arrived after midnight. The parents, extended families, and neighbors got out of bed to have a prayer meeting for the child. The child responded in what appeared to be a miracle. After breakfast the next morning I took them back home.

This visit with Dr. Burton was the first time I had seen them since then. I translated the story they told me about their child screaming day and night for several months until it finally died. As the bones of the child grew larger, the skin did not stretch to match the bone growth. Evidently this was the genetic defect the doctor had diagnosed at birth. The child's suffering had devastated them. Their faith was in crisis over what looked like a miracle but had turned into a nightmare. As a Christian geneticist, Dr. Burton understood their pain and did all he could to comfort them in their suffering.

The thing that impressed Dr. Burton the most was Phyllis's asking for his shoes when we returned late from traveling through the country. She cleaned them while we ate supper and rushed to church for him to speak while I interpreted for him. I was so tired that I started speaking to him in Portuguese and to the people in English. When he returned to the States, he spoke in many churches about his trip and told stories about his time with us while illustrating them with a slideshow.

Another VIP was my mother. I thought about my mother doing what some of the parents of our missionary colleagues had done—visit Brazil. After writing about this to my sister Ruth, she contacted the rest of the family and asked for everyone to pitch in and pay for her trip. Mother arrived in Rio de Janiero after a four-stop trip from Miami. We spent the first night with missionary friends in São Paulo and arrived home tired but happy the next day. She had never seen Susana, and four years had passed since she last saw the other three children. Her first disappointment was that they could understand what she said in English but would only respond to her in Portuguese. This meant Phyllis or I had to translate for them. Older missionaries had suggested we not force the children to speak English, but we should speak to them in English, unless we were around Brazilians.

In spite of the language barrier, Mom was a wonderful guest. She and Phyllis got along as good friends. The women of the church held some special social meetings for her. To show her more of the country, I planned a vacation trip to Sete Quedas (Seven Falls) and Iguazu Falls along the southern border of Paraguay and Paraná. We spend the first night in Campo Morano with the Coopers who had many years of experience as missionaries in Brazil. Mom was happy to speak English with someone besides Phyllis and me.

We traveled over dusty roads most of the next day and spent the night in a cowboy-style motel at Sete Quedas. The next morning we saw the impressive sight of the falls. One of the park workers showed me a rope-and-pulley system with a small board for a seat that they had installed a few days earlier to reach a section of flat rock in the middle of the river where no one had previously been able to go. He said he would pull me across if I wanted to go. Phyllis and Mom didn't want me to go, because they knew that a fall would mean certain death. I went anyway and took some beautiful pictures from the best view of the falls. The kids were either proud of me or scared, because they gave me big hugs when I returned. I'm glad I went because those beautiful falls no longer exist. The waters of the huge Iguazu hydroelectric dam at Iquacu now have completely submerged the falls.

After lunch we traveled close to the Argentine border toward Iqauzu Falls. Everything went well until we came to a fork in the road that had no signs to indicate which direction to take. Road maps were not common in Brazil at that time, so I had to guess which road to take. After traveling some distance, I noticed the road seemed to get narrower. I wondered if I had made the wrong choice when we entered an area where virgin forest had not been cleared. When we came to a junction two hours later, I stopped to ask directions at a bar. The owner confirmed that I had taken the wrong road at the fork in the road. He pointed toward a narrow side road and said we could use it to return to the highway, but the road was very hilly. It started raining when I got back in the kombi, and I knew rain meant trouble on those hills. I stopped to put chains on the two back tires. While putting them on, a young man who spoke more Polish than Portuguese, asked if he could ride with us. I agreed to take him if he would help push if we got stuck. When we arrived at his destination at the bottom of a hill, I told him I would only slow down and he would have to jump out, because I needed the momentum to get up the hill. He managed to keep his balance in the mud when he jumped. In the rearview mirror I saw he had landed on his feet, but he was waving wildly to let me know he had left his umbrella behind. Without stopping, I put it out my window and stuck it in the mud.

The road got narrower the farther we traveled. The first settlers were still clearing the virgin forest, and they were living in crude cabins with thatched roofs. My fear was that we would meet a truck on the narrow road, but instead we came to a stop behind a truck stuck in the mud in the middle of an up grade. Deep ditches were on both sides. I couldn't go forward and I couldn't turn around. It was getting late in the day. I wondered if we would have to spend the night inside the kombi with mosquitoes and no telling what kind of people wandering around us. Mom was clearly worried. Phyllis was busy keeping the children calm so they would not upset me. I got out to find out what the truck driver and his assistant thought about the situation. They were worried as they looked at the men gathered on the land on both sides of the road to stare at the stuck vehicles, fearing they might steal their cargo.

I returned to the kombi to share what I learned with Phyllis and Mom. As we sat in silence, I started thinking about the Brazilian expressions *dar um jeito* ("make a way") and *quebra galho* ("find someone to help"). I noticed the truck was in the middle of the road with five to six feet on each side before the road dropped off into the ditches. If the truck could be pushed three to four feet to the right, we might have enough room to get past the truck. I shared my predicament of having a family stuck there for the night with the truck driver and my idea and asked if he would allow his truck to be moved to one side. Then I asked him how much he wanted for a case of beer to give to the bystanders in exchange for their muscle power. The driver okayed the idea, and asked the crowd for their help.

With a great deal of excitement about getting free beer, the men got some ropes and poles to move the truck. Once they slid the truck enough to one side, everyone got out of the kombi except me. Some men used poles to keep my vehicle from slipping into the ditch while others pulled with ropes and pushed from behind. I put a little pressure on the gas pedal to turn the wheels forward as we slowly passed the truck. After paying for the beer and thanking the truck drivers, we were on our way again.

When Mom asked me how I got them to do what they did, I told her about buying the beer. She had never allowed alcoholic beverages in the house when I was growing up, because dad had a drinking problem before he was converted. She said, "Son, you did the right thing."

Soon after nightfall we reached the main highway at a small village. I stopped at a Dodge City–style bar-restaurant-motel that had only one Jeep outside along with several horses. The men at the bar stopped drinking to take in the sight of an American family on a rainy night in their town. The owners cooked us a delicious meal while we settled into five small one-person-cot bedrooms. We finally had a toilet and a place to clean up in the community bath at the end of the hall. Each person had a room, except Susana, who slept with Phyllis, and Walter, who slept with me. I was too tired to be uncomfortable with Walter.

The rain stopped during the night and the sun soon dried out the roads enough for us to travel the next day to the small town of Iguaçu. After lunch we traveled very slowly through clouds of large, beautiful blue butterflies on the forest reserve road that led to the large pink hotel at the Iguaçu Falls. We did not have reservations, but we lucked out when the manager of the hotel agreed to let us sleep in the unused section of the servant's quarters at a reduced rate. The next two days we hiked and marveled at the sounds and beauty of the falls. I quickly agreed with those who listed it as one of the Seven Wonders of the World. (The movie *Mission* is a good way to see some of the beauty of the Iguaçu Falls without going there.) The kids were amused at the birds flying through the falls to their nest behind the water. They said, "Look! These birds don't need to take a bath at night." Mom overheard a couple speaking English and soon developed a friendship with them.

We made our way home through Curitiba and traveled north on the recently completed Alliance for Progress highway to Apucarana. On the way, we stopped to see Villa Velho, huge rock formations formed eons ago by cascading water falls like Sete Quedas.

I drove back to Rio with Mom so she could catch her plane home. She was a sight going through the airport with a huge cow horn slung over her shoulder. It was a souvenir that she was taking to give to Jim Rowan, Ruth's husband and her favorite son-in-law.

I took care of some business on the way back through São Paulo. I was looking forward to seeing my family when I saw a couple resting on the side of the road next to a large cross. I immediately recalled reading in the newspapers and hearing people talk about the man carrying a cross from north Paraná to the Catholic shrine of Nossa Senhora de Aparecida, situated between São Paulo and Rio, a distance of over five hundred miles. Though I was excited about getting close to home to see my family, I turned around and stopped on the shoulder where the couple was resting. Crowds usually gathered as they passed through populated areas. People gladly provided food and lodging for these holy pilgrims. I wanted to learn more about them and why they were motivated to carry a cross so far. The man told me he had made a *promessa* ("promise" or "vow") to God that he would carry the cross to Aparecida if God would do something special for him. He would not say what that was, but he said God had done it. Now he was keeping his vow. I attempted to convince him of God's grace through the sacrifice of Jesus on the cross, which relieves us from the need to sacrifice ourselves. When I realized my words had no effect on him, I asked his wife why she was making this journey. She said, "To keep this fool from killing himself." Before leaving them, I asked if I could see how heavy his cross was to carry. He warned me that I might be able to lift it and insisted that I use his shoulder pad to keep the six-by-six-inch beam of peroba wood from cutting into my shoulder. I got my shoulder under the crossbeam and tried to lift it. As quickly as possible, I sat it down. Here I was, at age thirty-one, unable to stand up straight while lifting that heavy cross, but a man in his midfifties was carrying it over five hundred miles to fulfill a vow. Weeks later I read in the newspaper about the big celebration when the couple arrived in the city of Aparecida.

Phyllis and I had some wonderful missionary friends. They did not replace our families in the States, but they did fill in for them while we lived in Brazil. The children called the adults aunts and uncles and continued doing this after we returned to the States. We were fortunate to have a

Canadian agriculture missionary couple as our closest English-speaking friends. Lloyd and Carol Strachan and their three children lived at the rural institute about an hour north of us. Lloyd was a great help to my work with the farmers. We were concerned about the farmers not being able to feed their cattle during the dry season. We finally came up with an idea about how to help them develop pastures that would survive the cold weather. One day Lloyd took all but the front seat out of his kombi before leaving home to pick me up. We traveled several hours to the agriculture grassland experiment station in São Paulo. He had arranged with the manager of the experiment station to give us a load of Dr. Burton's costal Bermuda forage grass plant. The guards at the state border thought it was a strange cargo, but they let us pass through. The next year this grass had spread enough for me to take packets of it for distribution to the farms of our Methodist families. (When I returned to north Paraná forty years later, I saw costal Bermuda had spread over the whole countryside and into the cities, but I kept quiet about who was responsible. Good intentions do not always produce good results. But the cattle liked it.)

Lloyd presented me with an ethical problem one day. He said he had bought a donkey for one of his workers to use so they could plant soybeans and other legumes he was experimenting with. He said the donkey had the habit of working really hard about an hour and then completely stopped pulling the plow. No matter what the workers did to the donkey, he refused to do anything except go back to the pen. Lloyd said he had decided to sell the donkey, but he couldn't decide if he should tell the buyer about the donkey's work habit. I told him I had known a lot of full-time human jackasses, but I had never met a one-hour jackass. So I couldn't help him.

I had a great relationship with the Brazilian pastors. We did some effective evangelism work. In my third year, I reported ninety new members, most of them on profession of faith. We also had a lot of fun teasing and joking when we were together. When E. Stanley Jones came to Brazil to hold an ashram with the Brazilian pastors, I invited four pastors from my district to go with me. The first one arrived before daylight. After eating breakfast we started our nine-hour trip to Campo de Jordan, a retreat center in the mountains of São Paulo. An hour later we arrived in Londrina, where we picked up two more pastors. Then we stopped at Ourinhos, a border town in São Paulo, to pick up Pastor Antonio.

We got out of the kombi to greet his family and drink some water. I noticed he had not shaved or dressed to travel. When I asked for his suitcase, he announced he was not going with us. We tried to change his mind, but we couldn't convince him. I asked his wife for a glass of water and followed her to the kitchen. She told me she was worried about him because he was so discouraged from dealing with problems in the church. He was thinking about resigning. When I saw tears running down her cheeks, I had an idea. I asked her to pack her husband's suitcase. She warned me that he was a very stubborn man. If he said he was not going, he was not going. I called my two colleagues into the kitchen and asked them to help me forcibly take Antonio with us, even carry him into the kombi.

When we returned to the living room, I asked Antonio again to come with us. When he said he wouldn't, I told him that we were determined to take him with us whether he wanted to go or not. When he adamantly refused, we grabbed him. He yelled, "I can't go because I don't have enough money to pay for the retreat." My colleagues dropped him into the chair, but I yelled for them to take him anyway. I asked his wife where the church treasurer lived or worked. She told me how to find him at his downtown shop. So I told the others to haul Antonio into the kombi. The children were alarmed at seeing their father struggling against his colleagues, and their mother looked concerned, but she assured them that their Antonio was not being hurt.

We went to the treasurer's downtown shop. I introduced myself and convinced him to advance enough money to pay for the expenses of their pastor.

When we returned to the parsonage, the wife was standing on the porch with the children gathered around her and Antonio's packed bag beside her. I reassured them we would take good care of him and that we were doing what was best for him. We returned to the highway with a very angry hostage who refused to say a word to us. We tried reasoning and kidding with him, but after no response, we started singing. He had a great voice and often led the singing at our district meetings. When we stopped for gas and refreshments, I kept an eye on him to make sure he didn't try to get away. When he willingly returned to the kombi I asked him to sit up front with me. The other pastors soon went to sleep. After I apologized for forcibly taking him with us and expressed empathy for the tough times he was going through at his church, he started talking about the conflicts in the church that had been going on for years and how he was tired of dealing with them. When we arrived at the retreat center, I decided it was time to release him to the experience of being with E. Stanley Jones.

Antonio sat in the back of the room during most of the retreat. But on the last night I heard a familiar singing voice. Antonio's. Something important had happened to him. As we packed up the next morning, he was noticeably different. He was happy and wouldn't quit singing when we quit. He told us about confessing in his small group that he realized how he was responsible for many of the problems that he blamed on his people. As the group prayed for him, he had a new baptism of the Holy Spirit that transformed his life. When we arrived at his home, his family greeted us and hugged and kissed him. I reintroduced Antonio to his wife as her newly transformed and happy husband. Their joy over the change in his life and the hugs and expressions of appreciation they gave me were my reward for taking the huge risk of forcibly taking him to the ashram.

Perhaps the most important thing I did during my first term of service in Brazil was befriending pastors and leading them in the creation of the new Paraná–Santa Catarina Annual Conference (Sixth Region) of the Methodist Church of Brazil. I talked with the pastors in north Paraná about the need for better episcopal oversight of the growing number of churches. I told them that the new paved highway from Apucarana to the capital city of Curitiba, and paid for by the US-Brazil Alliance of

Progress, cut travel time between the eastern and western parts of Paraná from nine to twelve hours to five hours. This made it possible to combine the Methodist churches of the Fifth Region in the northwestern part of the state with the ones of the Second Region in the southeastern section. The original highways running north and south in Brazil made it easier to create the Second Region with churches in Rio Grande do Sul, Santa Catarina, and southeastern Paraná. I invited a kombi load of pastors to go with me as a delegation to an informal meeting in Curitiba, with pastors in the Second Region of Paraná to discuss the possibility of petitioning the General Conference, meeting in Rio in a few months, to create a Sixth Region out of Paraná and Santa Catarina. The major decision of that General Conference was the creation of our new region. Wilbur Smith, the son of US missionaries in the state of Rio Grande do Sul, was elected to be our first bishop.

We had many wonderful experiences as Brazilian missionaries from 1961 to 1965. All of our experiences were not happy ones. We faced conflicts, illnesses, suffering, and death. The World Health Organization was trying to inoculate people against smallpox, but people were still being deformed or dying from the disease. One Sunday morning I tried to rush a newly born baby to a hospital in Londrina because electrical power was disconnected to safely allow workmen to install new power lines to the city. The baby needed an incubator to survive. We did not make it in time.

Phyllis had a miscarriage after a problem pregnancy. Caring for the children because the maid was visiting her family and leading Sunday school and worship left little time to give much moral support to Phyllis in the hospital. Neither did I have time to do my own grieving. Before daylight that morning, the doctor put the fetus in a clear glass jar, placed it in my hand, and said, "You should take this to the cemetery to have it buried." I awakened the disgruntled cemetery custodian who then led me to the deceased children's section of the cemetery. He dug a hole and asked me to drop the jar with my dead baby in the bottom so he could cover it. I felt so alone, angry, and sad. I must have been traumatized, but I quickly put away my feelings in order to do what had to be done that Sunday. But

God did not let me get away with burying the grief over the death of my child inside of me. A few nights later I had a long dream about the death of the baby and being at a church funeral service with my family with me in the front row. When I awakened, my pillow was soaking wet.

Not all laypersons made good leaders. I thought Benedito would be a good treasurer because he was a bookkeeper. Other members of the nominating committee resisted. I asked them why he shouldn't be treasurer. They responded that he did not sing in church, and they did not trust any Christian who did not at least try to sing. I had seen many church members in the States not sing in church, so I insisted on nominated him anyway. A year later he left the church and embezzled the money.

As we approached the end of 1965, the time for our four years in north Paraná was almost over. I was sad to leave a place that meant so much to me, but I felt good about leaving the churches strong enough to be financially self-supporting and with trained lay leadership in place. Bishop Sucasas appointed a pastor to serve the new Ivaiporã charge before I left. Arapongas finished construction of a new sanctuary. Apucarana completed a new educational building. The parsonage was paid for, and the new pastor had a telephone and a kombi waiting to make his work easier. We left in time to get to Phyllis's home for Christmas; eleven years had passed since she had been there for Christmas. She looked forward to seeing snow again. The children were excited at the possibility of seeing it for the first time.

> Christmas is the keeping place for memories of our innocence.
>
> —Joan Mills

CHAPTER 8

Extended Stateside Furlough December 20, 1065—July 15, 1967

Our life stories are who we are. They are our identity. A life story is not, however, an objective account. A life story is a carefully shaped narrative that is replete with strategic forgetting and skillfully spun meanings.

—Jonathan Gottschall, The Storytelling Animal

We arrived at Phyllis's home in Pennsylvania in time for our children to see their first white Christmas. We purchased a vehicle for travel to Frostproof, Florida, for a big reunion with my mother and siblings and their families. My brother Ed was pastor of the newly constructed Methodist church in Frostproof. Randy, my oldest brother, and Pauline, my oldest sister, and their families also lived in the same town. They had a big reception for us at the church and a family reunion for the Dinkins extended family. Our children were wide-eyed at seeing so many relatives but closed mouths because they were not accustomed to talking in English, though they understood it.

One of the major responsibilities of a missionary on furlough is to speak about missions at supporting churches and other churches interested in missions. After speaking in my home church and several others around Valdosta, I left Phyllis and the children with my mother and flew to Memphis for a week of speaking engagements in the Jackson UMC District. Sunday evening a severe cold front with rain and snow left a sheet of ice on everything. Closed roads meant cancelation of my engagements for the remainder of the week. My host told me to stay in the hotel in Jackson and read the books I brought with me. I told him I had a better plan if he could get me to the airport so that I could fly back to Atlanta to look for a house for my family. With a little slipping and sliding on I-40, we made it to the Memphis airport. I caught one of the last flights to leave before the airport closed.

I looked for a real estate agent near Emory University as soon as I got to Atlanta. I soon found one, and he helped me find a house within two miles of the university. The next morning I drove to Valdosta, but stopped at a telephone both on the outskirts to call Phyllis and wish her a happy thirty-fourth birthday. She assumed I was calling from Tennessee. After a long conversation, I asked what she wanted for her birthday. She said, "If I could have what I really want, it would be to have you with me." So I told her, "I'll be there in a few minutes." When I arrived, she alternated between hugging me and punching me for fooling her with a faux long-distance call. The kids were surprised and excited that I got home to help celebrate mom's birthday. My mother was glad to have me there, because she needed help to cover the water pipes under the house since the freezing weather had reached the area.

It was crazy to buy a house in Atlanta instead of renting a place to live. We had no furniture and planned to return to Brazil in a year. With four children and Phyllis expecting another child in six months, house payments were cheaper than rent in an area close to a good school. The policy at that time was that missionaries would have a year of furlough for every five years of service on the field. The year in the States was intended to be used for rest and speaking engagements where needed. Since most speaking engagements were on weekends, I decided to enroll in the master's of pastoral counseling at Columbia Theological Seminary in Decatur. The seminary was only three miles away. I found the classes to be stimulating, and the library was a wonderful place to study. I enjoyed being a student again after several years of reading books but having no one to discuss my reading with.

One of the requirements for the degree was to pass the biblical language exam. I graduated with a BD (MA) from Emory without a biblical language course, but there was no way around it at Columbia, so I spent most of the summer of 1966 studying Greek. I managed to squeak by the final exam, but I failed to develop a working knowledge of the language because I did not follow up with any New Testament courses that used Greek.

Meanwhile, we were adjusting to life in the States. On many weekends the family went with me when I preached and talked about the churches in Brazil. Randy and Ruth soon were communicating in English at school and ceased talking with Phyllis and me in Portuguese. Walter was not saying much; he seemed confused about the big changes in his life. He was only four months old when we went to Brazil. His primary language was Portuguese. He understood English and shifted to English when he went from homeschooling with his mother to a public school kindergarten in January 1966. Phyllis was relieved to have the three older children in public school before giving birth to our fifth child on June 6.

Our family was happy to be in the States on furlough. I concluded that if I could choose a vocation it would be a missionary on furlough. I enjoyed speaking at the Valdosta District Conference and visiting in the Valdosta District churches. They had faithfully supported us by paying our salary and providing extra funds for the things we needed in our work in Brazil. We knew they were praying for us. I distributed to the members hundreds of silk Bible page markers, made by a young couple in Apucarana. The markers had an outline map of Brazil centered with praying hands and an inscription: Pray for the Dinkinses in Brazil.

In 1966, people's major concern was the Vietnam War. The most frequent question that came up during the Q&A time after my presentations was,

What do the Brazilians think about the Vietnam War? I said they didn't understand why North Americans felt they should travel thousands of miles to fight a war in a foreign country that had not attacked the United States. I dreaded the usual follow-up question, because so many Americans had husbands and sons fighting in Vietnam. I responded cautiously but honestly. I said that the war was not winnable no matter how many troops fought there or how many bombs were dropped because we were fighting poor people on their soil who want to make a decent living in their own country. The wealthiest Vietnamese landowners lived in Saigon but owned most of the land. Whatever crops were grown, 75 percent was taken by the landlords. The peasant sharecroppers kept only 25 percent to care for their families.

In Brazil, I was the pastor of many poor people, so I knew how they think. They are not concerned with ideology, such as communism or democracy. They care about justice for their hard work. The North Vietnamese promised the peasant farmers in Vietnam that they could can keep 60 percent of their crops if they would join the struggle against the North Americans, just as they did against French colonialism a decade earlier.

I told the people in the Georgia churches to prepare for a long, costly, unwinnable war. I told them I could be wrong, and what I said might cause them pain, but I had to respond as honestly as I could.

Randy and Ruth did well in school. Walter started first grade but said very little about school. His teacher called before Thanksgiving to tell us he was not learning the basics of reading. We told her about his five years in Brazil and suggested she give him some time to adjust to learning in English. I assured her that he would catch up, and I asked her to call me if he fell further behind. I talked with Walter and asked him to try harder with his reading. The teacher called again in February to report that his reading had not progressed. She wanted permission to have him tested to see if he had a learning disability. I became very concerned and started feeling guilty for subjecting him to the multicultural neighborhood in Apucarana with two languages at home and Japanese and Polish playmates in the neighborhood.

Waiting time for Walter to learn to read was over. I asked the teacher to give us a few days to think about having him tested. I told Phyllis about the teacher's concerns, and she said that she hadn't detected any problems when she was teaching Walter the English Calvert courses when he was four and five. We agreed I should have a talk with Walter about his school responsibilities.

That night, while Phyllis was a choir practice, Walter and I were bouncing on the bed. We knew this was a prohibited activity, but the one who prohibited it was at choir practice. After a while, Walter and I collapsed on the bed. I decided this was the best time to talk with him about school. I started by reminding him that his parents and his older siblings had learned to read English and asked him why he wasn't learning to read English? He said, "Because I don't want to learn to read in English. I want to wait until we return to Brazil so I can learn to read Portuguese. When I see all those books you have in English, I don't want to have to read them."

I was stunned by his reasoning but tried to encourage him by saying he could choose which ones he wanted to read once he learned English. His mother was not happy when I told her what I had learned. I was asleep before she arrived home. His teacher was not impressed with this new information, but she agreed to follow my suggestion that she show some interest about his life in Brazil to see if that would motivate him. I promised to discipline him if he failed to try to learn.

During dinner the next evening, I asked Walter about his day in school. He said, "Not much happened."

I pushed a little harder and asked if the teacher had talked with him.

He said, "Oh, she asked me to teach the class something in Portuguese."

I was curious about what he taught them, so I asked, "What did you say?"

"I taught them to say thank you."

I asked what Portuguese words he used.

He said, "Arigato."

I reminded him that word was Japanese, not Portuguese.

He said, "Oh, I know the difference, Dad. But those kids think they are smarter than me because they are learning to read English, but they don't even know the difference between Japanese and Portuguese."

I knew then that he was more Brazilian than North American because he loved to tease and pull tricks on others. With encouragement and threats of punishment, Walter soon caught up with his classmates.

I wanted to attend the South Georgia Annual Conference the second week of June, but I didn't think I could leave Phyllis and the children only a week after Paul's birth. Phyllis's mother had come to help, but she didn't want to drive in Atlanta. Another Brazilian missionary family on furlough lived about a mile from us. D. A. Riley was working on his PhD at Emory, and his wife and daughters agreed to help Phyllis's mother care for the family while I went to St. Simon's Island.

This was a fortunate decision, because at the conference I told Bill Hinson, a former Brazilian missionary, that I wished I could complete a master's in pastoral counseling before returning to Brazil. He said, "Why don't you send a request to the Mission Board field secretary that you be granted a six-month extension to give you time to finish the degree."

I hadn't though of making such a request. And much to my joy and Phyllis's relief, permission was granted. Phyllis wanted Paul to grow a little more before we took him to Brazil. She also wanted the older children to get as much education as possible at the Sagamore Hills Elementary School.

Dr. Tom McDill was my mentor and major professor in pastoral counseling at Columbia. He had an amazing memory. When I met with him to be examined on the assigned books in directed studies, he recalled not only quotes but also the page numbers where the quotes and specific ideas could be found. He took a liking to me because he had once been a counselor for a woman from Brazil. When I told him about having an extra six months in the States, he recommended I take a unit of clinical pastoral education (CPE) at the Georgia Baptist Hospital. He chose Gus Verdery to be my CPE mentor. My large family background and transcultural experiences came in good for the give and take of CPE. I grew emotionally and intellectually from the three months of interpersonal contact with supervisors, peers, patients, and hospital personnel. I took one seminary class that was intellectually stimulating, but no matter how much I prepared, the professor did not appreciate my assertive participation in class. I read more on the subjects we discussed than my colleagues, but he seemed defensive every time I spoke up in class and gave me a lower grade than others. I never figured out why he took offense. He was not the first person who didn't like me for some reason.

I loved the philosophy of Christian education class. The professor used a dialogical pedagogy, with the students choosing a philosopher and presenting the main educational position and defending it in class. I chose Martin Buber and presented his "I and thou" approach to teaching, counseling, and other interpersonal relationships. Buber became very influential in my thinking and approach to counseling. The professor and my class colleagues were thrown off guard at first when I modeled Buber's approach to education as treating the learner as a thou.

This same professor had us read Nikos Kazantzakis's *Zorba the Greek*. I took it with me while I was traveling one weekend. Once I started reading it, I didn't put it down. This book had a powerful impact on my life. I asked myself, Would I live like Zorba or like the boss? Was I living my life cautiously from my head or was I living fully and passionately?

Little did I know that by completing the course requirements for the degree in pastoral counseling before returning to Brazil would set in motion some major changes in my life and ministry. The last part of the degree required a major thesis paper. My advisor suggested I not write the thesis before returning to Brazil, because three Atlanta seminaries were considering creating a ThD program in pastoral counseling and other doctoral studies. He said I might be able to transfer my credits into the ThD program when I returned to the States on my next furlough. I took his advice because I dreaded not having enough time to write the thesis.

Randy and Ruth were doing well in school. Susana taught Paul to walk three months before his first birthday. It was fun to watch them growing and playing together. Our family enjoyed our extended furlough year, but it was over before we realized it. It was time to pack our suitcases and return to Brazil. It didn't take long to sell the house and the furniture. We stayed at my mother's home in Valdosta a few days while we visited a few supporting churches again. We headed south, stopping along the way to see my siblings in Florida, arriving in Miami to get our flight to São Paulo.

My brother Ed helped me purchase a three-horsepower outboard motor to take along so I could fish in the rivers. He had it tested to make sure it would run. While I was putting on some extra wrapping paper, I heard something sloshing around. I discovered I was about to take a full gas tank on the plane. I had to slowly pour the gas down a commode between multiple flushes to dilute it as much as possible.

As we approached the airport, Walter saw smoke pouring out of the back of the planes as they took off. He asked, "Why do they have signs in the plane that says 'no smoking' when the plane smokes?"

It took two vehicles to deliver the family and our luggage to the airport. I was afraid we would incur an extra fee because our luggage was overweight. We were taking a television, a small boat motor, and many personal items that were cheaper in the States than Brazil. I presented seven tickets to the ticket agent and stacked the luggage on the scales. The agent processed the tickets, looked at the scales, then looked at us, and said, "Your luggage is considerably overweight, but you have all these tickets, so I'm not going to charge you. *Boa viagem.*"

The first time we traveled to Brazil had taken fifteen days by ship out of New York. This time we were taking a ten-hour flight to an uncertain future but faith that God was in charge of whatever was in store for us. As the plane lifted off and settled into the long flight, I was filled with gratitude for the eighteen-month furlough. Family, friends, professors, supervisors, pastors, and the church people had been so good to us. I could only say, "Thank you, God, for giving us these eighteen months in the States." I rededicated myself to missionary service in Brazil. I was grateful that I could communicate in Portuguese at the start of this second term of service.

CHAPTER 9

Santa Catarina

WE ARRIVED IN SÃO PAULO at 11:30 a.m. on August 18, 1967. I asked Phyllis to sit tight with the children until everyone else had deplaned. I knew it would be lunchtime by the time our luggage could be checked by customs officials. I figured they would have gotten their quota of money for this flight from the passengers in front of us, and they'd be in a hurry to go to lunch. When we got to them, they quickly cleared our suitcases and —until they came to the box with the boat motor. I had to take it out and assemble it for several of them to admire. I complained to the agent who charged me a fifty-dollar customs fee. He said I was lucky to be last in line and they were in a hurry to go to lunch. I could pay the fee or leave the motor with them. It helped to know how Brazilian culture functioned.

We spent a few days in the apartment behind Bill Bigham's house in São Paulo to get our visa and residency documents in order before taking a bus to meet Bishop Wilbur Smith in Curitiba, Paraná. While we were in Atlanta, he had let me know my appointment would be close to the main highway near the two border towns of Mafra, Santa Catarina, and Rio Negro, Paraná. The day after we arrived in Curitiba, he took us to see a house he had found for us to rent and to see the church. The house was about ten yards from a fifteen-foot-high railroad track in a low-income neighborhood. It had no ceiling and dangerously exposed electrical wiring. I was deeply disappointed in the bishop's judgment and conflicted between protecting my family and frustrating him. How could I tell him we would not live in the house that he was so excited to find for us? But

I told the bishop we wouldn't live here. He warned me that I wouldn't be able to find another house to rent. Little did I know this was the first of many disagreements I would have with him.

The bishop took us back to Curitiba, and I called Bill Bigham to ask if Phyllis and the children could stay in their apartment while I searched for a rent house in Mafra and Rio Negro. After a bus trip to get them settled into the São Paulo apartment, I returned to Mafra. I slept on a cot in a small Sunday school room for a month until I found a house. Meanwhile, I had one of the worst sinus infections I've ever had and was too sick to get out of bed for several days. Though the house I found was not ideal, it was much better than the one the bishop had found. It was on a hill and at an intersection. There was a steep, unprotected drop-off on one side. The only advantage was that it was within easy walking distance of the church.

As soon as I signed the contract to rent the house, I went by bus to Curitiba to tell the bishop and then flew to Londrina. From there I traveled by bus to Apucarana to find a mover to transport our furniture to Mafra. A leaky roof on the building I had constructed in the back of the church to store the furniture caused some of it to get wet. The custodian family did not know when I might show up to move the furniture. I found them using our cabinet record player and records as well as other belongings. The wife was washing clothes in bread bowl a farmer had made for Phyllis. The soap had penetrated the wood, leaving it unfit for bread making. We have used it since as a magazine holder.

During the nineteen months we were away, I received no information about how the people were doing in the Arapongas and Apucarana churches. I looked forward to meeting the pastor and seeing the people again. My excitement turned to sadness and anger. The people in Apucarana had been devastated by authoritarian decisions from the district superintendent, who also was pastor of the largest church in Londrina. He had taken the kombi I had left for the pastor and given it to another pastor.

He moved the pastor from Apucarana back to Arapongas and rented out the parsonage I had worked so hard to buy and remodel. He sold the expensive telephone service that I left for the pastor. No one knew what he did with the money. My four years of careful and patient disciplining of the people to become a self-supporting church was completely undone. I went to Arapongas, looking for the pastor. I found him discouraged and depressed by the mess created by the district superintendent. Many similarly disappointed people had left the churches over the superintendant's changes. It took all my strength to keep my opinions to myself. I left for São Paulo without visiting Arapongas. I knew that one family in particular in Arapongas was behind all these problems and had convinced the district superintendent to move the pastor back to Arapongas.

After a month without any information from Phyllis and the children, I was anxious to see them and move them to Mafra ahead of our furniture. On the way through Curitiba, I expressed my anger to the bishop for allowing one of his district superintendents to wreck our four years' of work in Paraná. He claimed to know nothing about it and dismissed my concerns with pious assurances about God helping it all to work out for good.

Phyllis was glad we had a house and ready to settle into homemaking. She has always been a terrific wife, mother, and missionary. She never complained about our living situations and set about making the best of whatever circumstances we faced. But the rental house in Mafra pushed her to the limit. She was afraid one of the children would fall into the roadway below. Twelve-foot ceilings made it hard to heat the house, and the huge windows were impossible to cover. This meant constant daylight inside the house despite bedsheet curtains covering half the height of windows. The final straw came when the water supply failed to keep up with the needs of the family. She was at her wit's end, and then I heard that a sawmill owner planned to move. He agreed to rent it to us, and we moved as soon as we could get a truck. The house was across the river and on the main road into town.

Not much later a new Chevrolet Silverado station wagon arrived. I had ordered it as soon as I arrived in Mafra. It took over a month for the factory to deliver it to the dealership because demand was so high. As I look back at all the travel by public transportation and taxis the first two months in Brazil, I wonder how we did it.

The new house made a huge difference for our family. It was well build, with reasonable-sized windows and an iron woodstove that Phyllis quickly learned to use for cooking meals and keeping the house warm in the winter months. She still used the two-burner kerosene stove with the portable top tin oven for baking bread and cookies. The back of the house was professionally landscaped with garden paths and beautiful shrubs. On one side of the garden was an eight-by-ten shed that had served as a radio shack. I claimed it as my office and spent many hours there reading and keeping watch over the children when they played in the garden. We tried to find domestic help but were not very successful.

Phyllis did so many things well. Now that the children were safe and she had the necessities for homemaking, she was happy again. She was able to carve out time for homeschooling the four oldest children in English. Randy, Ruth, and Walter also went three hours a day to a Brazilian school. This was difficult for them at first. They had forgotten much of their Portuguese during their time in the States. We paid a young Brazilian teacher to give them private lessons after classes were over, and they soon caught up with their classmates. The teachers were amazed at how fast they learned and how smart they were.

Paul loved the new house, especially the challenge of escaping the front yard to investigate the sawmill. Several times the sawmill workers would bring him back home and warn us about the dangers of the busy road and the sawmill activity. We were terrified and mystified as to how a sixteen-month-old in diapers could get through a latched gate. One day I followed him around the back of the house and watched him roll a block of wood against the fence to help him climb high enough to reach the latch and open the gate. I had to put a padlock on the gate.

From my office one day I overheard four-year-old Susana supervising the mixing of dirt and water to make mud pies. Walter and Paul were doing most of the work while she told them how to get the mud just right. I decided to play a trick on them by tossing a small rock over the hedge to land in the large pan. The rock landed dead center in the pan.

Walter asked, "Where did that rock come from?"

Quick as a flash, Susana responded, "God did it."

Walter then asked, "Why would God do something like that?"

Just as quickly, Susana responded, "God did it to play. He likes to play just as much as we do."

I went quietly back to my studies with the assurance that I had learned an important theology lesson that day.

The children once complained that bees were bothering them. When I investigated, I saw something rare. A drone had won the competition to be the first to get to the queen bee. While the drone completed the one and only reason for which he had been born, I explained bee-mating behavior to the children. What a fortunate opportunity to have a live and rare situation to teach them about the birds and the bees. We had already seen and talked about bird's nests with eggs in them.

Regarding our missionary work, the bishop told me I had been appointed to be the pastor and to start new congregations in eastern Santa Catarina. Earlier Methodist missionaries had started many churches and schools in the southernmost state of Rio Grande do Sul. They also started churches in north Paraná and a few in western Santa Catarina. The mountainous terrain between eastern and western Paraná made travel extremely difficult, however. The churches in eastern Paraná were connected to the Second Annual Conference (or Region, as they were called in Brazil). It seemed there had once been an agreement between the early Presbyterian and Methodist missionaries that the Methodists would plant churches in Rio Grande do Sul and the Presbyterians in Santa Catarina. Since that agreement was no longer in force, the bishop wanted to fill the gap by expanding the new Sixth Region to the larger cities on the coast of Santa Catarina. The strategy for doing this was to appoint an American missionary leader and recruit Brazilian Methodist youth to give one year of full-time missionary service, similar to Mormon missionaries. He wanted me to start recruiting the volunteers soon after getting settled. I asked permission to use the first four months to travel to several towns to do some informal research regarding the best places to start and methods to use. I promised to report on my findings at the Annual Conference in January.

In the early days of the church in Mafra, they had made the mistake of buying cheap land on the edge of town. This condemned the church to be mostly ignored by the population. After thirty years, the congregation had only a dozen families. On good Sundays, we had twenty-five to thirty people in attendance. Following the example of my home pastor and mentor, Brother Dixon, I was known as a visiting pastor. I had to be careful in Mafra because I could visit all the families in one week. I didn't want to set up the next pastor for failure by visiting them too often. I realized the bishop was trying to meet two needs with one pastor without considering the consequences. The Mafra church had very limited possibilities for future growth.

About a month after we had settled into our home, the executive secretary from the Board of Missions for Eastern South America visited us. He confirmed my assessment that the towns of Mafra and Rio Negro were not a strategic place for us to live if we planned to start new churches in Santa Catarina.

My brother Ed and Dr. Wayne Hulse, pastor of a large Methodist Church in Madison, Wisconsin, came to Brazil on a Board of Discipleship preaching mission. The new station wagon came in handy as we spent a week traveling week to several churches. They alternated preaching responsibilities, and I was their translator. I took them to Apucarana and Arapongas to preach and see some of the work we had done in our time there before.

A few days later we almost had a serious accident. I was driving about fifty miles an hour on a newly graded dirt road. As we approached a crossroad, it looked like the road continued straight through. No signs were posted to warn motorists that a deep ditch was on the other side of the crossroad. I was in the crossroad before I saw the ditch. Immediately, I spun the steering wheel to the right to slow us down until the vehicle settled in the road going to the right. We stopped and got out to give thanks to God for helping us avoid an accident.

An hour later we checked into a rustic motel. I was hot, tired, and still nervous from the close call that day. I wanted to get a nap before we went to supper with a Japanese family and to church for worship. Ed woke me up to ask which of his several sermons he should preach that night. I responded that it really didn't make any difference, because I already knew what I wanted them to hear when I translated. I was kidding him because he was frustrated with depending on me to communicate for him.

Ed has always been a good big brother to me. I could write chapters about his many acts of kindness across the years to make life easier for me. I really enjoyed the week we traveled together in Brazil. His traveling companion was also enjoyable to be with.

The travel and research for future church planting in Santa Catarina was the most interesting part of my appointment to Mafra–Rio Negro. When I was traveling, I had no way to communicate with Phyllis. I trusted Phyllis to know what to do and trusted God to care for her and the children while I was away.

I traveled down the mountains on bumpy, dusty dirt roads to several town and cities. German and Polish immigrants had mostly settled these towns and built houses very similar to the ones they remembered from their homelands. What a surprise to see so much European construction and so many Europeans than I had previously seen in tropical Brazil. I also discovered beautiful, sparsely populated beaches and fishing villages along the coast.

After several days of difficult driving, I arrived in the seacoast village of Balenário Camboriú. I had been told this would be a good place to stay, so I got a room in a rustic hotel facing one of the most beautiful beaches I had ever seen. I wished so much that Phyllis and the children could be with me. Mostly fishermen were on the beach, with their dugout fishing boats. About two dozen vacation cottages were on higher ground along the beach. I wished I had saved enough money to purchase land along this beach. I knew that after the government paved a highway to this place, the price of land would rapidly rise. (Today, ten- to twenty-story condos and hotels stretch as far as one can see along this beach.)

I stopped in several towns to gather information about the best places to start the new churches. The light industrial and manufacturing towns of Joinville and Blumenau looked promising. Along the way I visited with pastors of other denominations to talk about the viability of planting Methodist churches in their towns. I visited government officials to collect as much demographic and economic information as they could give me. The farther south I went, the more I liked the looks of this area of Brazil. When I arrived in the capital city of Florianópolis on the coast, I could hardly believe my eyes. Mountains, lakes, and beaches surrounded the city. To me it was the most beautiful capital city I had ever seen. A Lutheran pastor there answered my questions about church planting very frankly. He told me religion was important to the people, but going to church was not. Most of the population headed to the beaches on Sundays. He said, "The people here think they already live in heaven, so they are dedicated to enjoying it. You will not find people who take time to go to church on Sunday."

A Presbyterian pastor told me his church had been here almost a hundred years and had only a hundred members. The Baptists had done a little better; they had been here fifty years and had only seventy-five members. The primary reason for the slow development of churches in this area was that German and Polish ethnic backgrounds were deeply rooted in Catholic and Lutheran cultures. This made the people extremely difficult to convert to another denomination. My trip to the coast of Santa Catarina provided many wonderful impressions but few ideas about where to plant Methodist churches.

Phyllis and the children excitedly welcomed me home each time I traveled. They listened to my reports of the beautiful cities and beaches with both interest and disappointment at not having been with me. We did make one trip so they could see some of the things I had seen and spend a few days at a beach hotel. Phyllis and I agreed that we would enjoy living in this area, that our appointment to live in Mafra–Rio Negro had been a mistake.

Only four months after we returned to Brazil, it was time for the Annual Conference of the Sixth Region. Leaving Phyllis and the children at home, I drove several hours through Paraná to Santo Antônio da Platina. The church was too small to accommodate us, so the conference was held in a school building nearby. We slept a dozen to a room on rusty cots that creaked loudly sounds when someone turned over in the night. We bathed in the school bathrooms and held meetings in hot classrooms. We walked two blocks to the church for our meals and worship services. The accommodations were not ideal, but no one complained. We were happy that we had our own Annual Conference. After almost two years away, I was excited to see my colleagues from north Paraná and meet new colleagues from the Second Region, now joining the Sixth Region. I was well prepared to report on my travels and research in preparation for planting churches in Santa Catarina. And I knew the bishop wouldn't be pleased to hear what I had to say.

I reported on the beautiful cities and the cooperation received from pastors of other denominations, but I recommended we not move forward with the idea of recruiting young people to go there for a full year of missionary service. I said the program would fail if the volunteers couldn't have significant success within a year. This was very unlikely to happen in an extremely conservative religious environment. Instead of sending youth, I suggested we recruit Methodist families from other regions to move here and work to support themselves while they developed home churches. I suggested the conference appoint an American missionary or a Brazilian pastor to a strategic location to help train and give moral support to the home churches. If we wanted to utilize the volunteer youth, they should be sent to the new towns rapidly developing in the western part of the state. The people there would be in a considerable state of flux. This would make them more open to new ideas and social relationships, which would create opportunities for evangelism. This, in turn, would offer a better chance of success for the short-term volunteers.

Though most of the pastors agreed with me, the bishop did not like my report because it did not substantiate his assumptions on how and where to start new churches. He tabled the matter and moved on to other business. The problem was resolved the next day.

I was trying to get an after-lunch nap in my hot and noisy bedroom when I felt a sharp punch on my side. I yelled "Shato!" which basically means "You idiot!" I turned to find my colleagues laughing loudly and Bishop Wilbur standing by my bed. He laughed and said, "The cabinet is meeting down the hall, and we want you to come right away to meet with us."

When I walked into the room, I saw the cabinet members smiling. I had no idea why I had been summoned. Dr. Otto Gustavo Otto, the president of the Methodist seminary in São Paulo was with them. I had seen him earlier in the day and heard him give a report about the seminary.

The bishop said, "The president of the seminary came here today to ask us to appoint you to teach pastoral care at the seminary. We want to tell you that we have agreed to do that."

I sat in silence, too stunned to speak. When we first arrived from the States, I had heard that anti-American seminary students had pressured the last two North American missionaries who had taught at the seminary to leave. Bill Hinson returned to the States to teach, and Bill Bigham became the treasurer for missionaries in Brazil. I begged the bishop and the district superintendents not to appoint me to the seminary. I promised to go anywhere but the seminary because anti-American hostility toward North Americans because of the Vietnam War spilled onto the missionary professors. The seminary president promised to protect me from them if I would go. He appealed to my need to be a useful missionary when he said he desperately needed me because there was no Brazilian Methodist available with an MA in pastoral care and counseling. He said I could leave after two or three years when a Brazilian student studying pastoral care and counseling in Canada would return to the country.

Word soon spread throughout the conference that I was going to teach at the seminary. Two delegates were seminarians. We had started to develop a friendship. They rejoiced that I was going to be one of their professors and said they would help me relate to the students. They also answered many questions I had about the students and the situation at the seminary.

With no telephone service at home, I had no way of communicating with Phyllis about this sudden change of direction in our missionary service. I alternated between warm excitement about becoming a seminary professor and cold fear of failure. When I returned home, after the excitement of seeing everyone and the evening meal, I told Phyllis we needed to talk out of the hearing of the children. When I told her the news, instead of being frustrated at another move, she hugged me. She told me how proud she was of me for working so hard on my counseling degree while we were in the States, and she was happy for this opportunity to use what I had learned.

We told the children the next morning. They helped pull out the four fifty-five-gallon steel drums and boxes to pack for the move to the seminary in Rudge Ramos, a suburb of São Paulo. This was our third move in five months.

The people in the church were puzzled that we were moving after only four months in Mafra–Rio Negro. Some asked me if I was moving because I didn't like living there. They had waited for me for eight months with substitute pastors between the time I was appointed in January of the year before until we arrived in August. Actually, I didn't like their towns after seeing the towns to the southeast, but I couldn't tell them that. Instead, I told them I had to go where the bishop told me to go.

Phyllis and I remember Mafra–Rio Negro each Advent, when the Christmas boxes are unpacked for decorating the house. The nativity set we bought from a skilled artisan in Mafra always has a special place in our house to remind us of the Christmas story.

CHAPTER 10

1968: The Year the World Went Crazy

> We had the experience but missed the meaning,
> And approach to the meaning restores the experience
> In a different form.
>
> —T. S. Elliot, *Four Quartets*

Starting again often means going somewhere to do something different—occasionally radically different—from what was expected. I never dreamed of being a seminary professor in Brazil. From the time I first heard about my appointment to the seminary in Rudge Ramos, my mind started churning about how I would approach the formation of future pastors with the disciplines of pastoral care and counseling.

The Methodist seminary in Brazil was established by missionaries of the Southern Methodist Church and Brazilian leaders and situated in the small town of Rudge Ramos, near the top of the mountain plateau of the eastern part of Brazil, a few miles from the ocean. The seminary faced the Via Anchieta highway from the port of Santos to the city of São Paulo. When we arrived in 1968 the administration and library building were to the right of the entrance through a guarded gate. Farther to the right was a large auditorium, and to the right of that a church was under construction.

A classroom building was slightly up the hill on the right. An all-important soccer field took up most of the center of the land. At the top of the property, facing the highway, were the dormitory and dining facilities. Along the left of the paved street were the married student apartment building and five faculty houses. We had been assigned the last house at the top of the drive. Today, the seminary is only one of many schools in the largest Methodist university in Brazil.

My fears about teaching at the seminary were confirmed the day after the truck arrived with our furniture. I was busy unpacking books in my spacious corner office on the ground floor when two students suddenly appeared at my open window to tell me that they and their classmates did not want another American as a professor at their seminary. They informed me that they intended to get rid of me just as they had run off the last two Americans.

I responded angrily, "I did not want to come here anymore than you want me here, but your president invited me and my bishop appointed me against my will. Now that I'm here, I intend to stay. Either you come in here and help me unpack or you get away from my window and find something else to do."

Shocked by my angry response, they left.

The seminary president came to my office a little later to tell me about my class schedule. First, he said that each faculty member had administrative responsibilities, and mine was to be the treasurer. I realized my lack of accounting experience would require a steep learning curve and a lot of my time. He said I was scheduled to teach classes in pastoral care and counseling and homiletics. I protested that I knew nothing about homiletics and that I had learned Portuguese mostly from communicating with rural and small town people in the interior of Brazil. I could not teach preaching in a refined, educated manner. I reminded him that he had invited me to teach pastoral care and counseling, and he had said nothing about homiletics. He said that pastoral care professors in Brazil had always taught preaching.

Standing there dumbfounded, I suddenly recalled a part of my Southern Methodist church history. I realized at that moment that the seminary was using the old theology curriculum the early missionaries had brought to Brazil. An experienced pastor taught the practical courses of preaching, pastoral care, pastoral counseling, visitation, and anything else pastors did in ministry. I felt trapped now that I had accepted this position and moved my family to the seminary. My assignments were considerably over my training and competence. I knew that missionary service required me to be flexible and to do things I wouldn't be expected to do in the States, but at this moment I felt stretched beyond the breaking point. This experience taught me a valuable lesson: before accepting a job, ask lots of questions.

I told the president that I would need office help and wanted him to pay for Herman Oberdik, one of the seminarians at our Sixth Annual Conference, to be my student assistant. Though funds were limited, he agreed to pay him a part-time salary. Herman was more than my student and helper; he became my advocate with the other students and a good friend.

Students began arriving on campus for the start of classes. This meant I had to hurry to prepare two class syllabi. I started in the library, checking out what textbooks were available for pastoral care and counseling. We had a small, well-ordered library under the management of Dr. Bowden, a retired Old Testament missionary professor, but there was nothing in Portuguese for my subjects. One English copy of Blackwood's classic book on preaching was the only resource for students to use in the homiletics class. A few students could read English, but they were not proficient enough to understand much of what they read. I was glad I had Blackwood's book and a few other English-language books on preaching in my personal library. I needed them to for lecture preparation, but this left me without a class textbook.

After a lot of thought, prayer, and revisions, the syllabi were ready. As I approached the classroom for my first homiletics course, I was confronted by some student leaders. They were in the hallway and badgered students to boycott the class. I tried to ignore them. Most of the students were curious enough to see who I was and what I intended to do before they walked out.

I started by telling them why I was there and admitted my limitations for teaching and the lack of didactic materials. I showed them the syllabus and explained why I had decided to use Brazilian novels instead of textbooks to help them learn to tell stories when they preached. I said that I planned to take them to the theater to see how actors communicated. In preparation for their practice preaching, they were to ride a bus to the end of the line and back as they talked with other passengers about the issues that concerned them. Then they were to use what they were learning in their Bible classes to prepare sermons that addressed the concerns they heard from people on the buses. After going over the syllabus, I asked if they had suggestions on how we could improve it to make the class as useful as possible to them. They had a few suggestions, mostly about the Brazilian novels, which I included in the revision.

The second meeting of the homiletics class started with all the students seated in the classroom, including the student who tried to lead the boycott of the first class session. The students who boycotted the first session started making suggestions for changes, but I cut them off by saying that the opportunity for suggesting changes had been given during the first class, which they had not attended. I passed out the revised copy of the syllabus and said that there would be no more changes. That put a stop to student resistance to my teaching at the seminary.

Herman told me later that the students accepted me because of my willingness to be vulnerable, open to suggestions, and firm against opposition. He said they had never seen a professor do this before. The students seemed excited about the class sessions, and I was surprised at how much I enjoyed teaching them. My appointment to teach rapidly became a calling. My relationship with the students inside and outside the classroom increased day by day.

Phyllis and the children loved living on the campus. The gated property provided protection and freedom of movement beyond our yard for the children to explore. The students loved playing with our children. Though he was less than two years old, Paul soon learned that the ringing of the dining hall bell meant the students were going to eat. He often made his way to the dining hall to mingle with them and wait for them to give him something to eat. They delighted in hiding him under their tables when we came looking for him.

Pollution from an asphalt plant behind our house often spewed droplets of tar when the wind blew in our direction. This happened at any time of the day. It was especially bad most evenings as the clouds moved in from the seacoast and up the mountains to the three-thousand-foot plateau where we lived. The sudden drop in temperature meant it was time to get a jacket or sweater. Phyllis has always loved hanging clothes on a clothesline, but she hated seeing drops of tar clinging to them when she took them down.

Randy soon befriended Wesley Veiga, a classmate from another faculty family. They traveled back and forth on a city bus to a private school. Wesley had a beautiful sister who developed a special relationship with Randy.

Ruth and Walter went three hours a day to a local elementary school. Phyllis continued to supplement their education with the Calvert home schooling courses in English. And she started Susana's kindergarten education.

Our arrival at the seminary coincided with the acceptance of the first female students. For decades women had studied Christian education at Chácara Flora, about an hour's drive from the seminary. The Brazilian Methodist Church did not ordain women at this time. Though the male and female students had been on different campuses, several female students had married seminarians to fulfill their calling to ministry. At the 1965 General Conference, a motion was made and voted on to save money by transferring the women to the seminary to take classes with the male students. The more conservative members of the conference tried to block the motion, but it passed and the all-female school concluded its long and fruitful ministry.

A dozen women arrived at the seminary at about the same time we did. They were housed in a former faculty house on the left side of our house. The male dorm was about a hundred yards to the front and right of us. This meant we had sixty men competing for the attention of twelve women. The conservative leaders claimed that mixing the genders on one campus would cause trouble, and I feared there would be considerable tension among the men regarding the outnumbered women. We often heard small groups of students playing guitars and singing beautiful religious music and folk songs on the front porch of the female students' dorm. Their singing and socializing reminded me of the youth camps I led in the States.

As treasurer, I was in a key position to see the rapidly declining financial situation of the seminary. The president told me he faced a great deal of opposition from more conservative pastors in three of the six Annual Conferences. Several things contributed to this:

1. A brilliant Catholic New Testament scholar had chosen to marry and leave the priesthood, and the president had hired him to teach Greek and other New Testament languages.
2. The graduating class from the preceding year had invited a popular liberal social justice Catholic archbishop to be their graduation speaker. This offended many conservative pastors who had a long history of anti-Catholic and antiliberal sentiments.
3. The conservative pastors were against women studying at the seminary because women could not be ordained.
4. The conservative pastors had heard stories about seminary students joining other university students in demonstrations against the military government for suppressing democratic rights for open and free elections.

President Otto told me about the conservative and pro-military leaders expressed their anger at the seminary by refusing to send their quota of funds from their Annual Conferences to pay for the students' expenses. Students continued to come to the seminary, but money to support them did not. This meant we were spending more on the students than we received to support them. With rising inflation, expenses rapidly climbed beyond the seminary's ability to pay the bills. President Otto tried to manage the public relations problems, and he frequently meet with conference leaders to try to convince them leaders to send the funds they owed to pay for their students. He cut expenditures, delayed payment of bills, and borrowed money to keep the seminary functioning. I saw the train wreck coming but could do nothing to stop it.

The crisis at the seminary can be better understood by taking into account the world situation. On February 1, 1968, I read and translated for E. Stanley Jones, the famous missionary to India, the news about the Tet offensive in Vietnam. His response was prophetic, "I believe that war is hopelessly lost." This year, 1968, was the year public opinion around the world turned against the United States regarding the war in Vietnam. On April 4, Martin Luther King Jr. was assassinated. Riots erupted in many US cities, and protests against the United States were launched in cities around the world, including Brazil. In the States, college and university students occupied several administration buildings to protest against the war in Vietnam. In Paris, student riots broke out. Sorbonne students and professors join the labor unions in strikes across France. In June, Robert F. Kennedy, while campaigning for his party's presidential nomination, was killed in San Francisco. Thousands of students in Mexico were killed or wounded as a result of protests against their government. In Brazil, university students protested in the streets against the military dictatorship. Many seminary students joined these marches. There was unrest, turmoil, and revolution among young people around the world.

If someone were to ask me when postmodernism started, I would say it occurred in the spring of 1968. This was the year when confidence in traditional institutions collapsed and societies began to fall apart. The legitimacy of powerbrokers was questioned and severely tested. Power flowing from the top down shifted to power in almost leaderless groups acting in cohesion to change the way society functioned. Reality changed. No longer was there one unified reality (*realidade brazilaira*) that could be assumed to exist and argued over; rather, multiple realities emerged, depending upon ideological positions and diverse communities of action. Theological reflection took a backseat to ideological assumptions. In 1968, conservative leaders were fighting desperately to maintain control and restore order, but it was too late to put the genie back in the bottle. At the seminary, this worldwide clash between old and new was an introduction to a season of confusion and suffering.

As my thirty-fifth birthday on April 30 approached, I was preparing lectures, grading papers, and trying to help manage an impending financial crisis at the seminary when Herman, my student assistant, told me that May Day (May 1) would be the start of strike by the students against the seminary administration. A few radical student leaders had gained control over the student body. They were inspired by the example of university students in several countries around the world who had gone on strike and, in some places, taken over the universities. Communication between the students, the administration, and the faculty suddenly ceased. The radical student leaders sent a list of demands.

The next day the students went to lunch but refused to eat. The president overreacted by telling the cooks to serve the same food cold for supper. This angered the students even more. They read poems, sang songs, and refused to attend classes the next day.

I finally managed to convince some of the leaders to meet with the president and faculty to hear their complaints. They let us know about their frustrations with the curriculum, the food, and other expenditures. This meeting gave the president an opportunity to inform them about the financial boycott against the seminary by the conservative leaders in half of the Annual Conferences. He warned them that by striking against the administration, they were giving power to the most conservative elements of the Brazilian Methodist Church to take over the seminary. The main complaint of the students was the dated curriculum that had been brought from the United States by the early missionaries to Brazil.

The meeting led to dialogue and negotiations for changes. This appeared to resolve the crisis; however, news of the student strike quickly spread across Brazil. Without communicating with the president of the seminary, the bishops, pressured by the conservative leaders, asked the trustees to correct the problems at the seminary. The trustees came and listened to the students, the faculty, and the president discuss the issues and agreed to help us make changes in the curriculum and do what they could to manage the financial situation. We did not realize how much the news of the crisis was being used by the conservative elements in the church to demand that the bishops intervene at the seminary.

Bishop Nathaniel of the First Region, and a former president of the seminary, took advantage of the opportunity. He had been so disliked by the students that they had forced him to resign as president. Now, he was a bishop and leader of the theological and political conservative Methodists. Pressure from inside and outside the General Cabinet led them to make the worst decision in the history of the Methodist Church of Brazil. The seminary president had pleaded for more time to resolve the crisis, but without visiting the students or faculty to listen to their concerns, the cabinet decided to close the seminary, send the students back to their families, assign ordained faculty to other appointments, and dismiss all lay professors and employees. They also dismissed the General Conference–elected seminary trustees. They thought they could take over the seminary by getting rid of some people not to their liking and keeping the people they liked. They did not realize their decision was like trying to thin a beehive by hitting it with a stick. Radical attempts to solve a problem often create bigger problems.

Early one Saturday morning, all six bishops appeared on campus to call a meeting at with the faculty. They first met with the president to tell him they were taking over the direction and administration of the seminary. When I arrived for the faculty meeting, the atmosphere in the room was extremely quiet and serious. The bishops announced their decision to close the seminary. We were stunned. Several moments passed before anyone said anything. The bishops rejected all discussion. They refused to explain why they were closing the seminary or reconsider the arguments against closing it. They were there to put their radical decision into action. They must have thought they could solve the seminary problems by starting over. They would not allow us to go to an upstairs conference room where the students were waiting.

After announcing their decision to the students, they told them that some would be invited back when they reopened the seminary but others would not. We heard a loud *boo* from the conference room, which I later learned was their response to being told that Pastor Alipio Lovoura had been appointed the legal counsel for closing the seminary. Everyone knew that Reverend Alipio, the pastor of Lins in São Paulo, supported the military dictatorship and was instrumental in pressuring the bishops to close the seminary.

After the meeting, Bishop Wilbur told me that he was appointing me to be a chaplain in the Hospital Evangélico de Londrina, Paraná. Though my new appointment was a surprise, I did not question his authority and prepared to tell Phyllis that we would be moving after living only five months at the seminary. But before I could tell her, I learned that the students met after the bishops left and decided to take over the seminary property. They felt misunderstood and disrespected by the bishops, so they were free to disregard the bishops' orders. They quickly choose leaders and planned how they would occupy the seminary and support themselves by looking for secular jobs to pay expenses.

The students' decision to disobey the bishops and remain on the seminary property created a crisis of conscious and calling for me. I was called to serve Christ as a missionary in the Brazilian Methodist Church. I was financially supported by churches in the United States, but I served under the authority of my bishop in Brazil. He had appointed me to teach the subjects of pastoral care and counseling at the seminary. Now, without consulting with me, he changed that appointment and ordered me to move to Londrina to be a chaplain.

In my short time of teaching at the seminary I had won the confidence of the students and became both their professor and unofficial pastor. How could I obey my bishop's order to move and leave behind the students when they most needed a pastor? I struggled with my tightly wrapped ball of theology called "Christ and the Church." Until now they had been one and the same. Suddenly, I could no longer keep them together. After a long discussion, Phyllis and I decided to stay with the students as long as they occupied the seminary. We realized our decision to disobey my bishop would have serious consequences for our future in Brazil. I knew missionary service would be difficult, but I never dreamed it would challenge my identity as well as my calling. I could not go forward to my new appointment, and I did not want to go back to the United States.

I sent a carefully worded letter to Bishop Wilbur and Mac McCoy, the Board of Missions secretary for Latin America, in which I told them about the students' decision to remain at the seminary against the bishop's orders. I explained my predicament as a pastoral caregiver to the students and how I could not leave them without a pastor as long as they remained at the seminary, especially since the recent integration of female students onto the campus. I said I would move to Londrina to serve as chaplain as soon as the seminary was reopened or the students left the campus.

Phyllis and I decided we would financially support ourselves by teaching English should our salary from the Board of Missions be discontinued. I still hoped that our refusal to leave would cause the bishops to reconsider and keep the seminary open. We were keenly aware that they could ask the military police to evict us if they wanted to force us out. Word soon got out that we should be careful what we said on the phone, because our lines were being tapped by the military police.

Herman Oberdik told me that the students had borrowed the master keys from the building and grounds superintendent to make copies for every building and room in the seminary. This worried me and made me more determined to stay on campus to keep them out of all buildings other than the dorms and dining facilities in order to avoid creating an excuse for the police to evict the students.

Three bishops were chosen to take over the administration of the officially closed seminary. One morning the president called to tell me the bishops were about to dismiss him. I said he should not be alone when they arrived and promised to be with him when they appeared. While we were waiting, I looked around his office. I saw a large picture of his seminary graduating class. Suddenly it dawned on me that this class of twenty to twenty-five years earlier had produced many strong, capable, and successful leaders of the Brazilian Methodist Church. This meant most of the leaders for and against Otto were in the same graduating class. His colleagues were still competing for dominance.

When the bishops arrived, they delivered the news that he was no longer president and they were taking over the seminary. It was a sad and humiliating experience to observe. He handed over his keys to the bishops. I followed his example by handing over my keys. To my surprise they gave my keys back to me and told me to keep them. They said I was the treasurer, and they needed my help with the accounts. I don't think the bishops realized that by returning the keys to me, they transferred authority from the seminary president to the bishops for me to be in the seminary.

Throughout the crisis I wrote long letters to Mac McCoy in New York to keep him informed about events taking place at the seminary and in the Brazilian Methodist Church and in Brazil. I did not know if he would respond by telling me that my service in Brazil was over ended and I was being recalled or that my salary would be terminated if I stayed in Brazil. The salary did continue. His only response to the many pages I wrote was, "We choose mature people to send as missionaries, and we trust them to make mature decisions." I assumed from these few words that he was prepared to support me but did not want to be accused of telling me what to do.

Writing to my mother and my brother Ed was difficult, because they had limited understandings of the complicated situation we were in, but they loved us, and I knew they were deeply concerned about us.

Perhaps it was most difficult communicating with our supporting churches. I wanted our news to encourage their missionary support, not cause them to worry about us and think our problems were not worthy of their support. I wrote about the craziness of our situation in the context of what was going on around the world.

The seminary students quickly found jobs. They organized rotating teams to do the practical tasks of maintaining the community. Twice a week I took two of them in my station wagon to the huge wholesale market in São Paulo to buy food. I had never seen so many truckloads of vegetables. One morning I counted fifteen trucks of nothing but gleaming yellow carrots.

I told the students that as long they were to have classes at night as long as they were at the seminary, and I would teach and facilitate the classes. In the midst of this crisis, the students were eager to learn. Attendance was 100 percent. As I look back over twenty-five years of teaching and I think of this time at the seminary as my most effective teaching experience. I was thankful for the class at Emory during Dietrich Bonhoeffer's sabbatical year. His books *Life Together* and *The Cost of Discipleship* provided the basis for the education of the seminarians during this time of crisis.

Meanwhile, the students communicated with their families and friends at home about the injustice of the bishops' decision to close the seminary. The dismissed trustees, elected by the last General Conference, also communicated with other church leaders about the authoritarian overreach of the bishops. The youth leaders all over Brazil met and protested the bishops' authoritarianism and supported the seminarians. The crisis at the seminary spread like a rock ripples in the water when a rock is thrown into a lake. A war of documents ensued, each side accused the other of being wrong.

The bishops were surprised by the reaction to their decision and the strong support for the student who remained at the seminary. They kept trying to figure out how to resolve the crisis. As Bishop Oswaldo and I were working on seminary finances, he confessed to me that they had made a bad decision by listening only to the conservative leaders, but they did not know how to correct it. Usually, three bishops came to campus together to work on the closing of the seminary.

There were no restaurants in Rudge Ramos where they could eat lunch. One day the bishops were in our living room, waiting for Phyllis to prepare a meal for them, when two students appeared at the front door with a large pot of milk. They had been heating the milk in the dining hall kitchen when the bottled gas gave out. They asked if Phyllis would heat it for them. She took the food for the bishops off the stove to heat the milk and told the students to go out the back door instead of through the living room. She then finished preparing the meal.

Students saw the bishops as their enemies and asked us how we could show hospitality to them when they were hurting everyone at the seminary. This gave me an opportunity to teach them about a higher level of love.

The bishops came to the conclusion that the students remained in the seminary because I had decided to stay with them. They summoned me to a meeting with the General Cabinet. As I was leaving my house, one of the student leaders asked where I was going. When I told him, he said, "You should not go by yourself. I will go with you."

I told him they would not allow him into the meeting, but he insisted that I should not travel alone and said he was going to be with me even if they wouldn't allow him to attend the meeting.

Though I was skeptical, I still hoped that the seminary could be saved if I could help the six bishops and three general secretaries understand the tragic long-term consequences of closing the seminary. I soon realized they were not there to dialogue. They had only one item on the agenda, and that was to convince me to leave so the students would do the same.

Bishop Almir dos Santos, who used to teach pastoral care at the seminary, told me that my theology of pastoral care was in error. I asked him to help me understand how it was wrong. He responded, "Obedience to authorities is the primary principle of pastoral care." I said that my definition was different. "A pastor cares for his flock, even to the point of sacrificing his life and does not flee when the flock is threatened."

We talked for three hours, alternating between my trying to convince them to change their decision and them using every kind of pressure to convince me to leave the seminary. I said that I stayed with the students because they needed an adult who cared for them in this crisis and would leave only when they did and not before. When they realized my loyalty to the students was greater than my respect for their authority, we stopped talking. As they dismissed me, I warned them that the issue was not my staying or leaving the seminary but whether the church would lose not only a large majority of the present students but the next generation of youth and future pastors. (This actually happened.)

When I returned to my car, the seminary student leader was faithfully waiting for me. I was exhausted and hopeless and I broke down and wept while he comforted me. His demonstration of pastoral care assured me that he had learned both the subject and spirit of what I was there to teach him. I also learned that I needed to receive care. (Two years later this student asked me to officiate at his wedding. When I saw him in 1998, he had completed his PhD and was teaching history at the Methodist University on the same campus where I had taught thirty years earlier.)

A few days later a member of the General Cabinet told a mutual friend that, after I left the meeting, a majority of the General Cabinet voted to ask the Board of Missions to recall me back to the States. The vote was changed, however, after the general secretary for social justice said the decision to close the seminary had created a general crisis in the Brazilian Methodist Church. By requesting the recall of a missionary, the crisis would spread to the Board of Missions in New York. He warned that asking for my recall could lead to a suspension of funds until the crisis in Brazil was resolved. He reminded them how dependent they were on this money for the administration of their offices and the Brazilian church in general. A vote was then taken to rescind the vote to send me back to the States; instead, they voted to call a special session of the General Conference in thirty days to make a final decision regarding the seminary.

Hope was restored on campus when news of the called session reached the seminary. Neither students nor professors had left the campus, though some professors decided not to align themselves with the student protesters. The students and I prepared our case for changing the decision of the bishops, proposing theological education reforms, renewal of the church in general, and reopening the seminary by restoring the faculty and students. The students and I developed several position papers on ways to do this. Rather than submit them directly to the General Conference, we invited key members of the suspended trustees to a meeting to discuss them. With their help, we made revisions and prepared final copies to present to the General Conference.

Among these trustees was the president-elect of the Brazilian Academy of Science. Dr. Warwick Kerr, a biologist, was famous for his research on bees. He's better known for importing African killer bees for research purposes. Dr. Kerr ate at our home when he visited the seminary. He was an outspoken opponent of the military dictatorship, and his family and friends feared for his life. The military dictatorship wanted to silence him, but they were afraid to arrest such a prestigious leader in the scientific community.

I was impressed with the students' sincerity and idealism. They considered leaving the seminary property a demonstration of good will, but canceled that idea when word came that the bishops had chosen Bishop Nathaniel to be the new seminary president. Two years previously, students had pressured him to resign as the seminary president; he was elected to the Episcopacy at the next General Conference as a compromise with the conservative delegates. The students were not about to let him slip back in as the bishop in charge of the seminary.

Tension was high when the General Conference met in Piracicaba, São Paulo, in late September. Hundreds of documents, both supportive and condemning of the seminary closure, had crossed paths all over Brazil. This war of documents was at the climax. The first order of business was two days of study and discussion to reform the church. The delegates adopted most of the ideas in the study documents prepared by us at the seminary and presented by the trustees. Few delegates knew their source. Then the fireworks started. Youth leaders from all the conference joined the seminary students in condemning the authoritarian decision of the bishops to close the seminary. To the consternation of the bishops,

Dona Otillia Chaves, a longtime delegate and unofficial matriarch of the church, sided with the students and confronted the bishops for their decision to close the seminary.

Though the students and I were not delegates, we attended the conference as unofficial guests. I was the only ordained clergy, or adult layperson, allowed into the students' strategy sessions. When a vote was adopted that only the position of the bishops would be presented on to the conference, the students decided they would force the delegates to hear their side of the story by taking over the stage and denouncing the injustice against the seminary, and then they planned to walk out and turn their backs on the United Methodist Church of Brazil. When word of their plan reached the delegates, the vote was changed to allow a former trustee to speak against the closure of the seminary. The delegates were shocked after the former trustee documented the issues against the decision of the bishops. Most of the delegates were unaware of the actions leading up to the General Conference.

I think we won the hearts of the delegates, but we did not win their minds. Some of the bishops threatened to resign if the vote went against them. This threatened the authority structure of the church. The final vote was to support the decision of the bishops to close the seminary, but their method was condemned and they were ordered to reopen the seminary as soon as possible.

Though the majority of the delegates to the General Conference voted to support the bishops, I knew the students would not accept that decision. Neither would they accept an invitation to return to the seminary under a new administration after a winnowing process. As I predicted when I met with the bishops, only five of the seventy-five original students returned for classes when the seminary reopened in February 1969.

Though I was deeply disappointed with the vote of General Conference, it had answered my authority question. When the conference ended, I sadly bid farewell to the students and other youth leaders. I told them that the general church had spoken, and we should leave the campus. I found Bishop Wilbur and asked him, "Am I to be a professor in the seminary, a chaplain in Londrina, or some other position?" He said, "You are appointed to be a chaplain in the Hospital Evangélico de Londrina." I acknowledged the appointment and said that I would be moving as soon as I could find a house in Londrina.

I dreaded telling Phyllis we would be moving for the fourth time in fourteen months. Two days later I drove to Londrina to find a rent house. Valdir Peres Martins, the pastor of the Central Methodist Church in Londrina, had suggested my appointment to the Hospital Evangélico de Londrina. He was the same district superintendent who had done so much damage to our work in Apucarana and Arapongas. He helped me find a nice brick house on the edge of the city in the unfinished subdivision named Shangri-La. The owner said he would repaint it and have it ready within two weeks.

Upon my return to São Paulo, I suggested to Phyllis that we take the children to see Rio de Janiero before we moved. After a five-hour drive to Rio, we checked into the Argentina Hotel, close to Colegio Metodista, a pioneer Methodist school and only two blocks from Botafogo Beach. That afternoon we took a railcar up the mountain to see the huge *Christ the Redeemer* statue overlooking the city.

The desk clerk at the hotel assured me it would be safe to park our vehicle on the narrow street in front of the hotel. I elected to do this instead of going to the private paid parking lot three blocks away to keep from having to walk back by myself in the dark. That was the last time I saw our Chevrolet Suburban.

I went to a police station to report the stolen vehicle and get a statement to send to the insurance company. When the officer at the front desk told me it would take five days to prepare the report, I asked to speak to the officer in charge. I explained my situation and showed him a picture of our family of seven persons. He led me to the police chief's office and gave orders to have the report prepared within the hour. I asked if I should give him some money, but he waved me off. I guess my predicament, the picture of my family, and the expression of gratitude was enough for him. I was so focused on the loss of our vehicle that I failed to consider Phyllis's losses. The half-finished needlepoint tablecloth that she had been working on for a long time was in the back of our stolen vehicle. She did not tell me until months later, because she did not want to increase my sadness from the loss of the vehicle. She never did needlepoint again.

Before leaving Rio, we took a taxi to the starting point of the two cable cars to the top of Sugarloaf Mountain. The bus trip to São Paulo gave me time to think about the logistics involved in getting the family from São Paulo to Londrina. We did not have a key to our house because it had been in the Suburban. When we arrived home and started looking for a way into the house, Randy discovered the house had a broken window in the back. Ruth volunteered to squeeze through the opening. We saw signs of a robbery. It must have been neighborhood kids. A few valuables had been taken, including some of Phyllis's jewelry and her award for being the most outstanding student in her school.

The last Sunday before we moved, I took the children to the São Paulo Zoo. We stayed until closing time. This meant a crowd had gathered at the bus stop. I was so focused on protecting the children from the crush of people trying to get on the bus, I was not aware that a pickpocket lifted my billfold with my Brazilian documents and some money. A *despachante* (a paid document facilitator) used photocopies of the documents to get new documents.

This must have been a confusing time for our children. We kept them as informed as we thought we should, but how much can confused parents do except assure them that we were taking care of them. We decided to leave Randy at the seminary to complete the school year in December. He was invited to live with the mother of his buddy Wesley; Wesley's father was in the States completing a doctorate in Old Testament studies. This left the father unscathed by the crisis at the seminary, thus his family continued to live there.

The movers said it would take two or three days to deliver our furniture in Londrina. I suggested to Phyllis that, instead of going by an eight-hour bus trip and staying overnight in a hotel, we take an eighteen-hour trip and travel via old-fashioned passenger cars connected to the freight train from São Paulo to north Paraná. Many times I had seen this slow-moving train meander next to portions of the highway and wondered what it would be like to travel like the early settlers. We were surprised at the train station by some former students, who gave us the last of many musical serenades. We tearfully said good-bye to them; they had experienced some of the most interesting days of our lives. In the years that followed, I was invited to officiate at the weddings of several of these students who had chosen other professions.

Thirty years later we met again at the seminary for three days of reflection, statements of repentance, and asking for forgiveness from the church leaders for the unjust decision to close the seminary in 1968. The students had gone on with their lives and had become outstanding leaders in other professions. I often wondered what the church would have been like had we not lost a generation of these promising leaders.

The children loved the train trip with the seats transformed into sleeping berths at night and a woodstove to cook meals in the dining car. The slow twisting and turning of the train, combined with frequent stops, made sleeping almost impossible for Phyllis and me. I felt relieved at the end of all the excitement and conflicts in the seminary, but I was anxious about starting over again. This time it was to be a new ministry of hospital chaplaincy in Londrina.

CHAPTER 11

Starting Over in Londrina, Paraná October 1968—March 1971

The cave that you fear to enter holds the treasure that you seek.

—Joseph Campbell

Two taxi drivers took us and our luggage from the train station to our new home. The truck hauling our furniture arrived a short time later. The three-bedroom brick house was well built and attractively painted. Large ornamental plants grew in the small front yard, and fruit trees stood in the back between the house and the maid's quarters. The lots across the street and to the left of the house had not been sold. Our neighbors lived in the four houses to the right of us.

We missed the freedom of our own means of transportation between the six months when our vehicle was stolen and the time when we could buy another. Fortunately the bus stop on the route into town was only a block away.

The children wanted to have a Christmas tree, though they were seldom seen in Brazil because Christmas came in the middle of summer. I usually found one at a nursery, but this year we had no way to transport it. I decided to cut a branch from the tall hibiscus bush in the front yard as a substitute. After we decorated it, Walter said, "Daddy, do you really believe that's a Christmas tree?"

Riding busses and taxis soon got old. It took the threat of a lawsuit to get the insurance company to settle our claim for the stolen vehicle, but the settlement we received wasn't enough to buy another Suburban. We had to settle for a Jeep station wagon.

The fact that I was not consulted before the bishop appointed me to be the chaplain in the hospital meant that I knew very little about what was expected of me. Neither had I asked too many questions after the crisis at the seminary.

My first day at work was full of surprises. No one introduced me. I asked to speak to the president of the hospital. He informed me that the hospital had never had a full-time chaplain; rather, the pastors of the four founding churches occasionally volunteered a few hours a week as part-time chaplains. Rev. Valdir Peres Marins, the pastor of the Central Methodist Church and district superintendent, saw this as an opportunity to have a free full-time missionary chaplain when he heard about the closing of the seminary. The president agreed to accept his offer since I would not be paid by the hospital.

The president told me the hospital was owned and directed by the pastors and lay trustees of the Methodist, Baptist, Presbyterian, and Independent Presbyterian churches. He added that 90 percent of the doctors and employees were Roman Catholic and about 95 percent of the patients claimed to be Catholic.

The president did not tell me that he had not consulted with nor had he informed the doctors and employees about my position as hospital chaplain. I ran into a buzz saw of questions and hostility as soon as I started visiting patients. No one understood why I was there or what I was doing visiting patients, though I had taken time to stop at the nursing stations to introduce myself. The doctors and nurses had not requested a chaplain, and they didn't know what a chaplain was supposed to do. They saw me as interfering with patient care. The fact that I was a North American only added to the resistance.

A few hours later I went home disoriented and angry. I felt used and pushed around by the bishop and district superintendent who had made decisions without including me. Missionary service was not supposed to be this difficult. Why was I in such a predicament?

The next day I confronted the president about the lack of communication and preparation for my position in the hospital. He apologized and reminded me that several months had passed since he agreed to the request for me to be assigned as chaplain and my arrival. He did not know for sure that I would be coming. He suggested I start slowly, with an hour a day in the hospital, and gradually increase the time.

Over a period of several weeks I discovered my problem was the culture of Brazilian hospitals. They had no experience with a clinically trained chaplain or frame of reference for my role in the hospital. I discovered I was the first full-time Protestant hospital chaplain in the country. Brazilian pastors had served as part-time chaplains in this hospital for a few hours a week. None of them had clinical training for the job. Doctors mostly avoided them, because the pastors were known for asking doctors for free medical treatment for their families and members of their churches. Pastors with little or no seminary training and little confidence in medical treatment over their prayers had created many negative impressions. There were few full-time Catholic chaplains in Brazil, but they also had very little education and no clinical training. They tended to frighten patients into thinking they must be dying, because priests usually visited patients only to administer the ritual of extreme unction before death. Catholic bishops often sidelined incompetent and trouble-making priests by appointing them to serve as hospital chaplains. No wonder I was having so much difficulty.

This led me to think differently about my ministry in the hospital context. Starting over requires a good look at the cultural context of the new place. I had to do much more than provide individual care of patients. If I wanted to succeed, I had to demonstrate with my life and service how a chaplain could make a positive contribution to the quality of care in the hospital. If I could do this successfully, it would transform the predominant understanding of pastoral care.

The fiduciary churches had created a hospital institution that was known to offer the best medical care in north Paraná, but they had not combined that with good spiritual care. They realized they were ceding control of the hospital to the medical profession and were looking for a way to change that.

Though I knew little about systems theory, I started thinking about my role as a creator and facilitator of a system of pastoral care. Martin Luther's theology of the priesthood of all believers helped me conceptualize my role. Everyone working in the hospital was there to minister to the needs of the patients. We had different training, experiences, roles, and responsibilities, but each person participated in the healing ministry of the hospital. This thinking led to a plan of action for a holistic ministry of pastoral care in the hospital. I decided it would be best to dedicate half of my time to patient visitation and the other half to caring for hospital personnel in the context of their work.

In order to create a more positive impression of a hospital chaplain, I had to start by creating a favorable impression of me as a colleague and as a pastor. I had to meet the hospital workers where they worked. I knew the toughest profession would be the doctors, some of whom had already made snide remarks when they passed me in the halls. I decided to show up without an invitation in the doctor's lounge when they met at 10:00 a.m. for coffee and consultations. Four evangelical doctors showed some interest in talking with me, but most of doctors ignored me. One by one, I started conversations until they responded in a friendly manner, especially when I asked for information to help with my patient visits. Before long, some doctors sought me out to ask questions and to invite me to help care for their patients.

The nurses were easier to get to know, because I had been stopping by the nursing stations to check with them before and after visiting with the patients in their units. Before long they were hearing good things about me from the patients. They started seeing me as an asset to patient care. Some asked me to help them with professional, personal, and family issues.

I made it a point to a least say *bom dia* ("hello") to all the employees each day I was in the hospital by expanding my visits to all areas of the hospital. I walked through all departments and work area such as admissions, the nursing stations, physicians break room, business offices, kitchen, laundry, custodian's workroom, and pharmacy. It took time to do this, but the effort paid off. There was a huge dividend from my effort to make everyone feel important enough for me to stop and speak to them each day. Sometimes I was stopped to ask for prayer or to share some concern. When I was away on a trip, they asked where I had been because they missed me.

Many of the teaching stories I used for twenty-five years of classes in pastoral care and counseling came from my experiences in the Hospital Evangélico de Londrina. I've told them so many times until the exact sequence of events may not be in order. Here are some of the more important ones.

I had a major breakthrough a few months after starting this ministry. The chief OB-GYN nurse asked if I would talk with her mother, who had been suffering severe migraine headaches each weekend for the past twenty years. She had been treated by several doctors in the hospital and taken a variety of medications. But none of this had stopped the weekend headaches. When I learned that she was over sixty, I didn't think I could help her. I had read Sigmund Freud's statement that patients over sixty rarely changed, but I had plenty time to try to help her.

During our first appointment, she told me her family history. I discovered she had ten children, one of whom died when he was eighteen. She avoided my attempts to get her to talk about his death. At the next session, I asked more questions about him, starting with when she knew she was pregnant with him and working through the developmental stages of his life. When I asked about when, where, and how he had died, she quickly changed the subject. Following my hunch that the headaches were related to his death, I picked up the subject the next time by asking about the clothes he was wearing when she last saw him and the lunch he took to work. She had complete recall of all of this.

Finally, she told me he was killed on a Friday afternoon. She learned about his death from one of his co-workers who ran to her house shouting the news that her son was dead. He said a chain had broken, and a log rolled off the truck and crushed him. I asked about her reaction. She said that she was so overwhelmed that she grabbed her head. Then an overpowering headache forced her to go to bed. She stayed there for several days. She missed the funeral the next day. She cried very little and didn't want to talk with anyone about her son. She returned to her household responsibilities during the week, but she had to stay in bed each Friday through Sunday when the migraines returned and made it too painful to get up. Her post-traumatic headaches had been going on for over twenty years.

After a time of empathy and silence, I re-created a mental picture of the scene when she heard about his death. Before I could finish the scenario, she suddenly burst into belly-wrenching crying. Her crying escalated into screaming and yelling, as if she were hearing the news of her son's death for the first time. It was painful to watch and listen to her, though I knew this was exactly what she needed to do. Her screams were heard throughout the offices in the building. I had to reassure several people who came to check on the noise that everything was okay and getting better. I sent for her daughter to comfort her. This mother had never visited the grave where her son was buried, which was very unusual for a Brazilian. I suggested that the custom was to bury loved ones the day after their death; therefore, she should invite her children to go with her to the cemetery the next day to be with her as she said good-bye to her son. Before she left my office, she thanked me and said she felt relieved and much lighter from talking with me. Her migraine headaches never returned.

When the story spread around the hospital, mostly by her daughter, I detected a more positive attitude toward me and my hospital chaplaincy ministry. This woman was the first person to teach me about the power of encapsulated grief. This is grief that is not expressed after a loss and remains bottled up, waiting for a later opportunity for release, which may take years.

Dr. Benedito da Rocha, a short, stocky neurosurgeon soon took an interest in me, because he had completed a short-term residency in the United States. Talking with me was an opportunity to practice his English. He had a negative reputation among the nurses because he had a temper and would throw surgical instruments in the operating room. He was unmerciful with nurses when he found fault with their patient care. On the other hand, he was highly respected for his skills as a neurosurgeon.

During a morning coffee break, he was telling the other doctors that he did not understand why a sixteen-year-old patient who tried Russian roulette and lost the gamble was not moving his legs. He said the gun was pointed upward, thus the bullet missed the section of the brain that controlled mobility. But the kid said he could not move his legs or sit up.

I said that I had observed both parents had been at his bedside since his surgery, with the mother on one side and the father on the other. I suggested he ask the mother to go home and rest, And then tell the father to make his son sit up and walk around the room. Dr. Benedito said, "What in the hell do you know about neurosurgery." I said that I knew as much as he knew about families.

He was desperate enough to try anything, so he went to the patient's room and sent the mother home, telling her not to come back until he summoned her. She left crying. (I told him there was a better way to deal with the family of his patients than to speak so forcefully.)

When Dr. Benedito made his patient rounds the next morning, he found the boy walking around the room. In the doctor's lounge he demanded that I explain why I suggested he send the mother home. I told him that I detected marital problems during my visit with this patient. From this I concluded the boy was triangulated in the marriage and was trying to provide a reason for his parents to reconcile their differences for his sake.

Before long, Dr. Benedito was inviting me to make the morning rounds with him and referring some outpatients who were not responding to his medical treatments for me to counsel with them. After several reports from his patients about how much I had helped them with their problems, the doctor suggested I resign the hospital chaplaincy and start a counseling practice with him and two neurologists. He said he could make me rich if I would quit this religion business. I resisted this temptation so I could fulfill my calling as a Methodist missionary. Had I accepted his offer, I would still be living in Brazil, and my children and grandchildren would probably be Brazilians today.

As I was leaving the hospital one day, the receptionist asked if I had seen a critically ill ten-year-old boy who had been admitted that afternoon. When she showed me the chaplain's information card, I knew that I had not gone by his room. She reminded me that spiritualists usually go to their spiritual leader for healing and seldom come to the hospital. I immediately went to the boy's room. I saw him lying either sleeping or in a coma, with many lines with fluids running into his arm and leg. I introduced myself to the parents as the hospital chaplain.

The mother asked, "Who in this hospital gets rid of the evil spirits that are making my son so sick?"

Without thinking, I responded, "I do." Fear ran through my body as soon as I heard myself. But I quickly added, "Let's pray."

There was nothing unusual about my prayer. It was similar to the prayers I'd prayed for other patients that day. But I left the hospital thinking that the boy wouldn't live through the night.

As soon as I arrived at the main nursing station the next morning, the head nurse told me that several doctors were waiting for me in the doctor's lounge. This was very unusual. I asked why they wanted to see me.

She said, "It's about the boy admitted in critical condition yesterday, and you visited him before going home."

I asked, "Did he die?"

She said, "Oh, no. He's completely well and waiting to be discharged. The mother told the doctors that the chaplain went to his room after he was admitted and got rid of the evil spirit. She said her son got well soon after you left. The doctors are waiting to hear what you did."

I couldn't believe this news, so I went to see for myself. The boy was dressed, sitting on the edge of the bed, swinging his legs, and looking perfectly normal. The mother, in a very simple manner, thanked me for healing her son. I left the room completely surprised. While I walked to the doctor's lounge, I was worried that they were thinking I had interfered with the boy's treatment by casting out an evil spirit. I said a quick prayer and remembered how Jesus often responded to difficult questions.

As soon as I entered the lounge, all conversation stopped. The admitting doctor said, "Chaplain David, yesterday that boy was almost dead when we admitted him. When he got sick, the parents had first gone to a spiritualist practitioner. They almost did not get him to this hospital in time. We were doing everything possible to save his life. Then you go in his room, and the mother tells us he got well as soon as you got rid of the evil spirit. What did you do?"

I said, "I prayed a prayer no different from the prayers I prayed for other people. If you will tell me how some people get well from your medical treatments while others do not, I will tell you why this boy was healed and others are not."

The doctor said, "We can't answer that question."

So I said, "Neither can I. I'm just as surprised as you are, but I'm glad he's well no matter how his parents explain his healing."

Another doctor said, "All I can say is that it must be a miracle."

The experience of this healing taught me that I am not the healer but the facilitator of healing. God is the ultimate healer. The mother's faith in getting her son to the hospital, in spite of her spiritualist beliefs, had as much to do with the miracle as the doctor's treatments and the chaplain's prayer.

At the hospital I met an elderly full-blooded Brazilian Indian named Ze. He lived at the hospital and claimed to be more than a hundred years old. But he had no relatives to verify his age. At one time he collected and sold used newspapers to help support the hospital. When he became homeless, a hospital administrator let him live in an unoccupied building in the back of the property. I visited him several times to listen to his stories.

One day Ze climbed on a chair to change a light bulb, fell, and broke his hip. The orthopedist did the best he could to repair the damage, but

Ze never walked again. He was moved to a hospital room and stayed there for over a year, though he was a nonpaying patient. I visited him as often as I could to provide a little company and to pray for him.

During one of these visits, as I was getting ready to pray with him, he asked that I pray for him to die. I had never prayed for the death of a patient, so I prayed a general prayer that he would live as comfortable as possible until the time came for him to die. After I said "Amen," he grabbed my arm and said, "You did not pray for me to die."

I tried again, with a prayer that God would be merciful until Ze was ready to die. As soon as I said, "Amen," Ze grabbed my arm more forcefully and said, "Tell God to let me die now."

I then asked, "Why do you want to die now?"

He said, "When you are so old that people no longer understand your stories, it's time to die. I want you to tell God that this time has come."

I did just that, and he died the next day. Ze taught me to be more specific when I prayed, but first to find out the motivation behind a prayer request.

The head nurse in the OB-GYN ward asked me to visit a woman brought in from the country who was having trouble dilating and would not give her doctor permission for a C-section to deliver her baby. I pulled up a chair and asked her what she was most worried about.

The woman said that this was her first hospital visit, and she was worried that her child would die if she gave birth. I asked if this was her first pregnancy. She told me that two years earlier she had given birth at home with the help of a midwife. She gave birth to twins, and one of them died soon afterward. She said she was afraid this would happen when she gave birth to this child. I assured her that her husband brought her to the hospital because he wanted her to have the best possible help and that she was in a safe place with the best doctors and nurses to assist her. I prayed a long prayer for her and her baby before leaving the room.

About an hour later I heard the emergency paging system summon the OB-GYN doctor. I went to the unit a little later. As the doctor was leaving the woman's room, he stopped and said, "Next time you help get the patient to the delivery room before you pray for her."

I told him, "You owe me half your fee for the delivery of that baby."

Hospital patients taught me a great deal about the power of prayer. Sometimes I thought they believed in prayer more than I did. From my experiences with them, I gained confidence and courage in asking patients and clients if I could pray for them. The Catholic religious culture helped me claim the priestly power of my ordination. Since the majority of patients and staff were Roman Catholic, I wanted them to know that, as a Protestant chaplain, I respected their beliefs enough not to force mine upon them. When a patient or family member requested a visit from a priest, I called the local diocese office. Usually, these requests were for extreme unction when a patient was dying.

The patriarch of a large extended Italian family was in his last hours of life on earth when the family asked for a priest. I called the diocese to ask that a priest come as soon as possible. When he arrived, I stepped into the hall to allow him to talk with the family and offer the ritual of extreme unction.

When he came out, I thanked him for coming. He asked, "Do you think that man is dying?"

I said, "Yes, he's dying. Didn't you notice his long, deep-throated breaths? The only thing keeping him alive this long is the oxygen tent."

He said, "I've never seen anyone die."

I asked him how long he had been a priest, and he said twenty years. So I grabbed his arm and led him back into the room to see the man die. The waiting made him very nervous, and I stopped him from leaving several times. He started over with the Lord's Prayer and other ritual sayings. I encouraged the family members to join in saying the prayers with him.

After another time of silence, he said, "Let's light a candle for him as he goes from this life to the next."

I objected, saying, "If you light a candle with him taking oxygen in this room, we will all go where he's going." I suggested he talk with the individual family members about their thoughts and feelings regarding the patient.

When the man finally drew his last breath, the drama of family grief hit full force with crying, screaming, and moaning. The priest was so frightened by this display of emotions that he tried to calm them down with platitudes about death and told them not to cry. When this did not work, he tried to leave. I stopped him again to teach him how to give pastoral care in moments of grief. I told him that it was best not to stop this explosion of emotional response to the loss of a loved one; rather, to encourage them to release their feelings. He was trying to shut them up while I was telling them to express their feelings.

After the family calmed down and started to leave the hospital, I walked to the door with the priest to check on how he was doing. He told me that ministering to the family this way was the most beautiful experience he had had in all his years of ministry. His face convinced me that he was in awe at being present at the moment of a death. I was pleased that he learned a new way of being a priest.

My theology of divorce was formed during these chaplaincy years. Brazilian law did not permit divorce until the 1980s. Thus, prior to that, divorce was not an option for troubled marriages. "Until death do us part" was a blessing and a curse for people trapped in a failed marriage. On the one hand, the prohibition of divorce stabilized the institution of marriage, but on the other hand, people who needed to get a divorce had no way out. Some men took advantage of the situation either by having affairs or by maintaining a family with their wife and financially supporting a mistress. Some unhappily married men simply disappeared, thus abandoning their family and condemning their wife to a future without marriage and financial support.

I was the pastor to a woman whose husband had disappeared. She was living with a widower who loved and supported her. She requested the sacrament of the Lord's Supper, and I gave it to her, though the church rules stated I could not do this when this couple was not married.

I noticed how patients, especially women, were often very sad instead of being glad when they were told they would be discharged. Some got immediately worst so they couldn't be sent home. In such instances, I would inquire about marriage and family issues and grasped the intimate relationship between problems at home and physical health.

I was puzzled by the frequent deaths of post-op middle-aged women. I started asking questions before surgeries to discover if there was a link between unhappy marriages and death from surgical procedures. If I encountered a woman who believed she would die from the surgery, I usually found that she was trapped in an unhappy marriage. I shared this finding with the surgeons. Some of them postponed the surgery until I had time to counsel the patient, and this included the spouse whenever possible.

One surgeon brushed aside my report that his patient was convinced that she would die from a hysterectomy. He operated anyway. When she died the next day, I unloaded my anger on him in front of other surgeons for not considering the emotional state of his patients before surgery.

When one critically ill woman was admitted to the hospital, she continued to get worse during a course of aggressive medical treatment. So I asked her point blank, "Why is it so important for you to die? What is going on in your life that you would rather die than have to face it?"

She told me how happy she had been as a wife and a mother of two children. Then she discovered her husband had fathered a child by another woman and refused to stop seeing the other woman. She said she would rather die than live with this problem.

The next morning I told her primary physician and the other specialist treating her what I had found out from talking with her. I told them she would die unless something drastic were done, and then I asked permission to confront her.

With their permission, I met with her again and said, "You are the worst mother I have ever met. You are planning to die because you realize your husband has another woman and they have a child. That may resolve your anger toward your husband, but it will not help your children. They will then go to live with this other woman as her stepchildren. This means they will have second-class status to her children. You are a sorry mother because you are condemning your children to unhappy childhoods. If you want them to be happy and successful in life, you need to live in order to raise them the way you want them to live."

She angrily told me how mean I was, and then she cried a long time. I sat with her until I heard her say, "I want to live for my children. Will you help me?"

I promised to help her talk with her husband. Then I asked, "Are you now ready and willing to let your doctors help you live so you can raise your children."

She said she would fight to live. When I told her doctors what she decided, they used more aggressive methods to control her infection and later discharged her to go home to face her family situation. I had two sessions of marriage counseling with her and her husband before she left the hospital.

During my chaplaincy, I discovered how important the emotional state, social relationships, and spiritual beliefs of patients are in medical care. At the same time, the hospital staff began to realize the value of a chaplain. Doctors frequently told me how much they valued my work with them. They said they missed me when I was on vacation or traveling on church commitments. They asked me what I did that was so helpful to patients. When I said I did nothing but be with them, listen, and prayer, it was hard for them to understand something so simple.

The doctors asked if I would do more marriage and family counseling in the hospital. I tried to put them off by claiming that I did not have the professional training to do this. And so they asked if I knew someone else who did have the credentials, but I couldn't think of anyone. Then they quoted a Brazilian saying that has become one of the most important principles of my life: when you want to go hunting, and you don't have a dog, get a cat. They said to me, "You are the cat here, so do your job." I have often turned to this saying when faced with a situation beyond my understanding and resources.

When a doctor's patient died after surgery, I first comforted the family, and then I looked for the doctor to express my sympathy for the loss of the patient. I knew how personally they took the death of someone they were trained to help. By showing my care for them, I gained authority to confront them when I thought they were wrong in the way they treated the nurses and their relationships with the patients.

One afternoon I discovered the nurses at one unit were upset because a surgeon said he was going to have one of them fired for stopping a blood transfusion to a patient who happened to be the nurse's mother. The surgeon had ordered the transfusion after doing an abdominal surgery. My first thought was that this nurse needed to be fired for violating the surgeon's orders.

I approached the nurse as she was crying by the bedside of her mother, who was still under the effect of an anesthesia. I asked for her side of the story. She said that everyone in her family was a Jehovah Witness, and they had strong convictions against blood transfusions. Her mother had told the surgeon that under no circumstances was he to give her a blood transfusion during or after the surgery. But he ignored her beliefs and ordered a liter of blood anyway. The nurse said that if her mother saw the transfusion, she would go into shock and want to die. Though she realized she could be fired for disobeying a doctor's order, her love for her mother compelled her to remove the blood transfusion before her mother saw it.

Though I did not agree with the family's beliefs, I thought this nurse needed an advocate. I met with the hospital president before the surgeon could see him. With the information I supplied, the president refused to fire the nurse and used the situation to teach the surgeon that if he could not follow the request of his patients, he should refuse to do the surgery.

The first baby of a young couple born into in a large extended family drew a crowd to see the child and congratulate the couple. During the night the baby died, possibly a result of sudden infant death syndrome. The family's joy immediately turned to mourning. The mother was inconsolable and refused to go home without the child she had held the day before. Her family and the doctor and nurses couldn't convince her to leave. I was called to help deal with the situation.

I had briefly visited the mother soon after the birth and then after the baby's death. I suggested we have a special worship service in the break room where I held chapel services once a week. She agreed to this if I would call her pastor to speak, which I did.

I officiated for the funeral service and introduced the pastor of the Independent Presbyterian Church to speak. In his attempt to comfort the family, he tried to answer the question of why the child had died. He said God took this baby to heaven because he wants people of all ages to populate heaven. Her baby was chosen as a rose would be chosen to be one of God's heavenly babies.

I was seated behind the pastor while he spoke and noticed my foot swinging up toward his butt. After the service was over, I confronted the pastor, grabbed him by his lapels, and lifted him up to my level to tell him that I would rather be an atheist than believe in a God who would steal a mother's baby. He looked shocked that I was so angry. I do not know if he reexamined his theology of death, but I do know that he was chosen to fill the position of hospital chaplain after I left Londrina. (Years later I learned that that Protestant chaplains in Brazil now receive their clinical pastoral education in the hospital where I started the chaplaincy program.)

My family life started to settle into a routine. Randy was still completing his school year in São Paulo. We enrolled Ruth, Walter, and Susana in a three-hour-a-day Brazilian public school. Phyllis supplemented their education with homeschooling in English. We were fortunate to find Da. Nunciata, a wonderful forty-year-old woman, to be our housekeeper. She had a husband and two children, but she needed to work since her husband didn't make enough to support the family. Neither did his boss pay his social security with health benefits. We paid hers so she and her family would have some resources for medical care.

About a month after arriving in Londrina, we heard clapping at our front door and saw Maria Lopes Baltazar, a young woman in the church we served in Apucarana, waiting to talk with us. When we lived in Apucarana, her parents had asked me to dissuade their daughter from becoming a doctor, because they could not afford that kind of education for her. I refused their request and encouraged her to pursue her vision with faith that God would provide the financial resources.

After greeting us now, she said she had completed high school with honors and needed a place to stay in Londrina to study for the entrance exams to the new medical school opening the next year in Londrina. Phyllis and I shuffled the children's beds so that six-year-old Susana shared Walter and Paul's bedroom, which allowed Maria to share a room with Ruth.

One day Maria saw the children playing with an old microscope, which had been given them by an ophthalmologist in Waycross, Georgia. Maria asked if she could use the microscope to study for her biology exams. She later used it to teach high school chemistry classes to help pay her expenses.

As the day of the entrance exams to medical school approached, she learned that twelve hundred applicants had registered for an entering class of forty students. At the end of the long two-week wait for the exams to be graded, she was told she had made the highest grade and was accepted as a medical student.

Her acceptance, however, created several new problems. Where would she live? Who would pay her tuition? Who would pay for her textbooks? The first was easy. Since she had blended into our family so well during the previous three months, we decided she could continue to live with us.

One day during a coffee break with the doctors at the hospital, I talked about Maria. With a tongue-in-cheek attitude, I told them they had been robbing people long enough and it was time to do something good for a deserving medical student by paying the part of her tuition that her scholarship did not pay and to provide her with textbooks. To my surprise, the doctors agreed to do so. All the time Maria lived with us, she was a quiet, dedicated student. The last I heard from her, she was working as a psychiatrist in São Paulo.

In December, at the end of the school year, Randy came to live with us. It was good to have the family together again. In the backyard was a small apartment for a live-in maid. We didn't use it for that purpose because Da. Nunciata had her own home and family. Since I had lived as a teenager in a separate room from the house on Forrest Street in Valdosta, I asked Randy if he wanted to sleep back there. He liked the idea of having his own room.

We thought life had finally settled down, but bigger surprises were in store for our family.

CHAPTER 12

Our Last Years in Londrina

Do not forget to show hospitality to strangers, for by so doing some people have shown hospitality to angels without knowing it.

—Hebrews 13:2

We now had eight people living in our home in Londrina. A few weeks later we added another.

Bob Davis, the treasurer for the Methodist missionaries in Brazil, called me one night and asked me to meet the 7:00 a.m. bus from São Paulo to pick up an overnight package. When the bus arrived the next morning, instead of a package, Clara Amelia, the president of the Methodist youth in Brazil, stepped off the bus and walked toward me. She said, "Let's get out of here." I asked about her suitcase, and she said she didn't have one. When she saw soldiers milling around the bus station, she asked me to put my arm around her as if she were my girlfriend. I felt her body shaking and noticed how frightened she was as we walked past the watchful soldiers.

Once inside the Jeep, she felt safe enough to cry. Between crying spells, she told me she was with a group of university students in São Paulo who were getting ready to distribute leaflets demanding the military government allow free and open elections. The leaflets were to be soaked in alcohol and strewn from the tops of tall buildings at major intersections for the wind to distribute. It was against the law to do this, but it was the only way to appeal to the people after the freedom of press laws had been suspended. The students knew they were taking a big risk if they were caught, but they felt it was their moral duty to spread the news.

Someone discovered the leaflets in a back closet of the Methodist bookstore and tipped off the military police, which was known for arresting people without warrants and for torturing them for information. The group was discovered as they soaked the packets of leaflets, and most of them were arrested. Clara Amelia and her boyfriend, Domingos, were among the few who escaped before the police could apprehend them. They went in separate directions to avoid capture.

Clara Amelia was afraid to go home because the police might be waiting to arrest her. She went instead to Bob Davis's house and told him her story. After a couple of days with Bob's family, he decided it would be safer to get her out of the city. They agreed that I was one of the few persons they both trusted to help hide her from the military police. She was in a life-threatening situation had she been caught. The military police was alleged to rape women to extract information.

When we arrived home from the bus station, Phyllis prepared breakfast for her. When Da. Nunciata came, we told the children to stay inside while Phyllis and I went outside with Clara Amelia to talk. Phyllis and I had no hesitation in taking her into our home to protect her from the military police, though we knew that by doing this we were compromising our own safety. At least we would have help from the US government should we be arrested, whereas, a Brazilian would have no such protection.

We decided to ask Walter to sleep in the room at the back of the house with Randy. We gave Ruth the option to either sleep in the room with Susana and Paul or to sleep on the living room couch. She chose the couch. We knew the children would want to know why Clara Amelia was living with us, so we told the children and our housekeeper that Clara Amelia had problems at home with her mother and had come to live with us for a while. We decided to call her Marta to further disguise her identity. We decided that Maria Lucia should know the truth or she would be suspicious. We trusted her to keep the secret, and we wanted Clara Amelia to have someone close to her age to confide in. No other person, especially other pastors and Bishop Wilbur, were told about her living with us.

At the first Annual Conference after the closing of the seminary, the bishop invited the military honor guard to participate in the opening ceremonies in order to intimidate those who opposed to the military dictatorship. Phyllis and I knew not to trust anyone, except Bob Davis and our Canadian missionary friends at the Methodist Rural Institute near Maringá. I asked Bob to inform Mac McCoy in New York in case I should be arrested for hiding a fugitive. We stopped inviting visitors into our home. When someone came to the house, Clara Amelia immediately went to her room.

The first days Clara Amelia was in our home, she rested. Since she had only the clothes on her back, Phyllis bought some things for her as well as material to make dresses. When Clara Amelia expressed concern about her family not knowing what had happened to her, I suggested she write letters letting them know she was safe and being cared for by a Christian family. She was not to describe anything that might be useful to the police in tracking her down, including putting a return address on the envelope. I dropped these letters in post offices at various towns so they could not be traced back to us. This meant her family could hear from her, but she could not receive news from them.

A few months later I went to Belo Horizonte, Minas Gerais, not as a delegate to the 1970 Methodist General Conference, but as a reporter for the Board of Missions. While there I roomed with Clara Amelia's brother, Sebastion. He was a clergy delegate from the Fourth Annual Conference. Since it was common knowledge about the imprisonment of several Methodist youth and the disappearance of others, I asked him what had happened to his sister.

He cautiously told me the family didn't know where she was, but they knew she was safe and being cared for by a Christian family. He told me that after the police roundup in São Paulo, two members of the military police had been sent to the family's home to arrest her whenever she might return. They remained in the house twenty-four hours a day, against the wishes of the family, for two weeks. His mother knew that Clara Amelia would be arrested, tortured, and possibly raped or killed by the military police if she came home while the officers were there. In spite of this, she decided to show these soldiers Christian hospitality by treating them as special guests. She fed them and gave them a place to sleep. One of the soldiers became sick, and Clara Amelia's mother cared for him as if he were her own son.

Sebastion also told me about the birth of a sister's baby and other family news. As we talked, my heart almost broke from the desire to tell him that his sister was in our home, but I couldn't risk the consequences of him sharing this information with the wrong person.

Mac McCoy attended this General Conference, and we had a chance to talk privately. He said that when he planned to discuss the leaders of the Methodist youth and the military police, because he wanted to know where each stood on the matter. Most of them were supportive of the youth, but a few said that the students who got away should be found and arrested by the police. Mac also gave me a two-thousand-dollar check to carry with me at all times; I was to use the money to help Dr. Warwick Keer escape from Brazil if he was threatened by the military police. Dr. Keer was the Methodist lay leader whom the bishops had dismissed as a trustee of the seminary. In spite of this, Keer had helped the students when they occupied the seminary after the bishops thought they had closed it. He had recently been elected president of the Brazilian Academy of Scientists. These were dangerous times, and they required extraordinary precautions to minimize the danger.

In the 1960s and 1970s Londrina was the most Protestant city in Paraná. Over 20 percent of the population belonged to Protestant churches. The establishment of the Hospital Evangélico de Londrina and the leading private school, the Instituto Filadélfia de Londrina, contributed to the growth of Protestantism in the city. The Presbyterian,

Methodist, and Baptist churches in the city elected trustees to govern the hospital and the school. The school was started in the late 1930s by a Presbyterian layman. With his leadership, the school grew to over three thousand students in kindergarten through high school. It was near the center of the city.

Soon after I arrived in Londrina, I heard about serious problems in the school, but I was too focused on the chaplaincy program at the hospital to pay much attention. This changed a year later when I was asked to serve on the school's board of trustees. The president had been asked to resign when financial mismanagement caused the school to go deeply into debt. Enrollment had dropped from to less than fifteen hundred. The morale of the teachers was in serious decline because their salaries were not being paid on time.

The chairman of the board took over the presidency of the school, but he soon discovered he could not be the president and serve as pastor of the largest Presbyterian church in the city. The board members asked me to be the president to restore financial responsibility and credibility. I think this was because they respected my ideas about restoring the prestige of the school and because I was an outsider who lacked any threat of nepotism.

I thought and prayed about the school presidency. Phyllis said she had no objections, except she didn't see how I could do a good job as president of the school and as chaplain in the hospital. I told her it would mean a sharp reduction of hours in the hospital, but I thought I could manage my time to do both jobs. The Methodist pastor and leading Methodist layman on the board of trustees at both institutions encouraged me to accept the invitation. I said yes, but I should have consulted with Mac McCoy and Bishop Wilbur beforehand. When I informed them later, they were not happy that I was taking on this much responsibility, but they did not ask me to relinquish the additional post.

With the support of the school trustees, I threw myself into the realities of the present situation in order to develop a vision for the future. I discovered that teachers were owed three months' back pay. I went to the bank to borrow the money to pay them. It cost 25 percent for a three-month loan, the maximum length of time banks would lend money when interest rates were over 100 percent a year. I planned to repay the loan with tuition payments when school started again in two months.

The campus buildings had not been repaired or painted in years. Neither had they been properly cleaned. I hired a young man to be the buildings and grounds superintendent; he had become a Christian in Arapongas when I was pastor of that church. His job was to manage the maintenance staff and school purchases. I told him not to dump any problems on my desk, but to think through the situation enough that he could answer seven questions:

1. What is the issue?
2. What needs to be done about it?
3. How will it help?
4. What will it cost?
5. Who will do it?
6. How long will it take?
7. Who will get upset when it's done?

He became a wonderful manager and supervisor. One day he told me he had discovered why the school was in such a difficult financial situation. The former president had several relatives in key positions in the school. One of these had been in charge of purchases and continued in this position until I dismissed him. He had arranged for school suppliers, contractors, and outside workers to submit two receipts. One was for the actual purchase price and the other was about 20 percent higher for him to submit for reimbursement from the school. As we dug deeper, we found other relatives on the payroll who did practically nothing but were paid a salary. I learned to hate nepotism.

These relatives of the former president did not go without a fight. Threatening anonymous phone calls started coming to my office, warning me that the caller was going to denounce me as a communist to the police or other accusations to get me into trouble. At first they worried me, then it made me angry.

I had to do something before these rumors turned into someone's reality. I decided to fight back by telling the academic director about the calls and how I recognized their voices and knew their names. I said I was going to report them to the police and ask the police chief for a certified statement that there was no record in Brazil of my being a Communist. When I got this certificate I planned to frame it to hang in my office so that the people who were making these anonymous calls could be sued and reported to the police.

I knew the academic director had come from Poland after World War II and had survived a concentration camp, probably by being a good informer. He was a good academic director, but he was just as good at triangulating people. Evidently he told the people who needed to hear about my plan to go to the police, because the calls stopped.

A relative of the former president called to tell me that his daughter had graduated from college with a degree in English, and he expected me to give her a job as an English teacher. I told him to send her over. When she arrived, I spoke with her only in English. As I anticipated, she didn't know enough English to converse with me. Her face turned red, and she got up and left.

So I asked Phyllis to teach the class. No one could argue with her ability to teach English, and I would not have to pay her a salary since the Board of Missions did not allow us to earn extra money.

To better understand the mood, concerns, and hopes for the school, I put together three surveys: one for the teachers, one for the students, and one for the parents of the students. I made out extensive questionnaires and distributed them to each group and imposed a deadline for returning them. I wound up with several stacks of papers to evaluate, and all this had to be done by hand. When I reported on the results three weeks later, everyone thought I was a whiz with research. What they did not know was how Clara Amelia (our fugitive) did all this for me. She had studied research methodology as a sociology major in college. With time on her hands, she loved doing it for me. The research was very helpful to me, the board of trustees, and our administrators. We were now able to focus on our primary concerns, set priorities, and plan for a more hopeful future.

One of the first things we did was to sponsor a contest to find the brightest students in the city. The first-place winner was a fifth-grade student. He had learned to read by teaching himself when he was only three years old. He had read all the volumes of an encyclopedia before age five. His prize was a scholarship for all four years of high school and a trip for two to Rio de Janeiro. Other prizes also were rewarded. Our reward was discovering many very bright students and creating a positive buzz about the school in the city.

We had a full daytime curriculum for K–12 and a night elementary and high school program for adults who had never been to school or had dropped out of school. By this time they were motivated to get an education in order to improve their economic status. The director of the program complained that discipline was a major problem at the end of each semester, because they had learned the subject matter for the grade level but they had to amass the same number of classroom hours as children were required to attend, though the adults learned much faster. The director said that the law mandated the number of hours, and there could be no exceptions, regardless of how quickly they learned the subject.

I decided to verify this, which required a trip to Curitiba, the state capital. I met with the state board of education and asked them to allow us to pass students based on their proficiency in a subject rather than a set number of hours of classroom instruction. This was rejected because the board claimed that the law in question was a federal law, and states had no authority to change them.

I long ago had incorporated the Brazilian saying *dar um jeito* ("make a way"). So if the state couldn't change the law, I would appeal to the education department of the federal government. While I discussed the problem at a meeting with the school board, one of the members said that he knew the federal deputy from our congressional district, and this man had been educated in Granberry, a Methodist school in Minas Gerais. He said he would introduce him to me the next time he came to Londrina.

A few weeks later I received word that the board member and the federal deputy were coming to the school to talk with me. When I explained the problem, the deputy agreed that the law should be changed. He told us he had helped the secretary of education get an important bill through the Congress. After a few moments he invited me to his office at the House of Deputies in Brasília. I was thrilled because I had never seen the country's capital city.

I arrived by plane the evening before my appointment. The next morning I walked around and admired the beautiful architecture. Then I met the deputy at his office, and we walked from there to the ministry of education.

At least thirty people were waiting to meet with the secretary, including Dr. Benedito de Nacimento, a Methodist pastor and the executive secretary of the Brazilian Methodist schools. As soon as we arrived, the deputy gave his card to an administrative assistant. After a short wait, she escorted us in to see the secretary.

For the first thirty or forty minutes we talked about subjects related to education in Brazil and the United States, and then the secretary asked how he could help the deputy. He listened intently to our presentation, and then said our request was very reasonable and he wondered why the law had not been changed before now. When he asked the deputy what he needed to do, the deputy produced two copies of an executive degree to change the requirements from time in the classroom to competency tests for all of Brazil. The secretary read it and signed it right away. He thanked us for bringing this matter to his attention. He gave me one of the copies and instructed me to take it to the Paraná State Board of Education for them to provide a document giving us permission to elevate competency over attendance.

I traveled to Curitiba as soon as I could. The state secretary of education was very surprised to read the document from the national secretary of education. I told him I would wait while he prepared a document giving our school permission to advance students based on their knowledge of the subjects. With the change of this law, we were able to shorten almost in half the time adults needed to advance from one grade to the next. As I look back, I think this was one of my finest contributions to Brazilian education.

In spite of the financial situation and personnel problems, I saw progress at the school. I visited five of the best schools, similar to ours, in other states to get ideas for improving what we were doing. I was working twelve to fifteen hours a day, but I loved the challenge of seeing improvement at the school.

On Sundays, Phyllis taught the junior-age Sunday school class and I taught the youth at our church until our pastor was moved and another was appointed pastor and district superintendent. He was an African Brazilian who had grown up in the southernmost state of Brazil, where there were few people of color. As a young man he had endured racial prejudice in our Methodist school and appeared to transfer his negative feelings about white people, especially missionaries, to me. He became jealous of my relationship with the youth. He must have given a negative report to Bishop Wilbur, because very soon I was appointed to be pastor of two small Methodist churches in poor neighborhoods on the edge of the city.

I knew this appointment was to get me out of the central church and my relationship with the youth; it had nothing to do with the needs of the churches. I already had more than I could do at the school and the hospital. I did not have time to provide adequate pastoral leadership for the people and to prepare weekly sermons. Phyllis was upset because the churches did not have Sunday schools for our children. I suggested she and the children continue going to the central church, but she repeated the words of Ruth to Naomi: "Where you go, I go."

The people in these churches knew I was unhappy about being their pastor, though they did not know why. I usually asked lay leaders to pray the pastoral prayer during worship, because I was too troubled to pray. One Sunday night, my heart almost broke when a layman prayed, "Oh, Lord, help our pastor to love us so he can serve us." I knew he was right and admitted it. After this, I tried my best to be their pastor.

Randy was a growing teenager. He loved being on the swim team of the club we joined. One day he challenged me to a race. I kept putting him off with the excuse that he could not swim well enough to beat me, but finally I gave in. I choose the short end of the L-shaped pool and surprised him by getting across before him. His mother saw how I jumped halfway across the narrow end, so she told him to race me the long distance, and he proudly beat me. His schooling, however, was not going as well.

Phyllis felt confident to teach the children in the elementary grades, since she had an elementary education degree. But she didn't feel as confident in teaching high school subjects. Randy needed more as a middle school student than she had been trained to do. They got increasingly frustrated with each other. Except for math, his Brazilian high school classes didn't offer a quality education. And he did not want to go to the school of which I was president. We decided to let him live in the hostel with the children of Lutheran missionaries in Campinas and attend the nearby American school. Though this meant he would be several hours from us, it turned out to be a good experience for him. We made the sacrifice because we knew this would help him have an easier transition to high school in the States. Ruth joined him when the next term began.

Walter came down with a very high fever and terrific earache. He was diagnosed with scarlet fever and given antibiotics, but the pain in his ears increased to the point that an ear doctor came to the house one evening to treat him. He should have punctured his eardrums to release the pressure, but he wanted to see if the antibiotic would reduce the pressure. It was a bad decision. Walter's eardrums burst from the pressure, and his hearing markedly decreased.

The doctor told us he could not help him, but an ear surgeon in Rio de Janeiro had developed a new procedure for improving hearing by cutting a piece of skin behind the ears and transplanting it to form substitute eardrums. Walter and I drove to Rio. On the day of appointment, I went to a bank to cash a check from our treasurer and got a briefcase full of cash to take to the hospital to pay for the procedure. At the admissions office it took another thirty minutes to count the stacks of bills to prepay the doctor and the hospital. After the surgery, the surgeon told me the operation went well and he would probably discharge Walter the next day; however, he wanted us to stay in Rio for ten days so he could monitor Walter's progress.

I had counted on being in Rio only four or five days, but as it turned out, I benefited as much as Walter did, because I needed some time to rest. As soon as Walter felt like walking, we went each day to walk along the beach. The sight of so many beautiful young women in very small bikinis began to get to me, and I knew that Walter was starting to think like a man as he commented on them.

I ran out of reading material but found a nearby bookstore with several books in English. One of them was by a sex therapist. Reading this book, plus seeing the women on the beach, stirred a deep desire within me. I called Phyllis and told her to leave the children with Clara Amelia and Da. Nunciata and catch the overnight bus to Rio. When she objected, I repeated the suggestion more emphatically and said that she was needed desperately. I got an adjoining room in the hotel for Walter so Phyllis and I could have some privacy. These days in Rio were the beginning of a passion we hadn't known before. I had been too passionate about my work and left loving for any time after work.

I learned some important lessons about administration while serving as president of the Instituto Filadélfia de Londrina. I learned to delegate authority and hold leaders accountable for positive results. I learned that employees need good, fair, tough, consistent, and growth-oriented supervision. Work discipline had been a serious problem because so little attention had been given before to supervision. Teachers often didn't show up to teach their classes, housekeepers did little cleaning, and the finance records were a mess. The one area that performed well was the registrar's office, but I soon ran into trouble there.

I discovered that the military police went straight to the registrar to ask for the school records of former students. When photos were found stapled in the files, they were removed without permission to be used to track down and arrest people wanted by the police for subversive activities. I put a stop to that by requiring that no one from outside the school could see any student files without first talking with me. When the police detectives arrived, I told them to wait in my office while I got the file. I angered the registrar when I went straight to the filing cabinet without asking her for her help. If I saw a photo attached to the file, I pried the staple apart and threw the picture in the back of the cabinet before delivering the file to the agents in my office. I ruined a lot of fingernails, but it was worth it to protect young people from arrest and torture.

The registrar retaliated by making my life miserable and trying to provoke me into dismissing her. I knew if I fired her, or any other employees for that matter, I would have to pay severance of one month's salary for each year on the job. The registrar would have received two years' salary for twenty-four years of service, and the school did not have the money to pay her. I decided to wait her out. And then someone at the university told me that I was going to lose the registrar because she had been hired as the university registrar and was to start in that job when the school opened for its inaugural class at the beginning of the year.

The experience of seeing how determined the police were in tracking down young people suspected of resisting the military dictatorship caused me to be more concerned about Clara Amelia's safety as well as that of my family. Along with these concerns was the reputation of the hospital and the school should I be arrested for hiding a fugitive in our home. I had become well known in Londrina through my positions at the school and the hospital. It would take only a slip of the tongue—or torture—to set many negative actions into motion. When we explained the situation to our Canadian friends in Maringá, they asked Clara Amelia to live with them. We said a sad farewell to her when Lloyd and Carol came to pick her up. She stayed with them several months. When word reached her that her boyfriend, Domingos, was in Chile, she decided to join him there. It was a huge risk, but love is a powerful motivation. The last we heard from her before we left Brazil was that she had crossed the border but had to leave her suitcase behind.

We were making good progress at the school once people realized I might not fire them, but I wasn't going to give them a raise if they failed to perform their jobs. The campus looked much better after the main buildings were painted. Of particular interest was our sports arena. At that time it was the largest sports facility in north Paraná, and it was in desperate need of repair (many windows had been broken) and paint. Meanwhile, newspaper articles about construction of a new city sports arena reported that the word had fallen behind schedule, which was crucial since the new arena was supposed to host a Pan-American judo contest. I drove by the site several times to see how the construction was going. I knew that if the building weren't completed in time, the only alternative for the city would be our school's arena. When an official from the mayor's office approached us with a request that we host the games, I had a list prepared of some things we would need the city to pay for in order to make the arena presentable for a television audience and spectators. As soon as the painters finished painting the whole building, I had a sign painter inscribe Instituto Filadélfia de Londrina at several places in large letters so they could not be missed, especially by the broadcast. During the days of the matches, I enjoyed the president's privilege of going anywhere I wanted, including where our children could see me on television.

I first noticed some numbness in the little finger of my left hand in September 1970, two years after we moved to Londrina. When it spread to the next finger and thumb, I decided to see Dr. Rui Viera, a vascular surgeon at the hospital. An x-ray failed to reveal the cause of the numbness, so he injected a contrast agent into the vein to get a better picture. These x-rays revealed a tumor in my lower arm that was putting pressure on the ulnar nerve, which controls feelings in the areas where I was feeling nothing. Surgery was recommended to remove the tumor as soon as possible to keep it from affecting more of my hand and arm. This meant my presence in the hospital temporarily shifted from chaplain to patient.

After the surgery, Phyllis and I were told the tumor was removed only after calling other surgeons to the operating room to consult with them. They recommended the tumor be removed along with a seven-inch section of the ulnar nerve that had been penetrated by the tumor in several places. They said the hemoangioma (blood tumor) made it impossible to save that section of the nerve in my arm. He told me I would have limited use of my hand since one of the three main nerves to the hand no longer functioning. He said he was sorry to have done this, but the tumor needed to come out, and there was no other way to do it without removing the nerve with the tumor. He had sent the tumor to a lab in Curitiba to find out if was cancerous. This was a blow, but I was determined to not let it stop me.

Three weeks passed without a lab report. So I made a special trip to Curitiba by bus to get it. And then I had to wait until my return to Londrina for the doctor to explain the results. I breathed a sigh of relief when he said the tumor was benign. He said it would have grown even larger had it not been removed.

A few days later I temporarily forgot about the surgery and used both hands to help slide the dining table to another position. Immediately pain shot through my left arm in the area of the operation. Evidently, by using the muscles in my arm to move the table, I pulled the sheath off the end of the nerve that had been cut in the surgery. After this, I experience intermittent pain like an electric shock every fifteen to twenty seconds, twenty-four hours a day.

The doctor prescribed pain medication and sleeping pills to allow me to work and sleep. Soon, though, my body adjusted to them, and they were of little help. He referred me to a physical therapist who used electrical therapy to relieve nerve pain and help nerves to grow back. I never knew the theory behind this, but it felt like torture when he hooked me up to some electrodes and turned on the juice. I heard it was the same instrument the military police used to torture people. After three weeks of these daily doses of extra pain, I called it quits and accepted my left drawn-up-like-a-claw hand as a permanent handicap. But I couldn't ignore the persistent stabbing pain. It was starting to wear me down. Before the surgery, I could manage twelve- to fifteen-hour workdays, but not afterwards with the constant pain and the loss of sleep.

When Dr. Benedito da Roscha returned from a six-month residency in neuro microsurgery in Germany and saw my situation, he was very upset. He told me about the new nerve-graft surgical procedures he had been studying. He warned me that the procedures were experimental, but I knew I needed the surgery or the pain would never stop and my left hand would be useless. He told me about a surgeon at Tulane University and another in Toronto who were leaders in microsurgery nerve transplants. Then he said jokingly but lovingly, "Americano, I've been trying to get rid of you a long time, and this is my chance to do it. I'm going to write a referral for you because you must go and do this."

I put off informing Mac McCoy and Dr. Devon Corbitt, the medical director at the Board of Missions, and Bishop Wilbur about my situation. I kept on working, but I knew I was on a fast track to burnout.

Phyllis finally made the decision to get help for me. I told her I had driven downtown for an appointment, but the car was gone when I came back to where I had parked it. I couldn't find it anywhere. Panic set in from the remembered trauma of the stolen vehicle in Rio. I was on my way to catch a taxi when I remembered I had started to park the car here but had changed my mind and parked closer to my appointment. The car was where I had left it, not where I thought I had left it.

"That's it!" Phyllis said. "Either you write to Mac and Dr. Corbitt to let them know about your condition or I will. Something's going to be done. I can no longer stand to see my husband suffer like this."

I asked Drs. Viera and da Roscha to write reports on my situation, and I helped translate them into English to send with a cover letter from me. Mac and Dr. Corbitt responded by telegram with orders for us to be in New York in two weeks. This was a stronger response than I had anticipated, but I knew not to argue with them—or with Phyllis.

We had to act fast concerning the logistics of such a sudden move to the States. Our first concern was what to do about Randy and Ruth, who were seven hours by automobile away from us. We were very concerned about taking them out of the American school in Campinas in March. They could lose the school year. A call to the director of the Lutheran hostel solved this problem. He said they could stay there until June, and he would make sure they would be on a flight to the States after that.

Phyllis sent a letter to her parents to ask if we could stay at the farm with them until we knew where we were going to live. We knew I would be going to New Orleans, and she would need a place to stay with the three youngest children.

I called the chairman of the school trustees to my office to start the process of turning the school over to him. The president of the hospital was not surprised that I was leaving, because word of my condition had reached him. He told me how much he hated to lose me, but I had demonstrated the value of a hospital chaplain, and he was going to include the salary of a full-time chaplain in his budget. He told me he wanted to have a special *despidida* ("going-away party") for me, which occurred a week later. The speaker for the physicians expressed their appreciation for my service and some things they had learned by having a chaplain in the hospital. He told the group that when they talked about me, they called me their "Protestant Padre." The speaker for the nurses also expressed appreciation for my pastoral care with them and the patients.

Phyllis and I took an overnight bus to São Paulo to work with a *despachante* (document facilitator) to arrange the necessary travel documents and purchase airline tickets. The next night we took the bus to Curitiba to inform Bishop Wilbur about the sudden change and the need to appoint another pastor to serve the churches we were leaving behind. Evidently our strained relationship caused him to be skeptical about my motives for leaving. A few days later he sent another pastor to Londrina to find out if I had told him the truth. I was in too much pain to be angry with him for doubting my word.

When we got home, we helped Maria Lucia move to a dorm and then started packing to travel. We discussed the pros and cons of storing our personal belongings or selling what we could and giving away the remainder. Randy encouraged us to get rid of the furniture with the Brazilian saying that three moves equal a house fire. A letter from Dr. Corbitt informed us that he had contacted Dr. Cline, the pioneer in micro neurosurgery at Tulane, and he had agreed to accept me as a patient for the experimental nerve transplant surgery. Dr. Cline said he wanted me to remain in the States at least two years to confirm the results of the surgery. This was a huge disappointment to me, because I loved living and working in Brazil. I realized, however, that with two years in the States and the pressing educational needs of our children, we were ending our missionary service in Brazil. There was not enough time or energy to say many *despididas* or grieve with so much to do in the little time we had before our flight.

We sold our furniture at a very low price and gave Da. Nunciata, our beloved housekeeper, the things we could not pack in the four barrels and boxes to be shipped to the Board of Missions in New York. We scheduled our flight out of Viracopos International Airport, which was near Campinas, so we could see Randy and Ruth before we left. It was painful to leave them in Brazil at the ages of fourteen and twelve. At the airport I gave the car keys and the car documents to the Methodist pastor in Campinas. I signed over the car ownership to the Annual Conference of the Sixth Region, but I never heard what they did with it.

We were on our way home, though we had no idea where home would be. I would be starting over again—somewhere. After this experience I had much empathy for refugees, though I realize their experiences are much more traumatic than ours. We were confident of the love and support of our families and supporting churches.

I will close this chapter with reflections on the lessons I learned in Londrina and how my life was changed during the transformative four years of our second term of service in Brazil.

In a real sense I grew up in Londrina. No longer could I depend upon the church to provide meaning, leadership, and authority. I was still under the appointment of Bishop Wilbur, but attributed him limited authority for control over my life. Leaders on the political right in the Brazilian Methodist Church considered me a rebel. On the left I was seen as a hero for standing up to the bishops and supporting the youth. The Board of Missions supported us financially, but it had limited information about my activities.

I was forced to form my own identity as a hospital chaplain because there were no models to follow. Working with the doctors at the hospital helped me to claim authority as a clinical chaplain and healing peer.

As a school president I had to transform a dysfunctional nepotistic system so it could survive and fulfill its purpose. I had serious doubts about the school's future even as I was doing everything I could to transform it. At one time it served many of the basic educational needs of the city. With the recent election of an evangelical mayor dedicated to using tax money to provide educational opportunities for children and youth, our purpose and mission were up in the air. Over the years we shifted to serving the families who could afford to pay tuition fees. I did not stay long enough to propose that we go out of business and turn the school property over to the city for a centrally situated high school, but I thought about it.

I learned that I could do many things and do them well, but I could not do so many at the same time without burning out. I could be a good pastor, a good leader, a good administrator, but I had to choose one instead of try to do all of them simultaneously. Stress from overwork finally got me. This, combined with the physical pain in my arm, brought a screeching halt to all of my activities.

I learned the importance of courage in facing a dangerous political situation. Hiding Clara Amelia in our home taught me the importance of strategy, secrecy, and cunning. It also motivated me to be more contentious about voting after living in Brazil under a military dictatorship.

The most important thing I learned, however, was that Phyllis and the children deserved more from me. I was so focused on my work issues that I had too little time and energy for them. We had some good times together, but they seemed to always take second place in my priorities. I decided to stay away from administrative positions after this, because I was too tenderhearted to make the necessary decisions that could hurt someone's livelihood. I vowed to stay away from educational institutions, especially teaching. I would become a chaplain or a pastoral counselor in the States by completing my doctorate, that is, after we dealt with my medical situation.

CHAPTER 13

Healing and Starting Again

Healing is a matter of time, but it is sometimes also a matter of opportunity.

—Hippocrates

You are never too old to set another goal or to dream a new dream.

—C. S. Lewis

The rapid change from Brazil back to the United States by plane on March 31, 1971, was very disorienting. I was asked to speak at the Board of Missions staff devotions in New York the next day. I thought it ironic that it was April Fool's Day. After devotions, Dr. Devon Corbitt checked the health of everyone in the family and gave me more information about going to New Orleans to see Dr. Cline. Two days later, Bob and Lois, Phyllis's brother and sister-in-law, met our plane in Pittsburgh to take us to the Diehl country home place, about forty miles east. At last, Phyllis and I could breath deeply in a safe place with her loving family. The farm in early spring became a beautiful temporary sanctuary after the turmoil and stress of leaving Brazil.

I soon discovered that people in the States were deeply divided over the war in Vietnam. News media reported intensifying protest marches as the number of battle casualties increased day by day. Public attitude was shifting to the idea that the war was not winnable. Outwardly, it seemed like nothing special was going on in the country. Besides newer automobiles, everything appeared as we had left it four years earlier.

We enrolled Walter and Ruth in school as soon as possible. Phyllis enjoyed walking with them down the lane to the catch the bus at the same bus stop she used during all twelve grades of her public schooling. She wanted to help care for me in New Orleans, but she needed to stay with the children at her parents' home.

I dreaded having surgery in a city where I had neither family nor friends. I did know one person: J. W. Hamby. We grew up in the same neighborhood and were both church members. No one was surprised that he was a homosexual in his adult years. His mother and my mother were friends, and both insisted I contact him. When I called his home, he asked that I meet him at 5 p.m. the next day in a bar across the street from where he worked at the Shell Oil Company headquarters. He introduced me to his friends and asked what I wanted to drink; I asked for a Coke. I quickly realized he and his friends lived a different lifestyle from mine; however, they were curious about my missionary experience in Brazil. I heard several years later that J. W. and many of his co-workers had died of a strange new disease: HIV and AIDS. Some believed the disease had been contracted in Africa by some Shell engineers and brought to New Orleans.

I met Dr. Cline at his office at Tulane University for a few days of testing before the surgery. This was the first time I ever saw a computer. The lab had a huge wall-to-wall bank of computers to test electrical nerve signals. Dr. Cline stuck some needles and wires directly into the nerves in my left arm to get some readings that would tell him where and how well the nerves were functioning. The intense pain from the needles felt like hours of torture.

When he finished, he told me he would be opening my left arm from top to bottom to move the ulnar nerve from behind my elbow to the front of it, thereby shortening the gap left by the surgery in Brazil from seven to five inches. Then he would take a five-inch length of nerve from above the ankle on my left leg to microstitch onto each end of the ulnar nerve gap.

He warned me that this was experimental surgery based on several years of testing on animals. I asked him about the possibility of success and was shocked when he said, "Only five percent, but it's your only hope of some recovery and the use of your hand." I remembered my mother telling me that prayer groups in many churches in South Georgia were praying for my surgery to be successful. I said, "Let's do it. You need a bigger monkey to work on, and I volunteer to be your human monkey. I believe you can make it work."

I went by the chaplain's office in the Baptist Hospital when I arrived to check in for the surgery. I wanted to let them know about my background and to request their pastoral care during my hospital stay. I had read some books on pastoral care written by Dr. Madden, the head chaplain and CPE supervisor of the hospital, and thought it would be interesting to meet him. I never saw him and had only one pastoral visit by a chaplain during my ten days in the hospital, but I didn't lack for pastoral care.

On the Sunday before the Monday surgery, I had gone to worship in a Methodist Church two blocks from the hospital. After church I told the pastor about my situation and double-binded him by saying, "Your bishop stayed in our home when he visited us in Brazil. If you don't visit me in the hospital, I'm going to call him to come see me." The pastor visited me almost every day and took my used pajamas home to wash.

My roommate was an African American in a coma from a stroke. His wife watched over him most of the time. She worked as a secretary in a Catholic seminary, but she had taken time off to be with him. We had some wonderful conversations. The thing I dreaded most was awakening after surgery with no one to help me throw up from the effects of anesthesia. In those days, almost everyone threw up after surgery. As a chaplain in Londrina, I had often held the pan and wiped the foreheads of patients who lacked family members to help them.

As I drifted in and out of consciousness after surgery, this woman stood beside my bed as Phyllis would have, holding a pan, rubbing my face with cold washcloths, and reassuring me with caring words until I was fully conscious and could care for myself. She was my guardian angel during those hospital days. My worry had been much greater than my faith. The hospital was in major conflict with Baptist pastors over integration of the races in the hospital, but in our room integration worked beautifully.

The surgery stopped the sharp fifteen- to twenty-second stabs of pain, but I still had a long way to go. I was transported back to Dr. Cline's lab for more painful needle testing of the nerves as they were recorded on his computer. He told me the nerve connections were working. He wanted me back in two months for more testing before a hand surgeon attempted to shift several tendons in my hand to help the fingers controlled by the ulnar nerve to open again.

The first and last time I rode in a wheelchair was at the New Orleans and Pittsburgh airports. My arm had been opened, sewn up, and bandaged. Ten inches of my lower left leg was cut to get a nerve to graft into the ulnar nerve in my arm. I looked like an accident victim.

A few weeks later I was back in the Baptist Hospital in New Orleans for the hand tendon transfer. The day before the surgery, a doctor entered my room with a group of residents. He introduced himself as Dr. Paul Brand. I recognized his name as a famous missionary in India. As a hand surgeon, he had developed some new procedures for helping leprosy patients recover the use of their hands and feet. At this time he was working at the Carville, Louisiana, leprosy hospital and at Tulane University as a teaching professor. He said another doctor would do the surgery, but he was there as a consultant for my surgeon and to show the orthopedic residents how to diagnose ulnar nerve damage. A few years later Dr. Brand wrote the best-selling book *Fearfully and Wonderfully Made.*

The residents seemed to be in awe of him. After they left, one of them came rushing back into my room to retrieve my chart that he had left on my bed. He said, "You should not be reading that," and tried to grab it out of my good hand. I pulled it back and told him that I was a hospital chaplain and had read more charts than he had.

I faced the same anxiety of awakening from surgery without someone in the room to assist me. The afternoon before my surgery, a new roommate was rolled into the room after an emergency appendectomy. He was an angry dentist who thought he was too busy to be bothered by an appendix. His wife said she was an RN, but I could tell she had a problem patient-husband to care for. He insisted on going to the bathroom on his own soon after coming from surgery. To show her he could do it without her help, he got out of bed on the side opposite from where she stood next to the window, but close to my bed. I didn't believe he would make it on his own, so I slipped quietly out of bed and planted my feet wide enough to catch him when he fell. I knew I could not use my left hand and arm so soon after my surgery, but I could use my good right arm. He took two steps and fainted. I slipped my right arm under his and lowered him to the floor.

When I came back to my room from surgery the next day, his grateful wife cared for me until I could function on my own. I asked God to forgive me for my lack of faith in his care for me. How could I have known that I would have an RN to hold and empty the vomit pan, wipe my face with a cold cloth, and talk me back into consciousness?

I remained in the hospital and at a downtown hotel until the stitches were removed and my hand was fitted with a metal spring-like apparatus to keep the fingers extended and usable. A few weeks later I flew back to New Orleans to see Dr. Cline and the hand surgeon. When I thanked Dr. Cline for helping me, he told me that he had shown slides of my surgery at several seminars for microneurology surgeons. He said, "God was with you during that surgery." (Forty years later I learned from another neuron surgeon planning to operate on my neck for stenosis of the spine that Dr. Cline was honored by hundreds of neurosurgeons at his retirement dinner for his pioneer work with nerve transplants.)

In May, as time approached the end of the school year, Phyllis and I wanted to get our family together and settled near Emory University in Atlanta. I flew to Atlanta to look for an automobile and a house. While I was at Emory to apply for entrance into the STD (later changed to ThD) program, Dr. Ted Runyon said he would sell me his Ford station wagon for a reasonable price, but he warned that the blue paint was peeling from it. I felt confident to drive with only my right arm. He suggested I see a Realtor he liked, and she soon showed me a house I liked, but I wished Phyllis were there to express her opinion.

After making a thousand-dollar deposit on the twenty-five-thousand-dollar price I had a terrible case of buyer's remorse. It started slowly and built to the point that I called the Realtor to cancel the deal. She had been through this with other clients. She talked my anxiety down to a manageable degree. Her main argument was that rent for a family of seven would be more expensive than mortgage payments.

The family selling the house said they needed two weeks to get out. They were amazed that we had no furniture and little money. We had five children, yet we both planned to go to graduate school. The man said he wished he could go to graduate school, and I said, "You can if you value getting more education and are willing to sleep on the floor."

Driving with one arm, I left Atlanta to see my mother in Valdosta for the first time in four years. She had been very concerned about us during our troubled second term in Brazil and the emergency return for my surgery. I learned that she had communicated with prayer groups all over South Georgia to pray for a successful surgery.

I also planned to rendezvous with Randy in Valdosta. As soon as the term was over at the American school in Campinas, the director had shepherded Randy and Ruth onto a flight to Miami. My brother Ed met them there. He put Ruth on a flight to Pittsburgh, where Phyllis's brother Bob and his wife met her and took her to join the family on the Diehl farm. Ed took Randy from Fort Lauderdale to Winter Haven to visit my sister Ruth and her family until I could get to Valdosta to meet him at the bus station.

I've always been proud of Randy and Ruth for having the courage to stay in Brazil to finish the school year and travel alone to the States. Randy was visibly relieved to be with me again. He had been very brave to face the unknown and look out for his sister. Now he could feel secure by being in my care again. He was also relieved to hear the good news about my health.

One of the first questions he asked was, "Who was Marta?"

So I told him the truth. He said he knew I wasn't telling the truth about her living with us, but he knew better than to ask.

When I asked how he knew, he said, "By looking at your eyes."

Randy and I went to see the new house in Atlanta and spend the night in a motel. The next morning we started the two-day trip to Pennsylvania. We were glad to have our family together again. Mother and Papa Diehl may have invented the phrase *boomerang kids*. Phyllis and our family were the fourth of five adult children to spend a significant amount of time on the farm after getting married. A few days later we packed the station wagon with five children, suitcases, and boxes to start the journey to a new life in Atlanta.

Our Atlanta neighbors wondered when our moving van would be arriving. It never did. Instead, we looked for furniture at garage, moving, and divorce sales. Phyllis and I slept on a cotton mattress my mother gave me when I was in Valdosta. The children had never lived with wall-to-wall carpeting, so they didn't mind sleeping on the floor until we could find beds.

One of the first things we bought was an aquarium. We went to a divorce sale looking for beds but didn't like what we found. But the children were fascinated with the fish in an aquarium. The last thing I wanted to buy was an aquarium, but the owner kept dropping the price and offered to dismantle, transport, and set it up again. Clearly, the children wanted it, and he wanted them to have it. I thought it would be cheap substitute for a television. In my mind's eye I can still see the children sitting contentedly on the floor for hours, looking at the fish.

A month later the fifty-five gallon steel drums and boxes arrived from Brazil. Unpacking our familiar belongings was like Christmas in June.

Upon our arrival in the States, Dr. Corbitt and Mac McCoy placed me on a six-month medical leave. The first two months were used for the surgeries and healing. When we moved to Atlanta, my request for permission to speak in churches was denied. I appealed the decision with the argument that my problem was only my arm, but that was denied too. I was told that I was to do nothing but rest and recover.

The first month in Atlanta was like a prolonged vacation. About the second month I was confused by the change from fifteen-hour workdays as school president, hospital chaplain, and pastor of two small churches to now be doing practically nothing other than a few things around the house. When the third month rolled around, I was angry with everyone and everything. Phyllis often invited me to go outside if I had to be so grumpy.

I finally realized I was angry with God for allowing my missionary career to come to a sudden stop. I was missing my friends and activities in Brazil and blamed God for this too. While sitting in the backyard one day, I had it out with God. During the silence after spilling my anger and grief, God spoke to me through my soul: *If you will allow me to be infinite, I will help you be finite.* It took me several minutes to figure out that I had been too busy doing ministry and trying to make things happen on my own. In a real sense, I had been too busy to listen and wait for God to act. That day I made one of the best deals of my life by accepting the offer to become finite and allow God to be infinite.

Soon after arriving in Atlanta, I contacted Dr. Tom McDill at Columbia Theological Seminary to inquire about the doctoral program in pastoral counseling. During my first furlough, he had told me about the ongoing discussion between Columbia, Emory, and the Interdenominational Theological Center about starting such a program. He reported now that the program had been approved and applications were being accepted. I told him I wanted to get my doctorate at Columbia, but Dr. McDill insisted that, since I was a United Methodist, it would be better for me to have a degree from Emory. He also suggested I do additional clinical pastoral education by applying for the full-time CPE internship at the Georgia Mental Health Institute. I applied and was accepted and granted a stipend.

Though my college and seminary grades were not as high as they would be required to be today, my acceptance into the ThD program at Emory was based on additional testing and missionary experience.

During my final interview, I was asked, "What do you want to do with this degree?"

I responded, "One thing I do not want to do is to use it to teach." This response came from my teaching experience in Brazil. God must have laughed that day, because I've taught seminary counseling courses for more than twenty-five years since then.

I convinced Mac McCoy at the Board of Missions to allow me to start the CPE program after five months in the States instead of six, per my medical leave, so I wouldn't miss the start of the program. He also agreed to keep us on salary for a year so we could keep our health insurance. In exchange for this, I returned my stipend to the board. Without his help, we could not have gone to graduate school and survived the cost of living in the States. Phyllis and I wanted to retool for ministry in the States and be prepared to make enough salary to pay for our five children's college education.

The first six months of the yearlong CPE internship was at the alcohol treatment center of the Georgia Mental Health Institute, which was situated in one of the homes of the Coca-Cola Candler family. I was the oldest of four men and two women in the internship program and had far more ministry experience than them—put together. It had been four years since I had completed my first three-month unit of CPE at the Georgia Baptist Hospital. I thrived in the intense interpersonal give and take of CPE. My supervisors and colleagues from other mental health disciplines provided many valuable learning experiences and seemed to appreciate my contributions in staff meetings. The direct patient counseling, reflections on patient treatment, and written supervision and evaluations contributed to my professional and personal development.

More was expected of me because I was the only CPE intern working toward a doctorate. I completed most of the academic requirements for the ThD during my last sabbatical, but I still had to take several courses at the three seminaries in the counseling program. I completed one or two each semester in preparation for my dissertation.

All candidates in the pastoral counseling ThD program were required to have personal psychotherapy while in the program. This was difficult for me, both timewise and financially. I'm glad my request to be exempted was denied, because I needed therapy. I was fortunate that Tom McDill suggested Dr. Tom Leland at the Atlanta Psychiatrics Institute. The psychiatrist in this practice was known for what was called experiential psychotherapy. They rarely used medication and depended on interpersonal relationship for healing and wholeness. They also differed from traditional psychiatry in that married clients were required to have their spouses participate in the therapy sessions. The theory behind this was that the personal growth of one spouse while the other remained the unchanged often led to divorce.

Therapy was difficult for Phyllis to accept. Pennsylvania Dutch culture has a low regard for normal people going to therapy. She was overstretched as a wife, mother of five children, graduate student, and full-time middle school teacher. She went several times to help me fulfill my requirement, but at one point the pressure caused her to rebel and refuse to continue going with me.

Dr. Leland said that if she didn't come with me, he would no longer see me. I struggled with this terrible double bind for several days and finally admitted to her that she did not need to have psychotherapy but I did if I was to complete my program of study. Then I told her I was going to continue to see Dr. Leland and she was going with me, even if I had to pick her up and put her in the car. To my surprise, she said she would go.

A few months later she was glad to have his help. She faced a serious case of injustice from a sadistic principal, and Dr. Leland helped her develop the courage to stand up to the principal. I believe the four years of therapy with Phyllis saved our marriage. Many of my pastoral counseling colleagues were not so fortunate. One reason Phyllis was concerned about my going into counseling was the high divorce rate among therapists.

The irony of doing CPE at an alcohol treatment center was the amount of drinking done by staff members at parties. Phyllis and I had never been around that much drinking. I soon learned that I was very sensitive to the effects of alcohol and either did not drink alcohol or drank a small amount out of fear of a DUI and a possible genetic addiction from my father's side of the family.

I also saw marital infidelity and the destruction of some marriages among my colleagues. I was not immune to temptation. When I realized opportunities were just waiting for me to make the first move, I had a good talk with myself about the moral implications and the consequences of compromising my marriage with Phyllis. I came to the conclusion that betraying her trust and putting my children through the hell of divorce was not worth the potential pleasure of being with another woman. This did not mean I was content with my marital relationship. Tom Leland helped me to be honest with the impasse in my marriage and find new reasons to be married. I discovered that Phyllis was just as ready for us to move from focusing our relationship on parenting to finding a new level of intimacy. I did not claim any moral superiority for my decisions and behavior; however, I am thankful for the investment of many people in my moral foundation. I'm also grateful I did not compromise my integrity when faced with serious temptations. Passing that test gave me the strength to navigate subsequent temptations with counselees.

As my cohort of six interns was completing the first six months of CPE, we were told that we would change supervisors for the next six months. We were asked to write down the names of three new supervisors in order of preference. All six of us listed Henry Close as our first choice. I was the only one to write his name three times on my list, so I ended up getting him.

Before we left the alcohol treatment center, I suggested that one of the interns not continue with us. The other four jumped all over me for saying this, but I stuck to my opinion that he was detrimental to the progress of our group because he could not tolerate the honest confrontations and intimate caring in the group. The two supervisors said nothing to defend me. I learned in my individual supervision session that the decision had already been made by the larger group of supervisors to discontinue him, but he had not yet been told. My supervisor confirmed my perception and affirmed my strength in confronting him and staying firm during the attacks of my peers.

I was assigned to the locked wing of the adult psychiatric unit for the second six months of CPE, with Henry Close as my supervisor. These were the days when the huge mental hospital at Milledgeville was being phased out and mental health professionals were being trained to treat patients from a multidiscipline perspective in local communities. We worked with supervisors from medicine, psychiatry, nursing, psychology, social work, physical therapy, occupational therapy, and chaplaincy training. I took advantage of the opportunity to learn to think from the perspective of each discipline. I also learned to be more precise in giving my opinion from a theological perspective. A patient I'll call Ann was an example of this.

Ann's family had he admitted on a Sunday. She was telling everyone she had gone to bed and had sex with Jesus. Laughter broke out when her case was first brought up in the Monday morning conference for developing a treatment plan. As I listened to admitting statement, I said that this patient had a spiritual intimacy issue, and I volunteered to be the lead therapist to develop her treatment plan.

She was very defensive when I first saw her. As I listened to her story of going to bed with Jesus, the song "I Don't Know How to Love Him," from the play *Jesus Christ Superstar*, started going through my mind.

Instead of trying to correct her, I asked, "Have you been to bed with many other men and was Jesus a good lover?"

She said, "He was the best. Other men have abused and used me, but Jesus really loved me."

In my report to the treatment team, I said that she had had a profound mystical religious experience and explained what this meant from a theological and psychological perspective. I told them that because of her past sexual abuse, sexual intimacy was the only language she knew to describe her religious experience. She had both a religious and a psychotic episode, therefore she should be given medication, but mostly she needed rest and a supportive environment as if she was normal.

A few days later, Ann said to me, "Perhaps I didn't have sex with Jesus, but I know that he loved me more than I have ever been loved before."

Ann's mystical/psychotic story became a valuable learning experience for her. She helped me and other staff members understand religious issues with our patients.

In the mental hospital I found more religion talk among patients than among Christians in churches. My academic studies, especially about the life and work of Anton Boisen, the primary founder of clinical pastoral education, came alive in the clinical setting of the hospital. I learned that religion and mental illness are next-door neighbors in the brain, and they sometimes visit each other without permission. I also discovered my common humanity with those suffering from mental illness. With a sufficient amount of stressors, I could become just like them.

As the internship was drawing to an end, we were told that this would conclude our four units of CPE training. We could apply for an additional year of full-time residency training. If we chose to continue, we had to indicate if we wanted to specialize in becoming a supervisor or a pastoral counselor. There would be a 40 percent increase in the stipend for the residency program. All five of us applied as well as several candidates not in our cohort. I was disappointed when told that my peers were accepted to train to be a supervisor, but I had not been accepted in the pastoral counseling program.

I later learned that I had offended too many supervisors by writing in Henry Close's name three times on my application for the second semester of internship in CPE. One supervisor had a special dislike of me because, in my interview with him, he presented a case of a female client (probably one of his) and asked me to describe her, give a diagnosis, and indicate a treatment plan. When I nailed every detail, he accused me of being a smart aleck. He was later fired on grounds of incompetency as a chaplain.

When one of the outside candidates declined acceptance into the program, Henry Close rescued me by volunteering to be my supervisor if the other supervisors would allow me to be accepted. They agreed, but only if my stipend wasn't increased to match the 40 percent raise of the others. Phyllis and I struggled with this offer, but we concluded I should continue with the second year in order to complete my studies and become a pastoral counselor. The difference in the stipend was unjust because the others were single or married without children while I was supporting a wife and five children. (Henry Close was a wonderful supervisor and has become a close personal friend. I would not trade our friendship for the extra amount of the stipend.)

I started the second year in the same office in the adult psychiatric unit. It was focused primarily on pastoral counseling. My confidence and competency as a counselor seemed to increase each day. I will limit myself to just one example of my many clients to illustrate how Henry was helping me to learn to think like a pastoral counselor. I'll call her Sarah.

Sarah was a beautiful young mother admitted after being stressed out while trying to mother her newborn. The staff tried to treat her as rapidly as possible with medication so she could return home to care for her child. When she was readmitted a second time, I asked to be her primary therapist. She seemed very fragile and emotionally insecure. As I talked with her about her life history, I discovered that her father had been burned to death in an automobile accident when she was five years old. Her mother showed her the burned car, which I assumed traumatized her and basically halted her emotional development.

The treatment plan I presented to the staff was that I was going to use a developmental psychology approach by relating to Sarah according to her emotional stages of development to see if I could help her grow up. When she was emotionally old enough, I would help her grieve the death of her father.

I started by reading to her age-appropriate books and playing games accordingly. Sarah responded to this re-parenting therapy by maturing at the rate of about one year per month. I had to be especially careful when she approached her emotional teen years and became very seductive. I kept the door slightly open to allow staff monitoring. After she grieved the loss of her father, we gradually gave her passes to be with her child and her mother.

She continued outpatient therapy with me after she was discharged. When I first met her in the hospital, she looked was unkempt and wore sloppy looking clothes. As she emotionally matured, her outer appearance changed accordingly. One day she came to her appointment dressed up and looking very beautiful. She said she enjoyed being a mother and was looking for a job to support her daughter. Then she announced that she was going to fire me as her therapist because she felt like an adult and no longer needed therapy and could make it on her own. The staff and I rejoiced with her.

Sarah taught me many lessons about arrested psychological development from trauma (now called PTSD), encapsulated grief, maturation during therapy, and the importance of experiential psychotherapy where the relationship between the patient and the therapist is the key for healing. I used the lessons learned from working with her to help many other clients. I also learned to accept the fact that successful therapy led to eventually being fired by the client.

The two years of CPE and personal therapy not only helped me retool for life in the States but also contributed to my transition from thinking of myself as a missionary to thinking and functioning as a therapist. The Valdosta district superintendent of the UMC offered me an appointment, but from my experiences during the second term in Brazil, I distrusted the appointment system too much to allow myself to be under the control of a bishop and a district superintendent. I loved and felt committed to the United Methodist Church, but only as a minister in an extension ministry.

Our family needed some years of stability after all the moves we had had in Brazil. As my time at the Georgia Mental Health Institute was drawing to a close I was focused on completing my degree. I thought about becoming a conference counselor for ministers and their families; otherwise, I had no idea how I would support our family. Phyllis planned to do her part by teaching.

CHAPTER 14

Counseling Ministry

Sacramental listening reminds us that current suffering isn't the end of the story.

—Richard Rohr

After we settled into Atlanta, the children were progressing in school, but I was worried about Randy. He was doing okay in school, but he wasn't adjusting to life in the States.

I was pleased with how well he had learned to drive. Soon after he passed his driving test, he asked a girl out for a date. As we gathered in the backyard to watch him leave to pick her up, I said, "Don't do anything I wouldn't do."

He responded, "Dad that's too wide for me. I'm just sixteen. Can you narrow it down a little."

Three months later his driver's license was suspended for six months. He had gotten a ticket for driving too fast while trying to get a friend home before his curfew. This crisis only added to his grief over being forced to leave his friends and his dog in Brazil. I was afraid he would drift into the hippy drug culture if we didn't do something soon.

Though finances were very tight, Phyllis and I decided to send him to Brazil for the summer. This turned out to be a good decision. He discovered that his sixteen-year-old Brazilian friends now were old enough to have full-time day jobs and go to school at night. The fun and games of childhood were over for them. Spending most of his time in Brazil alone in the daytime helped him realize that life as an adolescent in the States wasn't so bad.

He traveled to Londrina to visit our former maid and her family and say a final good-bye to his dog, now living with her family. Three months in Brazil also helped the time go by until he got his license back. He was ready to become an American. Had the war in Vietnam continued, I would have returned to Brazil to keep him from being drafted. Years later he told me that he didn't use drugs because he noticed the effects on his friends often led to broken families, and he didn't want to be the cause for his parents' divorce.

It was not easy living on a tight budget with Phyllis and me going to graduate school. One day Phyllis said we needed to get Ruth a new bathing suit. I cautioned her that we didn't have the money to buy one. She said that there were some expenses that could not wait, and this was one of those times.

When they returned from shopping, Phyllis said, "You need to see your daughter's new bathing suit."

When Ruth modeled her bathing suit, I was shocked at the realization that my little girl had matured into a beautiful young woman.

In our second year back in the States and the last quarter of my CPE residency program, I noticed some numbness in my right arm and hand. This frightened me. Memories of complications from the prior surgery on my left arm flooded back to me. I made an appointment at the Emory clinic.

The doctor listened to a few words of my description of my problem, and then he asked me to raise my right arm a couple of times while he listened to my upper right chest with his stethoscope. Two minutes after I had entered the room, he said I had thorax outlet syndrome. I asked what that meant, and he said, "Surgery." He would cut a piece out of my upper rib to allow better blood flow to the veins in my right arm. I was scheduled to be in surgery two weeks later. And two weeks later I awakened from the surgery in the Emory Hospital.

Several people visited me in the hospital. Everyone who asked if they could do something was given something to do, sometimes as simple as moving a vase of flowers. I learned as a hospital chaplain—and as a patient—that patients who accepted dependency and willingly received care healed faster than those who refused to be temporarily dependent upon others.

While I was recovering at home, Rev. Claude Smithmire, our pastor at Skyland UMC, visited me. He inquired about my plans. I told him that I was thinking about being a hospital chaplain or a pastoral counselor for an Annual Conference of the UMC.

He said, "We need you right here in the Atlanta-Emory District."

And I said I would walk right through that door if he opened it for me. He promised to talk with Bill Ruff, the district superintendent. Bill was receptive to the idea because he loved being an administrator but disliked counseling pastors with personal problems. He arranged for several pastors in the larger churches to contribute to my salary. I'll always be grateful for Bill's administrative gifts and for the way he helped me transition from a misplaced missionary to a place in his district.

In June 1973, Bishop Cannon transferred my conference membership from South Georgia to North Georgia and appointed me to be the director of pastoral care and counseling of the Atlanta Emory District. I became the first pastoral counselor appointed to a district in the United Methodist Church.

The primary goals of the District Counseling Center were (1) to provide pastoral care and counseling for pastors and their families, (2) to develop small peer support and professional growth groups for pastors, (3) to plan seminars to improve the pastoral care and counseling of pastors, and (4) to become a primary counseling referral resource for pastors to send lay persons in their churches. This last goal was to provide a source of income from counseling services to eventually pay my salary and the administrative cost of the counseling center. Charging a fee on a sliding scale according to family income made counseling affordable.

Norton Campbell offered to let me use a space in a house on the property of the Cokesbury UMC. It was within walking distance of my house. Phyllis and I were very relieved that we would not have to move again, and the children could continue their education in the same schools.

I asked the district superintendent to appoint a board of advisors to help me and provide oversight for the counseling center. He selected a superb group of capable people. We soon had the counseling center on a solid development path.

After a year of middle school teaching, Phyllis resigned because she could no longer endure the stress of working with a principal who had a habit of picking on one teacher each year to intimidate the other teachers. He thought Phyllis would be an easy target who would not fight back. He learned she wasn't so easy to pick on when she stood up to his manipulation, and the other teachers, students, and parents supported her against him, even with a threat to go on strike.

Instead of signing his two-page document that stated his reasons for suspending her, she took it to the director of personnel at the DeKalb County Board of Education. The director ordered an investigation that resulted in Phyllis being reinstated in her job and the principal was disciplined for his sadistic behavior. She used the next year to complete her master of arts in education at Georgia State.

I completed the academic requirements for the ThD in pastoral counseling and two years of full-time supervised CPE training at the Georgia Mental Health Institute (GMHI). Then I discovered I had not completed all the requirements, except the dissertation, to graduate. The Georgia Association of Pastoral Care (GAPC), based in the Central Presbyterian Church in downtown Atlanta, had a contract with the three seminaries to supervise clinical training in pastoral counseling. They refused to accept the supervision I had done at GMHI and required me to do it with them on a part-time basis. This meant I had to take off work from my full-time counseling job on Mondays to go downtown to do two years under GAPC supervision. But even this delay turned out to be a blessing.

One of the GAPC supervisors was Zeke Delozier. His toughness in personal relationships and wisdom in dealing with people challenged me to toughen up in order to be strong enough to stand up to the manipulations of counselees. After I completed this required supervision, the advisory board of the District Counseling Center approved the necessary expenditure for Zeke to continue as my counseling consultant for the next four years. I learned a great deal from his way of challenging me to look below the surface to deeper psychological issues.

The academic classes, clinical pastoral education, counseling under supervision, and personal psychotherapy were three of the four requirements for the ThD program. The last and most challenging step was the writing of a dissertation. I chose Dr. John Patton to be my advisor because he was the Emory coordinator for the ThD program. When I told him I was starting a UMC district counseling program, he warned me that it would take at least two years to build a full counseling load. But six months after starting the ministry of counseling, I had a full schedule of counseling appointments.

I was one of the first candidates to write a dissertation. The academic faculty was still deciding how to mentor a ThD dissertation. It was mostly a trial-and-error situation for me and my committee. John Patton approved my proposal to research the practices of counseling by seventy-five pastors in the Atlanta Emory District where I was working. Instead of using traditional written questionnaires to do the research, I asked my questions over breakfast or lunch with the pastors. As soon as possible after the meal, I recorded what I remembered from their responses.

Gathering the information by interviewing pastors and the start of the counseling program fit well together. The pastors had a vested interest in the success of the district counseling programs because their churches were supporting it. By getting to know them in a neutral setting, such as a meal, they talked freely with me. My interest in them, their families, and their ministry helped develop a personal relationship that gave them confidence to refer their church members to the counseling center. It also opened opportunities for several of them to seek my help with personal issues and to seek consultation for the counseling they were doing. I randomly chose the names of the seventy-five pastors to meet with. I soon realized that I was doing pastoral care with pastors going through tough personal and professional situations. Most of them paid for our meal. The following is an example of one of these visits. I'll call him "pastor Wilson."

One morning I had breakfast with Wilson. He asked why I had called him when his last name was toward the end of the alphabetical list of pastors. I told him it was a random choice. Then he asked what I knew about him. But when I said I didn't know much about him, he was skeptical. He thought someone had asked me to talk with him.

So he asked, "Did you know that I'm planning to kill myself?"

I assured him I didn't but would like to talk about it. He confessed that he had a loaded gun in his church office because he could not live with having fallen in love and having an affair with a woman at his church. His disappointment in himself came from finding out she also was having sex with another man in the church. He told me he felt guilty and disappointed with himself for being such a fool. He preferred death rather than tell his wife about the affair.

The suicide prevention training I had done at GMHI helped me to stay calm and develop a plan for helping him. As soon as I felt confident that he was telling me this because he wanted help more than he wanted to die, I got him to agree to not kill himself but to come to my office that day with his wife, so I could help him tell her. I asked if he wanted me to go with him to his office to get rid of the gun. He promised me he would not use it to harm himself or anyone else.

While they were in my office, I saw the strength of a wonderful wife as she struggled with her pain over the betrayal yet go into action to help save the life of her husband. I had never seen such emotional pain with crying, repentance, and forgiveness. It took several weeks of counseling to help them deal with the issues in their marriage and develop a much stronger relationship. Across many years we saw each other at Annual Conferences, but we never mention this early experience together. I'm grateful that he's alive as a result of that first breakfast conversation. Today, the resolution of the affair would be much more complicated with newly adopted professional ethics standards.

Ever since I'd returned from Brazil, I tried to visit my mother in Valdosta as often as I could. She complained for years about the noise from the increased traffic on Forrest Street. I helped her decide to move to a smaller house several blocks away. While packing to move, she had a serious heart attack.

After news of her heart attack reached me, I drove to Valdosta to be with her and my siblings. All ten of her children got to the hospital before she died on November 3, 1971, at age seventy-six. This was two days and thirty-one years after our father had died.

Rather than fight against death, she accepted it as she alternated between complaints about the hard hospital bed and a look of ecstasy as she exclaimed with the words I will never forget: "I am where I'm going, and it's so beautiful. I want all my children to go where I am going."

With her death I faced the problem of getting my family to Valdosta for the funeral. A member of our Sunday school class volunteered to bring them. While waiting for them to arrive, I walked around the corner to the simple frame house of Viola, an African American woman who was my mother's backyard neighbor and best friend. I wanted to thank her for the years she and my mother met in their backyards to check on each other and to share family news. I doubt they had ever visited inside each other's home.

It was the first time I had been in Viola's house. It quickly became a sanctuary where I freely shared my love for my mother and released my grief over her death. Viola told me several things I never knew about my mother and how much each cared for the other. Though I knew blacks had never been welcome in my home church, I invited her to my mother's funeral and said I would sit with her if she did. Shc thanked me and said she would not be going, because she and my mother had an "understanding."

It meant a lot to me to see the pastors of the Valdosta District of the UMC dismiss their meeting early to attend my mother's funeral. The drive to the Melrose, Florida, cemetery and the commitment service brought back a flood of memories. Upon returning to Atlanta I was glad to have Tom Leland, our therapist, to help process more of my grief.

I had a dream one night that helped integrate both the grief and the therapy process. I had gone back to the house where my mother had lived for thirty-five years. In my dream I was planning to move in Mother and had hired an interior decorator to prepare the house. While waiting for him, Mrs. Mary Love Tucker, my former Sunday school teacher, who was like a second mother to me, came to visit me. She was also a close friend of my mother. She had come to welcome me home and to wish me well. While we were talking with her, the interior decorator arrived. The decorator was my therapist, Tom Leland. I told him to go ahead and look around the house. After Mrs. Tucker left, I approached Tom and said that several pieces of Mother's furniture had been shared with my siblings. His said, "That's okay, I think we can use everything here, and we will need to buy only a few new things."

When I told Tom about the dream, he loved it and said, "I think you are about to release your mother and move on with your life." This dream gave me the idea for the article, "Therapy as Interior Decorating."

Upon completion of the required GAPC supervision for my doctoral program, I became a member of the American Association of Pastoral Counseling (AAPC). I enjoyed going to the organization's conferences, but soon I discovered that another organization, the American Association for Marriage and Family Therapy (AAMFT), had more to offer for the kind of counseling I was doing with couples. The pastoral counseling movement was philosophically committed to the medical model of individual diagnosis, psychodynamics, and treatment. AAMFT was more closely related to social psychology and systems thinking. My large family background, experience in church ministry, work in school systems, and my own marriage with five children led me to think primarily in terms of systems of relationships, not in individualistic terms.

Dr. Jim Kilgore invited me to attend AAMFT meetings and agreed to supervise my counseling to help me meet the membership requirements in AAMFT. We met in his Sandy Springs office one day a week. We agreed to split the counseling fees so I could make a little money as well as pay for supervision.

One case I vividly remember was a couple that walked into the office without an appointment. She was one of the most beautiful women I had ever seen. He was an ugly man and much shorter than she. I had as much trouble looking at him as I did at her during the counseling sessions. Her complaint was that he was too controlling of her activities, and he was afraid another man would take her away from him. His also complained that her low self-esteem from thinking she was not pretty enough kept her from enjoying physical intimacy.

I found out she married him because she though she must be ugly when she came in third instead of first place in a Miss America contest. I learned from working with her not to complement a woman on her looks, because she may think the complement requires something in return. I assured the husband that he was not paranoid in thinking that another men wanted to take her away from him, because they did. I suggested he could lessen this possibility by loosening his control over her activities. I suggested that she remove the mirrors in her house lest she think they are trying to lie to her.

I'm not sure I helped their marriage, but they helped me understand the importance of self-image in controlling behaviors.

The six years we lived in Atlanta after returning from Brazil were filled with a variety of learning experiences. Books have always been my primary resources for learning. Reading and writing papers to complete my academic requirements provided intellectual stimulus.

Writing my dissertation helped prepare me for something I never dreamed would be ahead—mentoring dozens of doctoral dissertations. Direct interaction with psychiatric patients and counselees, along with group and individual supervision in CPE, honed my clinical diagnosis and treatment skills. Marriage and family counseling under supervision with Jim Kilgore helped me to think in systems terms. Years of group therapy practice on Saturday mornings with Charlie Roper, an Episcopal priest, help prepare me for working with various kind of group processes.

But I was not the only one in the family taking advantage of learning while we lived in Atlanta. Phyllis completed her master of arts degree in elementary education at Georgia State. And the children were making good progress in their schooling while we enjoyed living in our home in the Leafmore Creek community.

At first, Phyllis was resistant to the idea of doing training in couple's communication and marriage enrichment programs, because she had little interest in psychological issues. She was concerned about possible negative consequences from my becoming a pastoral counselor. After socializing with other pastoral counselors and their spouses, she observed how many of them were divorced or had troubled marriages. I thought training in prevention programs would help our marriage and offer opportunities for us to work together to prevent marriage problems with couples as well as help build my counseling practice.

Our most important learning experience about marriage came from the years of therapy that we did with Tom Leland. Learning about our own marriage, leading marriage enrichment retreats for groups of couples in the district churches, and counseling couples with troubled marriages taught me a lot about marriage and family issues. I came to the conclusion that I would do everything possible to resist extramarital temptations and work through the tough issues with Phyllis to keep our family together, if not for my sake, then for the future of our children. I had seen the devastating effects divorce had caused the children of some close friends.

Upon completion of my research interviews with the pastors, I decided to continue my breakfast and lunch meetings with the pastors. I saw how I could do good pastoral care when we talked over a meal in a neutral setting.

To help the pastors improve their pastoral care and counseling, I started four district peer group meetings of pastors in my office. To solve the question of who was a peer, I decided to form the groups by inviting senior ministers of the largest church, a group of associate pastors, a group of Christian educators, and a group of pastors from new and rapidly changing churches. Each group met twice a month to discuss counseling cases and get consultations for dealing with people and issues in their churches. I enjoyed leading the four groups. Many stories could be told about issues we discussed, but I'll share just one. I'll say his name was Jim.

Jim was the associate pastor of a large church. One of his responsibilities was hospital visitation. He mentioned the case of a young man close to his own age who had been hospitalized with a terminal illness. Jim liked him and wanted to visit him, but he had trouble staying in the man's hospital room more than a few minutes. He wanted help with his tendency of avoiding going to his room or leaving as soon as possible after he got there.

As the group explored issues around this case, I asked "Jim if he had ever had a close friend. He told us that his father was a pastor and how difficult it had been for him to develop friendships with frequent moves from one church to another. An exception to this pattern was his four years of high school, when his family lived in one place. It was here that Jim had a buddy.

When I asked Jim what happened to his buddy, he tried to change the subject, but I brought him back to the question. He told us how both of them had been drafted into the army after graduation and sent for basic training. Jim was sent to Germany, and his buddy was sent to Vietnam. Again he tried to change the story, but I kept pressing by asking, "Then what happened?"

He said, "As my unit was getting ready to go on maneuvers in Germany, I opened and read a letter from my mother. Her last sentence was, 'Did you hear that John [his high school buddy] was killed in Vietnam?'"

Jim got up and tried to leave the meeting, but I blocked the door and had him sit down and tell us how he reacted the day he got the news about the death of his best friend. He said he quickly blocked it out of his mind because he was with a bunch of guys who couldn't understand how much John had meant to him.

At this point in Jim's story, I took a sheet of paper and folded it to fit into a small envelope. I gave it to him and said, "Here is the letter from your mother with the news of John's death. Read the last sentence again."

He paused a few seconds before opening the sheet of paper, and then he went into a full expression of grief as if he had gotten the news for the first time. All the years of encapsulated grief were released in a safe environment of colleagues who had become his friends. It was a powerful group experience.

After we sat with him well beyond our usual group time, I asked him where he thought his friend was buried. He told us the name of the cemetery but said he had never been near his grave.

I asked Jim to contact John's family to find the name of the cemetery and the location of the grave. Then he should let me know so we could meet together as a group at the cemetery and have a committal service for John. I asked a member of the group to bring flowers and others to plan the service.

We met at John's grave three days later, which happened to be a Sunday afternoon. We stood under umbrellas in a pouring rain to hold a symbolic funeral for Jim's friend. It was just as real as any graveside funeral service I had ever experienced, except for an open grave. With the closure from releasing his grief and symbolically burying his friend, Jim said he felt like a huge burden had been lifted from him. He was now able to visit his dying parishioner and be his pastor.

Meanwhile, Phyllis and I were busy parenting our growing children. One weekend a month we left them at home to look after each other while we were conducted a marriage enrichment retreat for a group in one of the district churches. We left them with the threat that if they did something wrong while we were away, the punishment would be doubled. Only once did we have to follow through with this threat.

Our best summer was when we had four children in their teens. During Randy's last year of high school, I arranged for him to have a series of vocational tests and talk about college recommendations at Columbia Presbyterian Seminary in Decatur. He chose to go to St. Andrews Presbyterian College in North Carolina.

One of the exercises at the marriage enrichment retreats concerned setting goals for the future. The goal that kept appearing on my list was, "I want to complete my dissertation." I had been working on the dissertation in my spare time around a more-than-full-time job. I had been discouraged from a setback caused by a know-it-all professor who argued that I had the wrong approach to a ThD dissertation. The two other committee advisors agreed with him and had me structure my writing according to the know-it-all's orientation. I worked on it for more than a year without making much progress. When my mentor saw how much I was struggling, he decided to consult with a sociology of religion professor, Dr. Earl Brewer. The report was that I should write the dissertation differently, which turned out to be exactly how I had proposed to write it in the first place. When I heard this, I was too angry over the wasted time and effort to talk about anything else that day.

In 1975 Phyllis and I were leading a marriage enrichment retreat. When we were doing the "what I want for me, you, and us" goal-setting exercise along with the other couples in the group, I repeated the same thing I had written several times at other retreats: "I want to complete my dissertation." As Phyllis and I discussed the importance of completing the dissertation so I could graduate, she suggested she would care for the children three weekends a month if I would dedicate my time to writing. Three months later, my wonderful secretary, Pat Chapman, finished typing the last chapter for me to submit for my dissertation defense. I was the first graduate to finish and walk across the Emory University stage to receive a ThD degree.

One of my counselees told me about her father purchasing two large houses at the DeKalb County Courthouse steps. The house were on Ridgecrest Drive in Druid Hills, within two blocks of Emory University. He gave one house to her and wanted to sell the other. I asked her to tell her father to show it to me, because I was interested in making an investment for our future income. When I arrived, I was amazed to see a very large apartment on the first floor and four smaller apartments on the second. They were rented to married university students. His asking price could be paid over the next twenty years by income from the renters, with enough extra to pay for taxes and upkeep. I tried to convince Phyllis to refinance our house to make the small down payment, but she did not think we should take that big a risk. I was disappointed and upset, because I knew the house would be a good investment for our future, but my marriage was too important to fight against her wishes. Had we bought it, we would have been tied down to managing it and kept from making a decision that completely changed our lives and had much to do with the choice of spouses for three of our children.

The bumper sticker on the car in front of me at the stoplight caught my attention. I had a strange but powerful negative emotional reaction as I read the words "Oral Roberts University." Why would anyone even think about going to a school like that, I said to myself. I was about to find out.

A few days later I received a call from Dr. Jim Buskirk in Tulsa, Oklahoma. He had been a colleague in the Emory doctoral program and was teaching evangelism in the Candler School of Theology. He recently resigned and moved to Tulsa to be the dean of the new Oral Roberts School of Theology. He was calling to tell me that another colleague in our doctoral program and pastor of a downtown Atlanta UMC had been recruited to be his professor of church and society and director of the field education program. Dean Buskirk said he wanted me to consider moving to Tulsa to be the professor of pastoral care and counseling.

I listened politely and asked questions before telling him I wasn't interested. A week later he called again. By this time I had thought of many reasons why I didn't want to teach at Oral Roberts University. Again I turned down the offer. A month later he called to ask if Phyllis and I would have dinner with him at the Atlanta airport during a layover. I agreed to meet with him but warned him that he would not change my mind.

Over dinner, he told us he wanted to pay for us to visit the university. We accepted the invitation, though I told him he was wasting the university's money because I wasn't moving to Tulsa. Phyllis and I left that dinner impressed with Jim's vision for the new seminary and his passion for what he was doing. A few weeks later plane tickets arrived in the mail for the agreed-upon visit.

Before going, trip we watched Oral Roberts's Sunday morning television program to get a better idea about him and the university. We arrived in Tulsa with more than our luggage. I was loaded with questions, but mostly I wasn't interesting in accepting the invitation to join the faculty. We arrived in time for two days of Oral Roberts's preaching and healing seminars. We were two curious people among several thousand guests. On Monday we had a tour of the campus and saw drawings of future construction. I had an interview with Dr. Carl Hamilton, the provost. I asked him many tough questions about academic freedom, tenure, textbook choices, and so on. Every question was answered to my satisfaction. Questions I asked God were answered with more challenging questions for me. My reasons for not accepting the position seemed to evaporate. It was up to me to decide if I wanted to continue with the job I loved at the district counseling center or take a huge risk and move to Tulsa to teach at ORU. I asked for a month to decide.

That month was filled with intense struggle. I prayed and consulted with several trusted friends. Their responses were equally divided between go and don't go. As the pressure built, I prayed, *God, just tell me what I should do and I will do it.* The response came like a clear voice to my spirit: *You're a big boy now. Choose to do what you most want to do, and I will bless you wherever you are.* This response both frightened and thrilled me, but it did not tell me what to do.

On the next to last day to decide, I told Phyllis that I was going to turn down the invitation. As we sat on the edge of our bed, I saw something

I had rarely seen. Tears started running down her face. I asked her what her tears meant. She said she had decided not to do anything to influence my decision but to be supportive of me no matter what I decided. She said she would still do this, but she felt I was about to miss a blessing if I didn't accept the invitation to teach in a school of theology.

That did it.

The next day I called Jim Buskirk to tell him I would accept his invitation to teach at Oral Roberts.

Then came the hard part: going public about what we had decided to do. We first talked with the children. Randy was in his second year at Saint Andrews, and Ruth had been accepted at Emory University. This meant we would be moving a long distance from them.

Phyllis and I went down the list of people who needed to know, then those we thought should know. The first call was to Rev. Malone Dodson, chairman of the District Counseling Center Advisory Board to let him know so he could start planning for how the board would find someone to take my job.

There was a wide array of reactions to our decision. Some responded with disappointment, others celebrated with us. The wife of one of our best friends had the most loving response to the news when she got furious with me and cursed me for leaving them.

We lived in the Leafmore Drive house for the longest time we had ever spent in any one house over twenty-two years of marriage. With six intense years of a broad range of education after returning from Brazil, I was going to be a theological educator, something I vowed in Brazil I would never do again.

We started preparing the house for sale at a time of a serious down market in Atlanta. I flew to Tulsa to find a place for us to live. With the help of Ken Jones, I had no trouble finding a house on the first day. It was directly behind the new ORU baseball field. Not being able to sell the Atlanta house meant I had no money for a down payment, but the seller was willing to sign a contract. Our pastor, Rev. Claude Smithmire, came to the rescue with a personal loan to be repaid on the sale of our house.

In July, I had to leave in time to meet the starting date for my job. We sold both second-hand cars that had given us so many repair problems and bought a new one. I flew to Tulsa before we found a renter for our Atlanta house and packed to move. This left Phyllis and the children to do the job of renting the house and moving out on a very rainy day. Then they started the two-day drive to Tulsa.

CHAPTER 15

Tulsa Stories

> If you want to understand religion, go where it's a white-hot heat, not where it's become a cold dead habit.
>
> —William James

Arriving in Tulsa to teach at Oral Roberts University in 1977 was as strange as landing in Brazil in 1961. This time it was not the climate, language, or customs but the charismatic culture at the university. I had very little understanding of the culture and ethos of charismatic Christianity, but I was interested in learning. One of my intellectual mentors, Gordon Allport, included the William James quote above in his psychology of religion book.

Immediately, I felt the energy of the charismatic movement led by the healing and educational ministry of Oral Roberts. Though I'm naturally skeptical of religious leaders, Oral was different. He looked and spoke like a great Indian chief. Indeed, he was one-fourth Shawnee. Even the architecture of the buildings had Native American motifs. His brilliant intellect, combined with visionary clarity, kept him focused on building a great university. He was the most unusual leader I have ever known. He had the good sense to gather around him extraordinarily gifted people with the talent and training necessary to help him achieve his vision. When he chose someone to lead a part of the university, he did not micromanage them or allow anyone to avoid them by going directly to him. I have never worked at a place with so many dedicated and gifted people.

Our decision to buy the house directly behind the university turned out to be a great blessing. I had a choice of walking a half mile up and down a hill and around the corner to get to my office or go directly. A chain-link fence, however, blocked the much shorter direct route. Remembering the Brazilian expression *dar um jeito* ("find a way"), I requested permission to put in a gate in the fence behind our house, but the request was denied. With *dar um jeito* in mind, however, I created another way to go about two hundred yards directly from our backyard to my office. I bent down several feet of wire at the top of the fence, leaned a short aluminum ladder on our side, and wired two horse stirrups on the university side, then went downhill to cross a creek on some flat rocks—when it was not raining. This reduced the walking time from fifteen minutes to three minutes.

We had a good view of the university from our dining room and kitchen. During the swing of the spring and fall solstice, the setting sun shone several days each year directly behind the Prayer Tower. From our dining table, we needed little imagination to think about the sun blasting the Prayer Tower like a rocket ship into space.

The year we moved to Tulsa, Randy started his junior year at St. Andrews College in North Carolina and Ruth started her freshman year at the Emory-at-Oxford campus in Georgia. Walter and Susana were in their junior and freshman years at Jenks High School, and Paul started the sixth grade in Jenks Middle School.

When we first told our children that we were moving to Tulsa, Paul thought it was a great idea. Within a few months, though, he no longer thought so. He unloaded his anger at me one evening for moving our family. Instead of getting defensive, I responded to him that he must be missing his friends and confessed how much I was also missing my friends. We sat in front of the fireplace that evening and cried together over the loss of our friendship systems. I learned that night that family and furniture can be moved, but a support system cannot be transferred from one city to another. I also discovered how being so busy and focused on moving and paying little attention to grieving over losses only transfers the grief to the next place.

Phyllis planned to teach school in Oklahoma to help pay for our children's college expenses. We had been promised help with finding a teaching position, but that did not happen. After many unsuccessful applications, she discovered that completing her master's in education before we moved made her overqualified for the salary the school system was willing to pay beginning teachers. Principals wanted to hire her, but the school superintendent wouldn't approve her application because he could hire four teachers with bachelor's degrees for the same cost of hiring three teachers with master's degrees. She tried working her way into a job by substitute teaching, but the pay was too low to be worthwhile. Meanwhile, our expenses exceeded my income.

I soon realized my mistake of agreeing to come to ORU for the same salary that I was making at the counseling center in Atlanta. In Tulsa, our mortgage payment was double. Added to this were college expenses that took big chunks of our limited financial resources. Phyllis was a very economical person, and she was doing everything possible to help us save money, but we still could stretch the dollars only so far. I started a garden in our backyard, but that helped very little. To pay our bills on time, we began borrowing money from the teacher's credit union and using credit cards.

I tried to use the office of a friend to bring in extra money through counseling, but I soon discovered that scheduling appointments was too complicated to continue. Then I had the idea of using part of our living room for a counseling office. I hired a cabinetmaker to install double doors, a desk, and bookshelves to help the room look appropriate for both a living room and an office. Extra income from counselees helped relieve the economic pressure, but it did not completely solve the problem. The older children helped as much as they could by working during the summer and Christmas holidays.

As Christmas approached in 19777, we realized our credit was maxed out and there was no money to buy presents. Phyllis had been collecting bingo-type prize cards at a supermarket. A few days before Christmas, she showed me her collection and how she had matched the numbers on the cards. When I asked her what they meant, she responded, "According to the way I see it, it looks like we won a thousand dollars." I responded, "Don't breath. Let's go right now and show this to the manager." When we got to the store he confirmed that she had won the contest and issued a check for one thousand dollars. And we were able to buy presents that year.

My first task at the seminary was to read the students' application documents and interview each upon their arrival on campus. From this information, I wrote a one-page descriptive summary to help professors and administrators know something about each student. I started by quickly reading all the files and separating the ones I thought should have been accepted and the ones who shouldn't. Just before getting to the end of the stack of applications, I realized the stack of students to be accepted was much smaller than the other. If my judgment had been the determining factor for acceptance, we would have very few students to teach.

While I was meditating on this predicament, I sensed God saying, *Read them again and consider them in comparison to what you were like when you applied to seminary, not by who you are today.* As I reread the files again, the students to be accepted grew much larger than the others.

I learned a great deal about the students, especially in regard to the religious experiences that led them to apply to Oral Roberts. The books, classes, and clinical experiences in hospitals were a great resource for interpreting what I was reading in their autobiographical sketches.

As a professor, my first goal was to help students understand the psychological and spiritual dynamics related to their religious experiences. All students were required to take my personality and religion course the first year of seminary. Though I was not a charismatic Christian, or Pentecostal in terms of speaking in tongues, I was not opposed to this form of spirituality. I wanted to understand it from both an intellectual and spiritual perspective, such as speaking in tongues. I also wanted to help students gain a deeper understanding of the benefits, problems, and limitations related to their transformative religious experiences. I wish I had copied many of the major term papers that hundreds of students wrote about the relationship between their personal history and their religious experiences. They would be a rich source of information for research.

One semester I sent a letter to President Roberts via Dean Buskirk, requesting that he teach a class session on how he understood the relationship between his family history, his personality, and his Christian faith. To everyone's surprise, he accepted. It was an amazing experience.

He started by asking me how much time he had. I said, "You're the president of the university, so you can take as much time as you want."

He was very organized and candid in his remarks about what he received from his half-Indian mother with her keen intellect and deep awareness of spiritual reality. At this time she was one of over four hundred persons in the continuum of care facility he had built close to the campus. He said he got his love for reading from her. He told us that he took, or sent, a box of books each week to her room, and they would discuss them when he visited. He said he read western novels to relax and had read almost every published one. (Hearing him say this helped me believe what I had been told about Oral having a photographic memory and how he could read a book about as fast as he could turn the pages.)

Oral contrasted the influence of his mother with his Pentecostal holiness evangelist father who struggled to make a living during the dust bowl days of the Great Depression. He told us how his father had to put cardboard soles in his shoes to walk the dusty roads to and from preaching appointments. He brought home very little money to support his family. His uncles, unlike his father, had held on to their farmland through the dust bowl years. When oil was discovered on their land, his relatives became wealthy. As he walked to school, his rich cousins drove by him in new cars without offering to give him a ride.

Instead of developing a sense of inferiority from living in a poor family and contrasting that with his wealthy relatives, Oral said he determined to do something great, like become the governor of Oklahoma. His success as a high school basketball player was cut short at age sixteen, however, when he was diagnosed with tuberculosis. The disease progressed rapidly to the point that the wall of his bedroom was covered with the blood he coughed up. He had to drop out of school, and his family thought he was going to die. His mother looked for an Indian woman known for her healing miracles. When the woman prayed for him, he was instantaneously healed, with no signs of having had the disease. He slowly regained his strength to went back to school. Soon after this, he was called to a preaching-healing ministry. From high school he went to college a couple of years, but his fame for preaching and healing miracles soon demanded his full attention for organization, travel, and tent healing services.

This was a class session my students and I have never forgotten. Afterward, Oral accepted an invitation to teach another class. This time it was in the cross-pollination or multidiscipline class of students from various professional schools across the university. I was one of a three-professor team that taught the class. Church historian Steve O'Malley taught the history of healing. Old Testament professor Howard Erwin taught the theology of healing. And I taught the practice of healing. Since there was no one with more experience with the practice of healing than Oral, I convinced him that he should help me teach the class. He was very humble in telling the story of his healing ministry. He said he had seen many miracles, but he has never claimed credit for them; rather the Holy Spirit has done all of these miracles through him.

One of the things that attracted me and thousands of others to ORU was Oral's education philosophy. He wanted students to have a classical liberal education in a healthy Christian environment, where the gifts and fruit of the Spirit were honored and practiced in a disciplined manner. Twice–a-week chapel services integrated charismatic music with speakers across a broad spectrum of disciplines. We heard most of the outstanding leaders in America, including Supreme Court justices, politicians, businessmen, bishops, pastors, and television evangelists.

When I was invited to speak in chapel, I was determined to choose a subject that would hold the attention of the students. I chose the ten stages of honoring parents. Halfway through my presentation, I paused to see if the students were sleeping or studying. All eyes were on me.

One year the commencement speaker was Jessie Jackson. The next year Bob Hope spoke. The most beautiful vocal music I've ever heard was when over five thousand people in chapel sang in tongues. It was like the sound of thousands of angels. Some speakers were controversial, especially those with a name it–claim it theology. Many times I had to deal with questions about what was said in chapel before I could begin my day's lecture. Chapel at ORU was never a dull religious requirement.

The unique thing about Oral's holistic education philosophy was an aerobics program. In the early days of the university, Oral had read Kenneth Cooper's book *The Canadian Exercise Program* and decided that he wanted everyone in the university—students, faculty, administrators, and employees—to be healthy by participating in aerobics. He called the provost, Dr. Carl Hamilton, off the golf course to tell him to read the book and invite the author to be the consultant for the design of the program and construction of a state-of-the-art aerobics center. The program was in full swing when I arrived in the fall of 1977. No one was exempt from a thorough physical checkup, with a stress test to make sure we were healthy. We were required to attend introductory classes to help us understand the purpose and procedures of the program. Some students came with letters from family doctors regarding medical problems and asking them to be excused from physical exercises. They were put in special classes, where they started exercising with finger movements and gradually progressed to more strenuous exercises. I saw students with problems such as severe asthma who had never exercised in their life. Over several months of coaching and progressive exercises, they were able to run three miles or more.

I credit the ORU aerobics program for giving me the understanding, motivation, and opportunities for improving my health through exercise. Oral was a pioneer in the development of the aerobics program. He was often criticized for requiring everyone to participate, but he influenced generations of health-conscious people. He built the first indoor aerobics track on a college or university campus. I often chatted with colleagues and students as we ran around the quarter-mile track. This helped me get to know them better. Sometimes carbon dioxide built up on the track from having too many runners at one time.

I found running in a semicircle boring, however. I suggested to Dr. Paul Brentenson, the program director, that we needed an outdoor track for the people who preferred open-air exercise. When he claimed there was no room for a track on the campus, I asked him to get his distance marker and follow me. I showed him how a half-mile gravel track could be laid out on the university property behind our house. Phyllis and I often climbed the fence, crossed the creek, and ran or walked on this track. It's still there.

We also walked many miles on the hilly streets in our Walnut Creek neighborhood. I credit the ORU aerobics program for making me as healthy as I've ever been. I was pleased to reach my goal of running fifteen miles in a race, the most I ever ran. Phyllis didn't enjoy running, but she liked to walk with me. This gave us time to exercise and talk. ORU gave us the information, inspiration, and accountability to take care of our bodies with regular exercise. We continue to put it to good use.

Oral was a member of the Tulsa First Methodist Church. He thought the bishop of the Oklahoma Annual Conference had transferred his clergy credentials from the Pentecostal Holiness Church to the United Methodist Church. The problem was that the category of lay clergy membership was discontinued at the next General Conference, and his name was not transferred to an updated category. And when that bishop retired, the next one refused to have anything to do with Pentecostals or charismatics, especially Oral. This left a great deal of tension between Oral and Oklahoma Methodism. Starting a seminary in Tulsa with a Methodist dean and twelve of fifteen professors who were ordained Methodist elders increased the tension. When I realized we were seen as a threat rather than an asset, I suggested to my colleagues that we attend different Methodist churches in Tulsa so we could develop personal relationships with as many pastors as possible.

Phyllis and I chose the Jenks UMC. Our children went to school in this town, which was across the Arkansas River about two miles from our house. After we visited the church several Sundays, the pastor, Rev. Kerney Graham, came to see us. He wanted to check us out. Evidently he had been warned by the bishop and district superintendent to be on guard against the influence of people from ORU.

After asking about our backgrounds, he asked, "Why are you attending my church?"

I said that we wanted to worship God and participate as members in a Christian community.

Then he said, "I've never been the pastor of a seminary professor. What do you expect me to do?"

I said that I expected him to preach and teach the word of God, to care for our souls, to correct me if I do something I should not do, to pray for us, and if I should die while here, preach my funeral service.

He seemed to relax and said, "Well, I think I can do that."

Before he left, I told him I would like to have lunch with him from time to time so we could get to know each other better. This we did over the next eight years.

Kerney and I developed a wonderful relationship. I was careful about how I participated in the life of the church by never saying anything critical about him to other church members or getting involved in church business affairs. One day at lunch he asked me what he could do to help bring some excitement to the life of the church. I suggested that we start a new church congregation where new houses were being built. He claimed that would be impossible because the church did not have the funds for such a project. I asked him how much money he could allocate, and he said, "No more than five hundred dollars." I surprised him by saying, "That's enough."

When he suggested Glenpool as the best place to plant a new church, I asked how many families at the Jenks UMC lived there.

"Three," he said.

I said, "That's a good start."

I volunteered to be the founding pastor and recruit three theology students to help me so I could train them to plant new churches. We used the five hundred dollars to pay five months' rent at a local elementary school and buy the nursery and pulpit furniture.

I made an appointment to visit with a woman coming to our new church when her husband could be home. During our conversation, I said that I wished I could get a better view of the Glenpool development from above. Her husband said that if I was serious, I should meet him at the airport the next Wednesday afternoon. He said he was the pilot of a pizza restaurant's biplane used to tow advertising banners. When I got there he greeted me with a helmet, goggles, and scarf, and then said I was to ride in the front seat. He told me that when we were flying over the city, I had to point toward the places where I wanted to take pictures, because we would not be able to hear each other over the engine noise. Then he asked me to keep my foot on the brakes while he went to turn the propeller and crank the engine. Soon I felt like Snoopy's World War I flying ace as we flew over the city. I landed with a good idea about the central location of this growing city. (Two years later a man gave the land to build the church only a hundred feet from the spot I had picked as an ideal location.)

I started the worship services by doing most of the preaching. Gradually I asked the students to alternate preach responsibilities. After a year of working with the three and their wives, I suggested to Kerney that we pick one of them, Kenny Newsome, to be the pastor until he graduated.

Planting the church in Glenpool created excitement in the Jenks Church, so much so that Kerney suggested we start another one across the river from Jenks, where some expensive houses were being built. We discovered that this area was lacked any potential meeting places, such as a school or a space in a strip mall. And then, one day, Kerney called me very excited. He had talked with Father White, the Catholic priest of a new parish starting in a closed Catholic girls' home in the area where we wanted to start a new church. The priest offered to rent us the school chapel that his congregation had outgrown.

We had a place but no money to get started. Kerney talked with Jack Featherstone, the Tulsa UMC district superintendent, about the relationship between his church, the ORU professor, and the students at the Glenpool church. When Kerney told me he could get only three thousand dollars from the district superintendent to start the church, I assured him that it would be enough to buy several truckloads of gravel for a parking lot and chairs. This would get us started. After worship services began, people's tithes and offerings allowed us to do more.

My seminary colleagues were interested in my story about starting a church in Glenpool. When they heard about the possibility of new church plant only two miles from the seminary, several professors wanted to help. Kerney and I decided to form a team of professors and students. I accepted the role as lead pastor, including pastoral care and administration. Larry Laccour, professor of homiletics, would be the primary preacher, and the professor of evangelism, Bob Tuttle, would be in charge of evangelism. We chose a very bright student to be my assistant so I wouldn't have to spend a lot of time with church administration.

We had over a hundred people in attendance at our first Sunday worship service. Our musician was Millie, Larry Laccour's wife. She was a former orchestra harpist. The sound of her harp in the chapel sounded like dozens of harps, and the singing was like the sound of hundreds of people. Then we discovered that any speaker's voice echoed in the room. Marble floors and walls, combined with glass windows, created a three- to four-second reverberation inside the chapel. In order to be understood, we had to speak very slowly and precisely to keep the words from overlapping. The Catholic priest understood our problem, because he had to deal with it when he led worship in the chapel. He gave us permission to install sound panels on the walls and floors. This made a huge difference. The people had a big laugh one Sunday when I announced that I was making appointments to hear confessions in the Catholic confessional booth attached to the front wall of the chapel.

Since we had no rooms for Sunday school classes, we met in small groups in homes. I organized potential leaders into task groups instead of committees to make it easier to add new people as new members joined. Within six to eight months we grew tired of the name "new church" and choose a group to select a name. We worked from a large list of potential names and decided on St. James.

Except for a small salary for my student assistant, everyone was a volunteer. Toward the end of the first year, I felt the responsibilities of St. James demanded too much of my time. I was a full-time professor, a half-time counselor, and a part-time gardener to support our family. The stress was getting to me. For the first time in our marriage, Phyllis and I were not going to church together. She had to be at the Jenks UMC because Kerney hired her to work there as the Christian education director. Neither of us wanted to continue this arrangement.

I decided to tell Kerney and the district superintendent that the church was strong enough to have a full-time pastor to take it to the next level. They agreed with me. We were excited to hear that one of our best graduates had been appointed to be the new pastor. But the Sunday I introduced him to the congregation, I knew we had made a big mistake. His wife was so sick she could hardly walk to the front to be introduced with him. I thought to myself, *She is going to die in a few months, and he will go into a crisis of grief that will take all his energy just to survive.* She died four months later, and he moved two years later. The church barely survived the chaos.

Before the young man left, he got crossed up with Father White and was told to take the church to some other place. They moved the congregation to the sixtieth floor at the top of the City of Faith. (A new pastor came and stayed a long time. While he was pastor, he led St. James to purchase twenty acres of prime land and build the first phase of a large building for worship and other activities. Today that property is worth over twenty-five million dollars.)

Our children were growing up very fast. Randy graduated from Saint Andrews College two years after we moved from Atlanta. He came Tulsa to work and enroll in the Oral Roberts School of Theology. But one semester of that was enough for him. He returned to Laurinburg to be with his college girlfriend, and then, after a year of working the night shift in a factory, he decided that going to graduate school was a preferable pursuit.

When we talked, I asked him if he was trying to be come a minister like me. He confirmed my hunch but said he didn't want to be a parish pastor. He said he had admired our Canadian missionary friend in Brazil and would really like to become a researcher in agricultural science. I pointed him toward Oklahoma State University in Stillwater. The department of agriculture eagerly enrolled him even though he didn't have a college degree in science. In college he had majored in philosophy so he could go to classes in the morning and play on the soccer team in the afternoon.

Ruth finished two years of college at Emory-at-Oxford and transferred to Emory in Atlanta. When I discovered that Walter had signed a contract to take Bell & Howell technical school courses because he didn't want to add to our financial stress, I was furious with him and with his mother for agreeing to do this. I asked him what he would like to do, he said he wanted to study electrical engineering. A year before Randy started at Oklahoma State in 1981, Walter enrolled there to study engineering and worked in a co-op program to help pay his own way through college.

Susana carefully went through all her things before she left home in the fall of 1982 to study at Emory-at-Oxford near Atlanta. Starting with our oldest child, we required that they completely clean their room by throwing away what they did not want, packing what they wanted to take to college, and storing in boxes what they wanted us to keep for them. This meant they would leave the room clean so that others could use the space while they were gone, but they would have a place to stay in the house when they came home for holidays and in the summertime. We felt like successful parents because our first four children were good students and cooperative with our family values and rules. That changed with Paul, our youngest child.

As I said before, the move to Tulsa when Paul was eleven had not gone well for him. He missed his Atlanta buddies and familiar surroundings. Instead of making new friends from healthy families, he found acceptance with problem kids from broken homes. They were neither good students nor well disciplined. Paul's creativity took a turn toward risky behavior that kept us on guard for trouble. The most positive thing he did was run for the school track team. I loved his beautiful running stride, but I did not enjoy getting up on Saturday mornings before daylight so he could compete in running club races.

High school was bewildering to him. He went to his classes without becoming a behavior problem, except when it came to taking exams. I often felt hypocritical when counseling with young people and their parents about low grades when my own son was not making any kind of grades because he refused to take any exams. His stated excuse was that teachers used exams to keep their jobs, but the exams were not designed to actually evaluate the intelligence of the students. I did not know until much later that he did not understand how to prepare for exams and how to do the best he could when taking them. He was fortunate that he was not suspended from going to school. The education philosophy at that time was social promotion from one grade to the next according to age rather than competency.

I tried everything I knew to help Paul, but I wasn't successful. We took him to a counselor. The counselor believed in the prevalent psychological myth that troubled kids were a symptom of troubled marriages. He dismissed Paul's problems and wanted to see Phyllis and me to work on our marriage. We tried a few sessions until I realized he was not helping us to help Paul. Nothing we did seemed to help him. I also tried to stop him from tearing the sleeves of his shirts, including new ones, into strips. Then I discovered that his classmates were copying his style of torn shirtsleeves.

A breakthrough came when Ms. Lewis, his typing teacher, called me one evening to express concern about Paul's refusal to do the drills she had used to teach typing for more than fifteen years. I remembered reading some of the poetry and creative stories Paul had written and allowed me to read. He said he had written them in his typing class. I thought the poems and stories were wonderful, especially the phrase "You know a word when you can taste it's meaning."

I asked Ms. Lewis which was more important, typing drills or learning how to type? When she responded that learning to type was the purpose of the drills, I asked her if he was learning how to type. When she said he could type as well any student, I asked if she had read any of the poetry and stories he was writing. She had not read them before our conversation, but when she did, she realized Paul needed more than her typing class. She showed his creative writing and drawings to the director of the gifted program. She had him transferred to the nontraditional student classes to write and draw for the school literary periodical. He found acceptance based on his unique way of expressing his gifts rather than with his grades. Paul and I give Ms. Lewis credit for rescuing Paul from failure in school and inspiring him to develop his gifts.

By this time, I was refusing to blame myself for not finding a way to solve Paul's school problems. I knew that drugs were involved, and his friends were a big part of using them. I told Phyllis several times that our experience with his brothers and sisters indicated that we were good parents and I believed he was a good kid, but he would have to find his own way to grow up. Meanwhile, I wanted us to stop spending so much of our time worrying about him. Thanks to the social promotion philosophy in the school system at that time, Paul finished high school in 1985, the last year we lived Tulsa. When I asked about his plans for the future, he surprised me by saying that he planned to go to college. When I inquired how he would do this without a high school diploma, he said he was going to take the GED and the SAT, which he did and had no trouble passing them. Then he got Ms. Lewis to write a letter of recommendation to St. Andrew's. Randy graduated from this college and knew which professors to contact, and that opened the door for Paul's conditional acceptance.

As an ORU professor, I took my professional development very seriously. I attended both the Southwest Region of the American Association of Pastoral Counselors and the annual national meetings of AAPC. I was very active in the American Association for Marriage and Family Counseling (AAMFC). The Oklahoma division of AAMFC elected president for a two-year term. During that time I worked with others to lobby the state legislature to license marriage and family therapists. I took advantage of the professional development funds of the university to attend these meetings. I enjoyed learning new ideas about counseling and confronting professional colleagues about their misconceptions concerning ORU. The seminary would not pay my expenses to attend the North Georgia Methodist Annual Conferences, but I went at my own expense, because I wanted to maintain my conference relationship. I enjoyed teaching at ORU, but it was never a long-term career goal for me.

Phyllis's mother suffered many years with dementia. She was not diagnosed with Alzheimer's disease, though she had many of the symptoms. In spite of the fact that money was very tight for our family, we had been sending as much as we could to help Papa Diehl pay a nurse to help him care for her. In August 1980 Phyllis and I traveled to Pennsylvania for a family gathering, mostly to discuss what more needed to be done to help care for her. The dining room next to the kitchen on the first floor had been turned into her bedroom. Saturday morning we overheard a brief conversation between Mother and Papa Diehl, not that we were trying to listen to them, but since both had hearing problems, they loudly.

Mother Diehl had barely spoken for several weeks, but now she spoke as clear as a bell, "Papa, what's wrong with me?"

"Mimi, there's nothing wrong with you. You're just an old woman."

"Papa, are you an old man?"

"Yes, Mimi. I'm an old man."

"Papa, am I going to die?"

"Yes, Mimi, you're going to die."

"Papa?"

"Yes, Mimi."

"Papa, why don't you die first so I can take care of you?"

"No, Mimi. You're going to die first so I can take care of you while you die."

"No, Papa, I want to take care of you."

"Listen to me, Mimi. I've asked God to help me take care of you, and I'm going to do it. Do you hear me?"

After a long pause, she said, "Papa, I love you."

"Mimi, I love you."

As far as we know, this was their last conversation. Their love story was much better than *Romeo and Juliet*. It was a story that caused me to change my view of death.

Mother Diehl died a month later. I bought a plane ticket for Phyllis to fly to Pittsburgh because I wanted her to be with her family as soon as possible. The children and I made the trip by car for the funeral and burial in Middletown.

Exactly a month later, Papa Diehl died from a cerebral hemorrhage. I was determined to support Phyllis by returning to her home for his funeral, but we had no money for travel expenses and our credit cards were maxed out. When a bank loan officer turned down my emergency loan application, I wanted to choke him but decided to walk across the street to our church to talk with our pastor, Kerney Graham. I spilled my frustration and grief in his office. When he heard how much I loved Papa Diehl and how desperate I was to go with Phyllis and our family to his funeral, he walked across the street with me and told the bank manager to let me have as much money as I needed and he would sign the papers to guarantee the loan.

Living directly behind the university had its advantages. The three-minute walk from home to my office made it easy to go home for lunch or to take care of other business between classes. When we moved here, the university was completing the last phase of construction on the best baseball field on any university campus in the country. I often watched games while grading papers on our dining room table or while working in the garden. The sound of the aluminum bats hitting the ball was the signal for me to look at the play on the field. Phyllis made a large GO ORU banner to hang on the backyard fence during games to encourage the team. Some night games we climbed up on our toolshed and sat in lawn chairs and watched the game.

We watched the continuous two-year construction of the City of Faith hospital from the back of our house. After a prolonged legal battle with other hospitals in Tulsa, construction started on the largest reinforced concrete building in the world. When it was completed in 1981, it had a sixty-story clinic tower, thirty-story hospital, and twenty-story research center. The first five stories of each tower were tied together to form a dish-like base for the complex. The hospital nursing stations looked like a *Star Wars* command center with a view of rooms on two floors.

One afternoon, while waiting for an appointment with Jimmy Buskirk on the dean's floor of the university, I told his secretary I would be in the large conference room where the hospital blueprints were spread out. As I examined the blueprints, I soon observed that the doctors and nurses had special rooms dedicated for medical care, but there were no rooms for prayer partners to talk with people. (Oral did not like the word *chaplain* because the ones he met had been too passive for him. He changed the name from chaplain to *prayer partners*.) I showed this to Jimmy Buskirk when he came to get me, and he later talked with Oral about it. Oral ordered the architects to modify the blueprints on all thirty floors to include a prayer partner room on each floor of the hospital.

Before the hospital opened, I was asked to speak at the university faculty chapel on the subject of healing through the ministry of chaplaincy/prayer partners. I was told the chapel service would be taped, but I was not told that Oral would be sitting in the front row. After I spoke, he warmly congratulated me on my presentation about the history of CPE and my theology of healing through clergy prayers. A few days later Oral told me that his wife, Evelyn, listened to the tape of my talk and was pleased by what she heard. Then I learned all this was a prelude to my being chosen to be the chief prayer partner (chaplain) of the hospital. When Dean Buskirk told me that Oral wanted me to do this, I asked for time to think and pray about it.

As Phyllis and I talked about my shifting from teaching to administration, I concluded that I did not want to give up teaching in the seminary to become a hospital administrator of what was planned to become a large staff of hospital pastors. This would require more of my time than all the other things I was doing and would pay less money than I was making as a teacher and counselor. I told the dean to thank Oral for considering me for this important position, but I could have a bigger influence for good at the university by continuing as a professor to prepare future pastors and prayer partners. I never heard any more about this, but I was glad that I turned down the invitation to take a very stressful job. Twenty-seven full-time prayer partners were eventually hired, and all lost their jobs when the hospital closed several years later.

By the time our first class of students graduated in 1981, I was feeling confident as a seminary professor. The dean, twelve of fifteen faculty members, and most students were United Methodist. Word spread across the country about what we were doing at ORU. It caused a fearful reaction among more liberal United Methodist leaders. The 1980 General Conference of the UMC created a university senate to control which theology schools would receive accreditation for educating Methodist pastors. My brother Ed was instrumental in helping me communicate with

Bishop Hunt, the episcopal supervisor of the Board of Ministry, to force the university senate accreditation committee to visit ORU and make a decision about accrediting us.

An interview with Oral as well as seeing so many United Methodist professors and students impressed the committee enough to get their approval. Once we got over the hurdle of accreditation, our students often surprised and pleased members of the boards of ordained ministry in the conferences where they were interviewed. Our graduates were often recruited to be pastors of large independent churches.

Discussions in our faculty meetings were healthy and challenging. Though the university had a charismatic culture and ethos, we had academic freedom to express different views, choose textbooks, and teach without interference from the administration. Professors and students from other disciplines had a great deal of respect for the School of Theology. Occasionally Oral visited our theology faculty meetings to discuss issues important to him. When chapel speakers said things that created questions in the minds of students, I felt compelled to shift my teaching plan to deal with the teachable moment. It was an exciting place to teach. The tension between various theological positions created an environment that forced faculty and students to define their beliefs and theological positions.

Oral was under a great deal of pressure as president of the university. He had to raise an enormous amount of money to build the City of Faith. He also had an extensive preaching and speaking ministry. His personal family tragedies, such as the death of his oldest daughter and son-in-law in a plane accident in 1977 and the suicide of his oldest son, took a toll on his emotional resources. His son was a Stanford University summa-cum-laude graduate and had been a top intelligence officer during the Vietnam War. Like so many Vietnam veterans, his son never found peace in civilian life. He started using drugs to deal with his confusion. He ended his pain by taking his own life. I attended the very sad funeral in the university chapel.

Reporters frequently misunderstood Oral's biblical, metaphorical thinking and took his statements literally. Things like "I saw a ninety-foot Jesus" were widely quoted in the press. What he really meant was "I saw a Jesus big enough to lift my burdens." One of his close associates told me that Oral suffered from what used to be called manic depressive disorder but now is known as seasonal affective disorder. His highs and his lows were much more pronounced than in most people. When he got exceptionally depressed, his wife, Evelyn, would convince him that it was time to go to the desert. I discovered that *desert* was a code word for their home in Palm Springs, California. She knew he would feel better after getting plenty of sun and rest as well as golfing with his neighbor, Bob Hope, and other people. We understood that sooner or later he could not keep carrying all these responsibilities. He needed to retire from the presidency of the university, but who would be our next president?

In spite of tight financial problems, I was determined to continue with our family vacation tradition that we had started in Brazil. Some of these vacations included the semiannual Dinkins reunions in Florida. Others were visits with friends and Phyllis's relatives. Phyllis and I went to Costa Rica to visit with Ruth while she served a year with the Alphalit literacy program. We also wanted to meet the Candler School of Theology boyfriend she had been writing about.

Our son Randy had fallen in love with a PhD candidate from Prince Edward Island, Canada. We enjoyed visiting with them in Stillwater and their visits with us. It was no easy task to get our family, scattered from Tulsa, Oregon, and Idaho, to Prince Edward Island for their wedding and some vacation time.

Phyllis and I decided that since our three oldest children had traveled more than the two youngest, we should take seventeen-year-old Susana and fourteen-year-old Paul on a monthlong trip to see the national parks in the West. We left as soon as Paul's soccer team played their last game. We stopped at the major parks as we traveled across Oklahoma, New Mexico, Arizona, California, and Oregon. Our original plans were to turn east once we got to Oregon, but six weeks before we left, Mount St. Helens blew up and spread a lot of ash across the area we planned to travel. Susana suggested that we continue north, along the Oregon coast, to avoid the ash. We went through Washington and made a big loop in Canada to get back into Montana and Wyoming. Susana turned out to be a very good planner, navigator, and driver.

We had to cancel more than a week of our reservations to change our route. This meant we traveled with the hope of finding places to stay. We spent the first night in a wonderful forest resort in Washington and the next night only three miles from Butchart Gardens on Vancouver Island. Since our plan was to skip major cities, we only drove through Vancouver toward the Canadian Rockies. When we got to Lake Louise and stopped at the Dear Inn near the lake, the manager couldn't believe we had risked traveling to this resort area without a reservation. She told us she had just received a cancelation for two rooms. The highway to Banff, with glaciers and blue-green lakes, was the most the most beautiful drive I had ever seen. We drove to Glacier National Park in Montana in time to continue with our reservations from there on to Wyoming to see Yellowstone.

On most of the trip Paul acted like a typical fourteen-year-old in the process of transferring his attention from family to friends and books. I was frequently irritated at him for pulling his cap so low over his eyes that he could not see the beautiful landscapes we traveled. While he was sleeping at Glacier National Park, I hid his cap in the bottom of his Phyllis's suitcase. The bubbling hot springs and geysers at Yellowstone got his attention, as did the dinosaurs at the Dinosaur National Park. I'm glad we made that trip. It was money we didn't have, but it was well spent.

When word got out that I knew how to start new churches without a huge upfront investment of money to buy land, buildings, and pay a full-time pastor, the pastor of the Broken Arrow United Methodist Church asked me to help him start a new church in East Broken Arrow, where several families in his church were living. He said the district superintendent suggested I might help do this, and he would find both district and conference money to help us get started. We chose a general location but couldn't find a place to meet. The district lay leader was a commercial real estate broker, however. He found a house on the corner of the road that was designated to become a four-lane highway.

When I saw the four-bedroom house with a three-car garage and a swimming pool, I immediately saw how the garage could be transformed into a sanctuary, the bedrooms into Sunday school rooms, and the pool into recreation for a youth program. I did not tell my seminary colleagues about starting this new church until after the first worship services, because I knew some of them would volunteer to help me. I wanted to preach and pastor a church again. I recruited a student to be the youth pastor so I could be with my family Sunday evenings. I spent one night a week visiting and training the various task groups.

The New House Church was soon outgrowing the space. I insisted that we not name or charter the church until we reached one hundred members. And before the year was over, we had reached that goal. I led the leaders through choosing a name, and then we were ready to charter the Heritage United Methodist Church. We started the search for land to build a church facility. I couldn't understand why I had to struggle against one leader who insisted on buying land close to a creek until another leader told me about the vested interest she had in the land and how much she could profit by us buying it.

One day I noticed an empty plot of land at the highest level in the area and thought it would be a wonderful location for the church. A few weeks later the district superintendent and lay leader asked me to meet them at a location they were interested in purchasing from an overextended land developer. When I got to the location, it was the same land I had found earlier. In my prayer of gratitude, I said, *God you must have overheard my thoughts.* I looked forward to continuing as pastor of this church because it had so much potential, but I then realized that too many other things were going on for me to have time to continue. I recommended to the district superintendent that he appoint one of our best graduating students to become the next pastor.

I was pleased to hear Jessie Jackson speak at the 1984 graduation. But I wasn't glad to see Oral give a liberal arts degree to his youngest son, Richard, when I knew he had not done the academic work to deserve the degree. Richard had mostly played when he attended the University of Kansas. As I watched hundreds of other students receive their hard-earned diplomas, I realized my time at Oral Roberts was coming to an end.

I knew Oral would soon retire, and it was uncertain who would be his successor. Jimmy Buskirk and most of us believed he be the new president successor, and then Richard Roberts become more visible on stage in chapel than Jimmy. Oral told Dean Buskirk that he needed the money that had been reserved to start a PhD program to pay expenses in the City of Faith. Jimmy realized he wasn't going to be the next president, so he accepted an invitation to become pastor of the Tulsa First Methodist Church. Our colleague Mike Miller was chosen to be the interim dean until Bob Stamps, the beloved longtime university chaplain, completed his PhD in England.

Our son Paul was finishing his last year of high school in 1985. I decided to talk to Bill Ruff, my former district superintendent in Atlanta, about an appointment to a church in North Georgia. When I saw him at the Annual Conference in 1984, he was not very encouraging about an appointment above the first or second salary level. A few months later he must have told Malone Dodson, the chairman of the Board of the Counseling Center where I worked for the Atlanta-Emory District, that I wanted to come back to Georgia. A few months later I received an invitation from Malone to join the staff at the Roswell United Methodist Church as minister of pastoral care and counseling. After several letters, Phyllis and I decided that I should accept. We kept the decision confidential until I had to tell the Dean Buskirk in March so he could start looking for a replacement. I learned a few days later that he was also planning to leave, as well as five other United Methodist professors. Oral's decision for Richard to succeed him caused many professors to move. Years later

I learned that Oral offered the presidency to several capable persons, but everyone turned down the offer when they saw how much money they needed to raise to pay the enormous cost of the City of Faith and the university.

Our last six months in Tulsa were a mixture of excitement about moving back to Atlanta and grief about leaving friends, colleagues, and a teaching career. Phyllis was more excited than me, because she hadn't been able to get a teaching job in the Tulsa school system. The minimum salary jobs she did find paid less than I could make in one hour of counseling. When I offered her the choice of staying home to take on some of my responsibilities, such as managing counseling and family finances, she gladly accepted and gave all her teaching materials to Susana, who had started teaching at a private school in Atlanta.

It was one thing to want to move; it was another thing to sell a house in a severely depressed housing market. Sales were so bad that an agent said he didn't want another house to list for sale. Our faith that it would sell and our efforts at personal marketing paid off on the day before the moving van arrived. A widow wanted to move to Tulsa to be close to her son and had cash to pay for the house. Our son Randy and his wife, Judy, helped us pack while I did the paperwork with the buyer at the lawyer's office.

I spent several hours that last night in Tulsa, about as tired as I had ever been, in a seat at the Oklahoma Annual Conference, waiting to receive a special award from the conference for my ministry of new church development. We stayed the last night in Tulsa in the home of the Hewitts, my closest colleague and our best friends. Instead of sleeping, I wept over the loss of the vision that led us to move to Oklahoma. Tears of grief were mixed with tears of anger at the Roberts family for opting for Old Testament nepotism instead of New Testament gifts regarding the leadership of the university. When their son Richard was chosen to be president of the university, I knew he was not prepared and there would be nothing but a troubled future ahead. I did not want to invest my future in a leader I couldn't respect.

By 1985 we had learned a few things about moving. After announcing our plans to move, we used every opportunity to say good-bye to the people who were important to us. When someone tried to brush away the reality of our departure by saying they would be seeing us again, I thought that might be possible, but it will never be the same. We started the custom of expressing gratitude not only to people but also to our experiences in each room of the house. After the last things were packed in the car, Phyllis, Paul, and I went inside the house and held hands in the living room as I offered a prayer of appreciation for eight years of life in this house, the longest we had lived in one place. We also started a custom of staying some place overnight between where we had lived before moving into where we were going to live. This helped ease the transition from one place to another.

CHAPTER 16

Roswell, Georgia, 1985–1992

The quality of our lives depends not on whether or not
we have conflicts, but on how we respond to them.

—Tom Crum

We spent a night in an Arkansas motel, which helped with the emotional transition from life in Tulsa to a very different life in Roswell. Our daughter Ruth had moved back from Chicago to Atlanta after completing her master's in Spanish at Northwestern University. She found a basement apartment in the home of a couple who taught at the Candler School of Theology. (No one realized at the time that the apartment came with a potential husband for her.) We were glad to be living closer to her. Susana graduated from Emory University with a degree in education and was hired as a middle school teacher. She lived with us until she saved enough money to move to an apartment near Emory with some friends.

I was excited to join the pastoral staff at Roswell UMC, one of the fastest-growing churches in North Georgia. The senior pastor had been the chair of the advisory board at the counseling center when I had worked for the Atlanta-Emory District before moving to Tulsa. I was pleased he wanted me on his staff and that my salary would be 30 percent more than at ORU.

When we moved to Roswell, the church was in the process of buying several small houses at the end of the street next to the church for construction of a new sanctuary. The senior pastor said that Phyllis and I could live in the house directly across the street from the house where the counseling offices were located. This gave us time to find a house to buy before construction started at the church.

Growing up in a large family prepared me for working with staff colleagues. I soon felt at home in my new work environment and enjoyed the give and take of staff relationships.

The senior pastor took my suggestion that he extend his vacation time from two weeks in the summer to a whole month now that he had another pastor on staff. I was asked to preach on one of the four Sundays he was away.

My first words were about how much I loved the beautiful RUMC sanctuary. I told them a story about worshiping in the sanctuary eight years earlier on the Sunday before we moved to Tulsa. As we left the church back then, I had said to Phyllis, "I wish I could preach in this sanctuary some day. God must have overheard my silent prayer, because this is the day that prayer is being answered."

I thoroughly enjoyed preaching to about seven hundred people in each of the two worship services. After the last worship service, I was feeling great from the warm welcome of church members until an old retired highway patrol officer who lived next door to the church shook my hand.

He said, "I hope you enjoyed preaching today because you probably will not get to preach very often after this."

His words took me off guard, so I pressed him to explain.

He looked me in the eye and said, "Because you're a damn good preacher, and that will not set well with the senior pastor. It will be a long time before he will let you preach again."

When the senior pastor returned, I talked with him about what I had been told without revealing the identity of the person who told me. The senior pastor admitted that he had not asked his other associates to preach very often. He said the reason he had taken only two weeks for vacation was that attendance and giving dropped off whenever he was away. He told me he was pleased with what he had heard about my preaching and wanted me to do my best to outpreach him. Our conversation and his reassurance went a long way toward relieving my anxiety and strengthening our relationship. Though I preached only three or four times each year at Roswell, I became a better preacher because I had plenty of time to work on my sermons. It's easier to preach good sermons occasionally than to prepare a good one every Sunday.

During the interview visit to RUMC, I met and talked briefly with the director of the counseling center. The senior pastor told me he was a clinical psychologist and had started the center. The issue of leadership in the counseling center would be resolved after I moved to Roswell. Instead of assigning our roles, the senior pastor told us to work it out and let him know what we decided. I thought it would be best for the founding director to continue as the administrator and I would be the clinical director; both he and I would report directly to the senior pastor. This arrangement would give me direct access to the senior pastor and keep the counseling center director from becoming my supervisor. And such an arrangement would help me keep the vow made in Brazil that I would never again be an administrator. Our decision was accepted and it worked well for several years. Later, it became the worse mistake I ever made at Roswell.

Paul worked at odd jobs during our first summer in Roswell before going to St. Andrew's College in the September. He asked his mother and me what we planned to do when he left for college, since his departure meant there wouldn't be any children living full-time in our home. I told him, "We are going to burn down the house and get us a place too small for any of our children to return to live with us." He looked shocked but relieved to learn that we were looking forward to becoming empty nesters after thirty years of full-time parenting.

It didn't take long for the son of Ruth's landlord to discover he enjoyed visiting with the new renter in the basement. When they fell in love, Phyllis and I got more serious about finding a house to buy in case they decided to get married. We found one we could afford on Coleman Road, just one mile from the church. After Ruth brought Bob to help us paint the rooms, I asked her what we needed to do to help her kidnap him. She assured us she didn't need our help. A few weeks later they were engaged. This meant we needed to get the house ready for the wedding.

Ruth and Bob's wedding was a wonderful occasion for both families. Bob's father and I officiated. The church sanctuary was beautiful, and the reception in the social hall was simple but wonderful. The families enjoyed the afterglow from the wedding in our new home.

A few months after moving into our new house, I was standing in front yard, feeling satisfied with myself, the house, my job, and life in general. I thought, *I like this house. I'm tired of moving. I plan to live here until I retire and years into retirement.* Suddenly I heard an inner voice, *You will be here for a season.* I couldn't believe it. I'm tired of moving and starting over. I wanted to settle in one place. I wondered how long a season was supposed to be. How long was I going to live here? I was deeply shaken by this experience but kept it to myself out of concern for upsetting Phyllis as much as I was upset by the inner voice. The answer came six years later.

Meanwhile, Walter was working on a master's in electrical engineering and another in industrial engineering at Oklahoma State. He was getting more serious about his girlfriend, Becky. Two days after Christmas 1986, Phyllis, Ruth, and I flew to Kansas City and drove to Marshall, Missouri, for Walter and Becky's wedding.

The lay leadership of RUMC realized the church needed to move forward with the construction of the sanctuary because all three Sunday morning services were overflowing the present sanctuary. The building committee was chosen from key lay leaders and pastors. I was surprised to learn I was expected to serve on the committee. Though it was a lot of work, I will always be grateful for the experience. I learned a lot about all phases of a church building program from going to meetings every Monday evening for over four years. I enjoyed the give and take of committee discussions as I watched the chairman, Fred Shell, use his skills as a master negotiator to lead us through innumerable difficult decisions.

One of the major decisions was the physical direction of the sanctuary. Most committee members wanted the building to face toward the south, where most of the people would park and come up the steps to enter it. I did some research on the history of church sanctuary construction. I discovered that a majority of churches were oriented toward the east, the direction of the coming of Christ in the Final Judgment. The problem for us was that the homeowner of the property directly between the new and the old sanctuaries refused to sell her property; this meant the sanctuary would face a narrow driveway to the right of her house. I argued that she wouldn't live forever and the house would be on the market some day for the church to buy and connect the older buildings with the newer. (I returned to teach a class at Roswell twenty-five years later and discovered that the church finally bought the property. The house was gone and in its place is a beautiful garden with a green lawn and gazebo that are used for weddings and social events.)

The construction of the sanctuary with ground-floor education rooms continued at a rapid pace. It appeared that we would meet our schedule to be in the new sanctuary several Sundays before Easter, but then construction problems caused delays. When the final date was set for the move, the senior pastor realized he had to attend the national meeting of the health and welfare organization of the UMC on the last Sunday we were scheduled to hold worship services in the old sanctuary. But he was president of this organization and had to preside at the annual meeting. I was asked to preach the last sermon in what was to be called the chapel after we moved.

I built my sermon around the most common expression of people who saw the new sanctuary under construction: "It's awesome!" Then I tried to help people connect their awesome experiences with God from the past in the present sanctuary to anticipated awesome experiences with God in the future sanctuary. I wanted to help everyone say good-bye to the old sanctuary before facing the challenges of adjusting to a new, unfamiliar place to worship. After the sermon, several people told me they had dreaded the move until hearing this sermon. I learned from this experience that emotional transitions from one place of worship to another need special attention and are as important as emotional transitions when a family moves from one house to another. I also learned that multiple complaints about the unfamiliar space of a new building are part grief over the loss of familiar space and part discomfort with the adjustment process.

We thought everything was on schedule to move to the new sanctuary on Palm Sunday when word spread at a Wednesday evening fellowship meal that we had a serious construction problem that could cause another postponement. The two-ton wooden cross, cut from a huge popular tree that had to be removed before starting construction, was in the way of installing several large wood panels between the organ and the choir. I was asked to meet in the new sanctuary at 7:00 a.m. on Thursday to help solve the problem.

Early the next morning, two architects, two contractors, two metal frame subcontractors, two lay members of the building committee, and two pastors poured over blueprints and assessed the situation. When tape measures came out, I decided my knowledge was too limited to be of much help. I took several steps back from the group to get a better look. While staring at the cross, it dawned on me that the cross has always been a problem. It stood in the way of Jesus and has stood in the way of countless persons since the Resurrection, not as a technical problem, but as a spiritual reality. This cross standing in the way was nothing new, but it needed a different solution.

The committee chairman walked over to ask what I was looking at so intensely. I shared with him my brief meditation about the cross and asked him if he thought the tradesmen would be able to fix it before Sunday.

He calmly responded, "Oh, yes. They will fix it after they decide who is to blame and who is willing to pay the cost to fix it."

Evidently the architect had not correctly calculated the width of the crown molding on the wood panels and the distance required to hang the cross in front of the paneling. The cross needed to be unbolted from the frame, hoisted down, and a four-inch extension welded onto the steel frame support behind the cross in order to bring it far enough forward to install the panels behind it.

This was done in time for several lay volunteers to help the construction workers get the panels in place. Volunteers worked until late Saturday night to complete the preparations in time for our first worship services on Palm Sunday.

I chose to be one of the liturgist in the second worship service on Easter Sunday, because I wanted to sit with the congregation in the first service to experience worship as they did. Phyllis sang in the choir.

When a soprano soloist sang, tears ran down my face. At first I thought they were tears of joy, but that didn't seem right. When the service ended, I walked up to her to thank her for the beautiful solo. Again tears started flowing down my face. I realized they had something to do with her. She asked why I was crying.

Words I had not previously formed in my mind came out of my mouth: "When I heard you sing and thought about you, your husband, and your children, I saw your beautiful family being destroyed."

She was as surprised as I was. She said, "How!"

A one-word answer came immediately out of my mouth: "Alcohol."

She asked, "Do you think my husband's drinking is that serious?"

"It must be or I wouldn't be crying."

I felt rather foolish saying what I did. I immediately walked away to prepare for the next worship service.

Early Monday morning the secretary said I had a phone call. It was the soloist's husband.

He said, "I understand you talked with my wife yesterday. When can I go to your office to talk with you?"

This frightened me. I was afraid he was offended by what I had said. I responded that I would see him, but only if he came with his wife. I had learned in my clinical training how frequently alcoholics lie about drinking if family members aren't present.

The couple came the next day. As soon as they sat down, he asked how I knew so much about his drinking.

I said, "Only a couple of times I smelled alcohol on your breath at social occasions."

He confessed he was getting concerned because he had been arrested and given a DUI citation for drinking. He said his mother had tried to talk with him about his drinking. Then he said he was going to stop drinking.

I had heard these words too many times from alcoholics who never quit their addiction. I tried to convince him to get into a treatment program, but he wouldn't agree to go.

Then he said, "When my pastor, a man of God, weeps over my family because he looks into the future and sees my family being destroyed because of my drinking, I ought to be man enough to quit."

He extended his hand and looked me in the eyes, "I promise you I'm going to quit."

As I shook his hand, I said somewhat doubtfully, "I'll take your word that you will quit, but only with the understanding that you will go to a treatment program if you have one more drink."

I then told him that he should let me know that he had kept his word by showing me a thumbs-up each time I see him. (During the years I worked at Roswell, his thumb was always up whenever we saw each other. After I moved, he sent a card once a year to let me know he had kept his promise.)

Most Sundays I taught an adult Sunday school class during one worship service and served as a liturgist in the other. I liked the policy of having each associate pastor participate with the senior pastor in at least one of the services. This kept us visible before the congregation and helped us to be accepted as a pastor when we did hospital visitations. I took my turn with hospital visitation at least one day a week.

My major responsibility was to serve as minister of pastoral counseling. Some counselees couldn't afford to pay and others paid based on a sliding scale according to their income. I received a fixed salary and benefits that were paid by the church so that my time could be flexible enough to serve the people in other ways. The other ordained counselor and I had the same work and financial arrangements. We also had a female therapist and a full-time administrative assistant in the counseling center. We kept together many marriages and families in the church by helping them through some difficult times. In the long run we contributed more to the financial strength of the church than the church paid for our salaries.

Phyllis volunteered in several ministries of the church. She also was my co-leader for several marriage enrichment seminars. We continued taking as many mini-honeymoons as time would allow.

Many of my best stories from ministry at Roswell are about counselees, but it's best to keep those stories confidential rather than describe them here. The written notes from my counseling sessions have long since been destroyed.

I enjoyed working with the church staff and outstanding lay volunteers. There were many things I admired about the senior pastor. His long tenure and countless acts of ministry created a strong sense of respect and authority for his leadership. He was recognized as one of the most effective pastors in the North Georgia Annual Conference. He had the good fortune to arrive in Roswell in the midst of a demographic explosion. To meet the demands of a rapidly growing church in an affluent area of metropolitan Atlanta, he recruited senior level staff and paid above-average salaries to motivate us to help him develop a high-quality ministry. He made our staff Christmas parties special by personally presenting bonus checks to each staff member. Advent and Lent seasons at Roswell were the best I have ever experienced. We had one of the best music programs in the state of Georgia.

I enjoyed our clergy staff retreats where we planned several months of future activities, expressed concerns, solved problems, ate together, and bonded as a collegial pastoral ministry team. The majority of my work time was spent counseling. I taught the parents of the confirmation class each year with a female co-teacher. This helped our confirmation class to grow from approximately thirty-five to over a hundred each year. Many new families joined the church through the confirmation program. I supervised the mission program of the church, assisted the mother's morning-in program and the widow's support groups.

The church had a wide range of ministries and programs. Our Wednesday night dinners were the best I have ever known. The senior pastor insisted that the food service manager prepare high-quality food. We planned a variety of programs that motivated church members to attend.

My background in church ministry had been in new, rural, and small churches in Brazil. Working on the staff of a large church expanded my understanding of what a church could be. We could not have created this scale of ministry without the vision and leadership of the senior pastor. He set a high standard for all aspects of our various ministries. I learned from working with him the importance of thorough decision-making processes. He made sure that leaders were consulted and informed about decisions related to their responsibilities before changing or starting something new. He had little patience with staff members who did not meet his standards for excellence.

His major problem was that he did not know how to supervise us to help us do a better job except to show his displeasure with a generalized "shotgun approach" in staff meetings when things did not meet his expectations. Instead of letting go underperforming staff members or helping them to understand what they needed to change in a one-on-one conversation, he created an atmosphere of anxiety in staff meetings by throwing out generalized criticisms. We usually knew the intended target of his displeasure, but the whole staff experienced it together. I tried to help him stop doing this by talking with him about more healthy ways to supervise, but he never changed.

Several staff members talked with me about their personal and work-related problems with him. I had to be very careful with these dual relationships in order to keep confidentiality, remain loyal to the church, and maintain ethical boundaries.

The rapid growth of the church membership and the staff, along with increased pressure to raise more money to support an expanding ministry, caused the senior pastor to become increasingly anxious. As his anxiety increased, he became increasingly critical of a few staff members but continued to make general criticisms of the whole staff. He seemed to choose one staff member at a time to express his indirect displeasure. Once he turned against a staff member, there was nothing that would change his attitude. When staff members came to see me because they were suffering his direct and indirect anger, I tried to help them to find ways to talk with him directly or help them make a decision to look for another place to work.

One female staffer said she planned to sue him, but after talking with me, she decided to leave quietly rather than risk potential problems in getting another job. One male staffer told me he planned to physically assault the senior pastor the next time he criticized him in the presence of other staffers. I warned him about the consequences and suggested he find another place to work as soon as possible. I also told him that he would have to go over my body to get to the senior pastor, because I would do everything I could to stop him. After our conversation, I either sat next to him in staff meetings or between him and the senior pastor until the staffer left the church for another job. I could not justify the senior pastor's behavior, but I probably enabled it by trying to keep peace in order to maintain the ministry of the church. The lay leadership probably never knew about the tension in the staff, because everything outwardly seemed to be running well. I often thought about the irony of a church that did so much wonderful ministry could also cause several staff members to leave as wounded souls.

Instead of looking for another job, our Christian education director withdrew into the safety of her office when she became the target of his criticism. The education ministry was suffering from her lack of leadership in recruiting volunteers. I led a task group to develop a document about a Christian education, a vision statement, a strategic plan, and the necessary qualifications for a director. We used this to evaluate her performance and force her resignation. The decision that only the women on the task group would communicate with her fell apart when she appealed the decision to the senior pastor and he revealed his negative feelings about her. She left terribly wounded.

I became convinced of the value of creating a clear vision statement, developing a strategic plan, and listing the qualifications for leadership of a ministry when something happened a few weeks later. A former faculty colleague at ORU was traveling from Illinois to Florida with his wife and stopped to spend the weekend with Phyllis and me.

I told them about the changes in the Christian education program at RUMC, and he asked to see the document our task force had created. After he read it, I was astonished to hear him say, "Do you think I could apply for this position?"

He told me how he loved being a pastor, but he was unhappy with the Annual Conference where he had been serving since leaving ORU. When I realized how serious he was about making a change, I called the senior pastor at his home to tell him about my friend and asked if we could have lunch together after the Sunday worship services. When they met, I could tell how much they liked each other. It didn't take long for the staff–parish relations committee to invite him to join our clergy staff. Everyone was excited to have a PhD in Old Testament as our new Christian education minister.

The senior associate pastor had been at Roswell longer than any of the other staff members. He was probably the best associate pastor the church has ever had. His unselfish spirit, together with his pastoral skills, provided a model for the church motto, We care. Everyone seemed to like him, but very few realized how he bore the brunt of an overanxious senior pastor with unpredictable behavior under stress.

The pressure increased as he did more and more to care for an expanding membership and deal with the demands and criticisms of the senior pastor. He had tried to leave several times, but he was talked into staying because the church needed him so much.

When he was at the point of complete burnout, he asked to talk with me. After listening to his concerns, I asked him about his options to get relief from this stressful situation. He told me about an opportunity for ministry as the owner and CEO of a parachurch Christian radio ministry. Though it was a huge risk, he decided to make the change. I hated to see him go and was concerned about the kind of associate pastor that would be recruited to take his responsibilities. I soon found out I had reasons to be concerned.

My time to preach came only a few days after the fall of the Berlin Wall. I preached about turning spears into pruning hooks and swords into plowshares. I had a piece of the wall in one hand and a piece of barbed wire in the other that had recently been taken from the Berlin Wall. After the benediction, the senior pastor walked with his arm over my shoulder to the front door for us to greet the people. I wondered what was going on, because I had never seen him act this way to any of his associates. Before we left the church, he said he wanted to have breakfast with me on Tuesday morning. A few hours later it occurred to me that he was planning to ask me to be the new senior associate.

Before leaving home on Tuesday morning, I asked Phyllis to pray for me, because I was afraid serious trouble would start when I turned down the invitation to serve as the senior associate of the church. I told her that I had prayed and thought a lot about the impending decision and shared with her the reasons for saying no. I had worked long and hard to get my doctorate and credentials to become a pastoral counselor and a marriage and family therapist. I wanted to remain in the counseling center, where this training was most useful to the church. I reminded her that psychological testing and years of therapy had helped me realize I have the gifts for organization and administration, but I didn't have the emotional resources to endure the pressures of a second-in-command position. I had turned down several other opportunities to be an administrator because I did not want to be anyone's gofer. To accept an invitation like senior associate pastor would be a demotion, not a promotion, even with an increase in salary.

I was concerned the senior pastor wouldn't understand or accept my reasons to turn down the invitation to be his senior associate. He would likely turn against me for saying no. He would think I was being a poor team player, and our relationship would begin a downward spiral.

When he offered me the position, I did my best to say no as gently as possible. But he was visibly upset. He did, however, follow through on my suggestion that he recruit an ordained clergywoman to fill this position. I reminded him that the church had five male pastors. I said he needed a female pastor as his senior associate to provide a broader perspective and better quality ministry with the church membership. In the end, the woman chosen to be the new senior associate was an experienced pastor and a competent administrator.

I made the mistake of trying to develop a friendship with my clergy colleague at the counseling center. I needed a friend more than I needed a professional colleague. We did a lot of jesting, kidding, and sharing of confidential information the first couple of years. Then I began to notice he didn't demonstrate the knowledge and expertise expected of a clinical psychologist. As the clinical director of the counseling center, I tried to hold staff clinical case conferences, but he would either be absent or contribute very little when present. He lacked psychological knowledge and clinical skills. Clients seemed to like him enough to return for more sessions.

After he experienced several personal or family crises, I noticed a pattern: they occurred every four to six months. These would distract him from some of his church responsibilities yet garner sympathy for him. I noticed how he frequently missed appointments and compromised boundary issues with vulnerable female counselees, but he always had excuses when confronted about his behavior.

One Sunday morning I found one of his female clients using the computer in the counseling office. When I asked her why she was there—this was, after all, a restricted area where we kept confidential case files—she reported that my colleague had given her a master key to the building. I knew that key opened all of our offices. The next day I confronted him about this. I told him how I was concerned about him seeing this woman in his office when no one else was in the building. I suspected they were having more than a counseling relationship. When his behavior did not change, I reported his behavior to the senior pastor and the district superintendent, but nothing was done to stop it. Finally, I demanded that he cease seeing this client or I would take my concern about his behavior to the bishop.

By this time I had lost respect for him and stopped sharing any information more than necessary about my clients. His behavior toward me became physically belligerent. He often walked up to me, puffed up like a bantam rooster, as if to physically challenge me. I puffed up in return to show that I could be just as belligerent as he pretended to be. He would then laugh and walk away. I think he realized that, though he had technical authority to be the director of the counseling center, I would never allow him to intimidate me or have authority over me.

While looking for a form in the counseling center files one day, I came across his curriculum vitae and discovered that his PhD from Notre Dame was in educational psychology, not clinical psychology, as he claimed and as was printed on information about him at the church. I reported this to the senior pastor because I was concerned about the potential legal implications should a dissatisfied client sue him and the church. Evidently my concerns were not taken seriously, because brochures continued to be printed that claimed he was a clinical psychologist. I knew it was only a matter of time before his lack of clinical training and boundary issues would cause serious problems for the church.

I felt tension building in the counseling center as well as between the senior pastor and me. When the opportunity to become the pastor of a church in 1988 failed to materialize, because the candidate from North Georgia was not elected bishop, I decided to find new ways to enjoy to my job at Roswell.

As part of my responsibility for supervising the mission program of the church, I went with a team of laymen to Costa Rica to assist in the construction of a church building. Marion, a retired missionary, had a small bus ready to pick up the team members and equipment. He, however, was driving an old pickup. I asked if I could travel with him so I could learn more about Costa Rica and the church's ministry here.

About three hours in our journey, I noticed he was getting sleepy and driving erratically. Though I didn't have an international driver's license, I figured it was safer to drive than to ride with him asleep at the wheel. He was soon snoring in the passenger seat. I discovered what it was like to drive without a rearview mirror. The side mirrors had been knocked off, and the rearview mirror was blocked by a cement mixer in the truck bed. I had to dodge deep potholes by sometimes going into the left lane on the poorly paved road while cars that I couldn't see passed us at a higher rate of speed. I discovered the importance of a rearview mirror for safe driving.

The senior pastor called me to his office one day to tell me the staff parish relations committee (SPRC) wanted to pay for Phyllis and me to go to Israel. This was a complete surprise to us. We thoroughly enjoyed our trip with Bishop Fitzgerald and a bus full of North Georgia UMC pastors and spouses. The ways my mind had pictured historical biblical places were radically revised after seeing them in person. I was turned off by the elaborate religious construction that had been built across the centuries over the historic places of Jesus' ministry. Actually being at the places where so many famous Bible stories happened in Israel enriched the descriptive language of my narrative preaching and Bible teaching.

Our five children were born over the first ten years of our marriage and were in their twenties and thirties during most of the seven years that Phyllis and I lived in Roswell. Paul enjoyed his studies in philosophy with some challenging professors at St. Andrews College. In his third year, he was told to leave the school dorm after a Saturday night disturbance. He moved into a tent in the woods on school property. I went to check on him after becoming concerned about his safety and his health. I felt better when he reported that moved his tent to the backyard of a farmhouse rented to several other students after some kids destroyed his tent and damaged his belongings.

Ever since reading all fifteen books of Nikos Katazansakis, my favorite author, I wanted to travel to Greece. When Paul's favorite professor recruited students for a trip to Greece, Paul asked us to pay his travel expenses. I really struggled with the decision to give up my trip to pay for him to go first, but I decided it was more important for him to go. At his graduation, several women who worked in the dining hall and other low-paying jobs on campus, gave him a graduation card and a small amount of money. They made a special effort to quietly thank Paul for his friendship and care for them. I was as proud of this as I was of his diploma. It's one thing to get a degree in philosophy, but it's a better thing to live like a Christian philosopher. After graduation, he moved to Athens, Georgia, to be near his girlfriend.

During Susana's third year of teaching, she asked to speak with me, but she took a chair and had me lie down on the living room couch. Randy had suggested to her that it was best to get me out of the counselor mode by reversing our sitting positions. She broke the news that she was not happy teaching without the freedom to be creative in how she taught. She said she had applied to join the Peace Corps and would be going overseas as soon as the school year was over. I remembered how my mother heard me tell her that I was taking my family to Brazil as missionaries. How could I do anything but give Susana my blessing? She left for Honduras in 1988 to serve as an environmental education specialist to train rural teachers.

Phyllis and I traveled to Honduras to see Susana and to meet her boyfriend from Nevada; they had met during the first weeks of training in Tegucigalpa. She was assigned to work in the mountain town of Dulce Nombre del Culmí, and Ray, her boyfriend, had been sent to a coastal village. We enjoyed meeting him and traveling with Susana to see Mayan ruins and her adopted city. I was pleased at how she had so many friends and had made an impact on her adopted town.

A year later she called to tell us that Ray wanted to speak with me. I knew he was going to ask to marry her. When we talked, I asked him a question: "If you're using a hoe in a field and break the handle, what would you do?"

He said, "Susana warned me that you would ask me a question, but I never imagined you would ask that. I guess I would go get another handle."

I said that he was almost right, but not good enough to marry Susana. When I was satisfied that he was sufficiently anxious and could not think of a better answer, I said, "The best answer would be that you would go to your house to get a hoe handle that you had previously prepared and stored to use when you needed one. I guess I'll give my permission for you to marry my daughter."

Susana got on the phone to defend him. I told her that I liked him and was glad he wanted to marry her. When their two-year term of service in Honduras was over, they came to Roswell to live with us for a few months so they could save enough money to get married and apply to graduate school. Ray loved Phyllis's cooking. No matter how much she cooked, there were never any leftovers. We were sad to see them move to Indiana after their April wedding.

They were offered the weekend caretaker job in exchange for an apartment above the offices of the First Methodist Church in Bloomington, Indiana. The church was within easy walking distance to Indiana University. They worked for a year to qualify for state residency. We enjoyed being there when Susana received a master's in public administration and finance and Ray received his law degree.

After completing his studies at Oklahoma State, Walter and Becky moved to Lawrence, Kansas, where he had a full-time engineering job. Later, they moved to Atlanta for Walter to get a master's degree in materials engineering at Georgia Tech. We were glad we could see them more often while they were living near us.

After their wedding in 1986, Ruth and Bob moved into the first of three houses, and Ruth started teaching at Paedaia School, a private school that Bob and his two brothers had attended. Kelly, the first of two daughters, was born in July 1991.

The crisis that I feared would flare up at Roswell finally happened when the church received a certified letter in 1991 from the attorney of a former counselee, charging my colleague with sexual misconduct and suing the church for negligence in protecting her. Everything changed overnight. What my counseling center co-worker had been doing in secret was shouted from the rooftops by the news media.

Instead of a thorough investigation to find out if the charges were true, damage-control measures were put into place. To keep us from saying anything about our concerns regarding his behavior, we were told not to say anything to anyone. I felt alone and isolated because no one communicated with me and I could not to talk with anyone in the church about the situation. The biggest disappointment came when the senior pastor told the congregation that there was no truth in the woman's allegation of sexual misconduct by my co-worker and that she was suing just to get money from the church. I knew that he knew better, because I had told him and the district superintendent about the boundary-violation behaviors of my colleague. They had done no more than ask him if it was true, and he denied any wrongdoing.

All sexual predators lie about their behavior. Sexual misconduct and lying go together like a hand in a glove.

Now that the lie had spread to the whole congregation, I was helpless to stop it without seriously damaging the church. I made one last desperate step to do something about the situation by driving to Lake Junaluska to inform the bishop in the presence of the district superintendent about the way I saw the situation. I wanted their guidance, and they told me to keep quiet and let the legal process run its course. I realized this would take a very long time.

Meanwhile, the senior pastor no longer invited me to meetings I had been attending previously. I discovered that the church leaders had been told that the problems in the counseling center were caused by my inability to get along with my colleague. When I was asked to report directly to my co-worker instead of the senior pastor, I refused to be under the authority of someone I considered to be unethical.

I asked the district superintendent to appoint me to be the pastor of a church in the conference. He responded that since I had not been in the chain of appointments, I would be getting only a second-level appointment, which would pay less than half my present salary. With this information, I lost all confidence in the appointment system. When he told me that he, too, would lie if faced with a similar church lawsuit, I lost all respect for him.

This made me want to leave an ethically compromised church organization. I considered turning in my conference credentials and opening a private counseling center in the Roswell area. Two things, however, held me back. The first was the vow I had made at my ordination and my commitment to the Methodist church. I could not push my identity aside in response to the behavior of ordained leaders in the church. The second reason was that I had just finished paying the college tuition of the last of five children and had not built sufficient savings for a shift from a salaried job to pay the expenses of transition to self-support.

My brother Ed was a big help during this time. I talked with him because he understood my predicament from his ordained ministry leadership background. Phyllis, though, was my primary support. She could not tell me what to do, but she patiently and lovingly listened to my concerns. When I started having trouble sleeping because I felt so trapped, I scheduled appointments for Phyllis and me with a therapist to help keep us emotionally balanced.

I got to the place where I dreaded worship and serving as a liturgist in the Sunday worship services. The joy I had felt in the first years at RUMC disappeared as tension increased between the senior pastor and me. I no longer wanted to be here. Evidently, leaders in the congregation sensed something was wrong. The lay leader asked to take me to lunch. He knew me well because we had worked together on various committees and I had helped his family through some difficult times with their teenage sons.

He said, "Burrell, I can look at you at church and can tell that you aren't happy. What's going on?"

Up to this point I had not communicated with any lay leader about the issues I was facing. I knew several of them had heard negative things about me from the senior pastor. I admitted that I was not happy and told him a few of my reasons. I also told him that I planned to leave, but I didn't know how or where to go.

When we got back into his car that cold January morning, he asked, "What would you most like to do?"

I said I would like to get back into theological education. Then he asked if I had applied to teach in a seminary, and I told him about getting a letter from the School of Theology at Duke University, requesting that I submit information for the position of professor of pastoral care. I said I had sent the information, but I was not hopeful about getting this job, because most new seminary teaching positions were being given to women and minorities. I said they have several positions to fill, and they had informed me to be patient, because they were doing the faculty searches one at a time.

He said, "Well, let's pray." And he prayed a very sincere prayer for me personally and asked God to fulfill my heart's desire.

Talking with him helped me feel that someone in the church really cared and was concerned for my well-being.

In January, I was called to the staff parish relations committee for the annual conversation about my appointment in June. I asked to speak first and told them I planned to leave at the end of my appointment in June.

When they asked what I planned to do, I said, "I don't know, but I do know that I will not continue at RUMC and neither will I cause trouble by saying why I'm leaving."

They tried to persuade me not to resign until I had a place to go. I told them I was determined not to work under the pressure I had been feeling. I wanted to tell them how I had helped several other wounded staff members leave quietly and how I thought it would never happen to me, but I was mistaken. Nor did I tell them how I was working in an ethically compromised church and living with a mixture of anger about the present circumstances with fear about leaving a salaried job without knowing how I would support my family.

The answer to my predicament came a few days later in the form of a letter from the provost at Asbury Theological Seminary. She said that David Seamands, the professor of pastoral care and counseling, planned to retire, and my name had been submitted as a candidate to fill his position. She asked that I send my résumé, information about my present position, and references.

I received the letter at the same time my sister Ruth was visiting. As soon as I read the letter out loud to her and Phyllis, I knew the season of life in Roswell was ending and we would be starting a new one in Wilmore, Kentucky.

I called the provost to find out if I was just one of many candidates and how serious they were from what they had heard about me.

She said, "From the recommendation of Dr. O'Malley, your former colleague at ORU, we're waiting to see you before doing a wider search."

I was very careful about choosing my references and kept very secretive about the possibility of teaching at Asbury. I was fearful that if the senior pastor found out about it, he would sabotage my acceptance at the seminary, though I knew he wanted me to leave.

As I was packing to leave for an interview at Asbury, Phyllis said, "Tomorrow is Valentine's Day. I cannot be with you, but I want you to wear this tie with hearts on it so you'll remember how much I love you."

In the free time between five interviews at Asbury, I asked students why they had chosen Asbury and their experiences in the seminary and was pleased with their answers. In the most important faculty interview, I was asked questions about my theology. I started by using an analogy to describe the relationship of my love for God to a story about the tie with the hearts that Phyllis asked me to wear. I related how I had walked across the street between interviews a few hours earlier to the spot on the Asbury College campus where she and I had first kissed forty years earlier. I then remarked that if I could remember that place so well, I could surely remember when and where I had fallen in love with Jesus. The story satisfied them enough that they asked very few additional questions.

The last interview was with President McKenna. His first words took me by surprise: "I liked what I saw on the tape of your sermon." It took me a few moments to remember that I had sent a letter and a tape of a sermon that I preached in Roswell to a pastor I had known in Tulsa. He was now the first director of the new Beeson Pastor Program at Asbury. The president said he wanted me to give two-thirds of my teaching load to pastoral care and counseling courses in the school of theology and one-third of my time in the Beeson program.

I felt confident from my conversations with the president and the faculty that I would be teaching at Asbury. It took only a week for a letter to come with the official invitation. I was excited to accept. After writing to Asbury, I wrote the dean at Duke to let him know about my decision.

After the senior pastor at Roswell knew for sure that I was planning to leave, he kept trying to guess what I was going to do and telling others what his best guesses were. I wanted him to be the first person in the church to know that I was leaving to become a professor at Asbury Theological Seminary. Outwardly, he acted as if he was glad for me, but I could tell he was surprised and disappointed to hear that I was leaving for a better job.

I went to Roswell with professional integrity and planned to leave with my integrity intact. This was not easy to do under the circumstances of being the latest scapegoat for what was wrong in the church. The effectiveness of the counselor being sued for sexual conduct was over, and he left for a job in another state. The female counselor and I had to take on extra responsibilities, even as I was preparing to leave.

I was sitting on the floor of my office, cleaning out the bottom drawer of a filing cabinet, when the secretary walked in with the attorney handling the lawsuit against the church. She had come to talk with me about the lawsuit.

At the beginning of our conversation, I asked, "What took you so long? It's been over a year since the lawsuit was filed. I know more about the situation here than anyone in the church, but you are the first and only person to talk with me about it."

She sat quietly a long time after I answered her questions. And then she said, "I felt all along that more was going on than I was being told. I didn't think I was getting the full story. Your information helps me better understand the situation. The church is in more trouble than it realizes."

I heard months later that the church settled the lawsuit out of court by agreeing to accept responsibility and to compensate the woman who brought the charges. I never knew the amount the church paid. Nor did I hear how much my former colleague paid for his conduct.

The sadness of leaving the people in the church I loved, mixed with the excitement of my future theological education ministry, created a great deal of ambivalence in me. The senior pastor was on vacation when I preached my last sermon. I preached an upbeat sermon about the ministry of the church and positive reasons for my leaving to prepare future pastors for ministry. Many people spoke sincerely of their appreciation for my ministry at Roswell at the reception afterward.

I had never like the organizational philosophy of the church business manager, hired a couple of years earlier. He shifted the model of shared pastoral leadership to the model of the senior pastor as CEO of a business organization in charge of much lower paid staff. He became the point man for treating me disrespectfully in the last months I was at Roswell. I refused to respond in kind.

As I turned in my keys to him on the last day, I said to him, "I'm just the latest staff member to leave this church deeply wounded. There have been many before me, and there will be others after me. Your time will come before long, and you will then know how I feel right now." (He left a few years later a very wounded man.)

Working with the senior pastor of Roswell was a valuable experience. I admired his ability to develop a successful church in an affluent area. I learned both good and negative things from his leadership and personality that would make me a better teacher of seminary students, though I never mentioned his name or the name of the church. He was an extremely competitive person at golf and at church leadership. His motto was "I never lose." His drive for quality and growth catapulted him into leadership positions outside of RUMC. Two times he was chosen to be the candidate from North Georgia to be elected bishop, but he never got what he wanted the most. He lost his most cherished goal. I grieved when leaving Roswell because I had gone there when we were friends, and I left with deep sadness from the loss of that friendship.

This time we hired a real estate agent to list our house instead of trying to sell it ourselves, as we had done before. When it sold, she told us my little garden was the primary reason the family bought it.

Phyllis and I were exhausted as we packed the last items in the house the day before we left Roswell.

Late in the day I suddenly stopped and said, "Do you know what day this is?"

When she couldn't recall the significance of the day, I said, "It's our anniversary."

We hugged and cried because we had been so busy getting ready to move, we had forgotten the important date of our marriage.

The next morning I looked back at the house before getting into the car and said, "God, you were right. We lived here only for a seven-year season."

CHAPTER 17

Wilmore, 1992–1999

If you are giving a graduate course you don't try to impress the students with oratory, you try to challenge them, get them to question you.

—Noam Chomsky

Between my first interview visit at Asbury Theological Seminary and our move to Wilmore, Phyllis and I made a trip to look for a place to live and for me to finalize my faculty responsibilities. I was pleased to see that my request for an office with a window was honored by assigning me to what had been a small classroom with a large window overlooking the center of the campus. I had made a vow at ORU that I would never again have a windowless office, and I have kept that promise to this day.

We also enjoyed several social occasions with the faculty and their spouses. Before returning to Roswell, we took some time to walk across the street to the Asbury College campus and reminisce about the days when we first met. We left Wilmore excited about returning and looking forward to making it our future home and setting for ministry.

At the same time, we were disappointed that we couldn't sign a contract for the house we liked so much in Lexington, because the seller wouldn't accept it conditioned on the sale of our Roswell house. And then the Roswell house sold just before we had to move. In Wilmore we had to settle for temporary seminary housing. We turned down the first apartment because it was in awful condition and situated only ten feet from the backstop of a community lighted softball field. I appealed to Wade Pascal, my friend from Tulsa and the founding director of the Beeson Pastor Program, for his help to allow us to move into one of the new campus apartments that had been built for students in this program. The dean of students agreed to let us live there our first year or until we found a house to buy.

I realized I was confronting a huge challenge by taking the teaching position of David Seamands. He had been the beloved longtime pastor of the Wilmore Methodist church before becoming the professor of pastoral care and counseling at the seminary. Both students and faculty warned me that I was taking on a big task by teaching the same subjects he had taught. But I was determined not to compare myself to him or to compete with him. I wanted to use my ORU teaching experience to teach the way I thought students needed to learn in order to be good pastoral caregivers. After looking at the syllabus and textbooks previously used by Professor Seamands, I thought some changes were needed to make the classes more relevant to the needs of church members and the students who would be serving them.

The seminary required new professors to teach only two or three classes per semester their first semester so they would get accustomed to teaching. My classes were small at first, because when the students heard that Professor Seamands was leaving, many signed up for his last semester rather than risk breaking in the unknown new professor. After the first few meetings of my classes, word spread about my teaching methods, and several students said they wished they had waited to take my classes. Students liked my step-by-step practice sessions with their taking on the roles of counselor, counselee, and consultant.

I had a wonderful fall semester getting to know the students and my faculty colleagues. I felt at home at Asbury. Phyllis and I enjoyed the simplicity of apartment living and did not miss our furniture in storage. She sat with me in chapel twice a week. With extra time on her hands, Phyllis read a lot and started what turned out to be a four-year cathedral quilt project. We got back into our exercise program by exploring all the streets in town.

As soon as my final papers were graded before Christmas, I prepared the syllabus for the one-week Beeson doctor of ministry intensive class titled Pastor and People. Since it was an even year and our children were visiting their in-laws, Phyllis and I celebrated Christmas alone in Wilmore. A few days later Randy called to say he was in a major crisis. His wife, Judy, waited until after Christmas to tell him she no longer wanted to be married to him and asked that he move out of the house. This took everyone by surprise and started a profound grieving process. I suggested that he question her about the possibility that she was in love with another man. He immediately guessed who it would be. When his suspicion was confirmed, he went into an even deeper crisis.

I asked Randy to come spend some time with us. He flight to Lexington was canceled, and so he had to fly into Louisville. Phyllis and I were almost killed on our way to pick him up. We were driving on a rainy night on an unfamiliar highway when I entered the right lane on the opposite side of a four-lane highway. We narrowly avoided a head-on collision.

Randy and I talked and cried most of the week. We drove to Atlanta for my niece's wedding. I asked the other four children to meet us in Atlanta to show their love for Randy and for us to have some family therapy with Henry Close, my former supervisor, and his wife. That two-hour therapy session was very important for our healing and rebonding of Randy with the family.

A real estate agent told us about a large vacant lot in Wilmore about a mile from the seminary. We bought half of the lot and worked with a builder to plan and construct our first and only custom-made house. It was on a high elevation in one of the newer sections of town. We had a large backyard that was soon a productive organic garden. Behind the garden were rolling hills and pastures with grazing cattle. This was the same land where I had worked on the college farm in 1952. An interior decorator helped make our new home look very special. Our eyes feasted on the landscape and the cattle. When winter came, we pulled our chairs closer to the fireplace to read and listen to music—when I wasn't grading papers.

For several years I had wanted to use a computer, but I had never taken the time to learn. The seminary provided computers for the faculty and technicians to teach us how to use them. I soon discovered just how technologically challenged I was with a computer. I took enough lessons to learn the basics. When Maxie Dunnam became president, he negotiated with a major donor in Memphis to give several million dollars to provide a first-class computer technology system to enable ATS to become the pioneer seminary to teach theology classes online. When the offer was made to give us a new computer and three thousand dollars if we took special classes and taught at least one course online, I jumped at the opportunity. I learned a lot, but I didn't continue teaching this way when I discovered my typing was too slow; I typed only with my right hand. I had lost all lateral use with the fingers on my left hand after the surgery in Brazil on my forearm. It took me twice as many hours to teach online as teaching a traditional class of students.

I loved my one-mile walk between my home and my ATS office across campus, though my enjoyment was tempered with feeling like a fraud for having the privilege of teaching at the seminary. Often I asked myself, Why should I have the privilege of teaching at ATS? I wasn't the brightest student in either my college or seminary classes. After several months of I enjoying something so much I felt I didn't deserve, I asked God to help me understand why I was here.

One day on my walk across campus, I felt God's loving presence and heard a still, small voice say, You're right in thinking you don't deserve to be teaching at ATS. I chose you, not because you're worthy, but because you're willing to take risks that others more capable than you won't take. You have the training, credentials, and experiences that have prepared you for teaching others how to be good pastors, and you're willing to put my callings before financial security.

Afterward, a great sense of peace and confidence came over me. A sense of calling and being led by the Holy Spirit replaced my feelings of inferiority. Never again did I doubt why I was teaching at ATS.

As Randy's year of postdoctoral research at the University of New Brunswick, Canada, came to a close, he faced the painful decision of leaving his girls behind in order to find work in the United States. Before finalizing their divorce, he and his wife went to counseling to develop a parenting plan to lessen the detrimental effects on their children. Phyllis and I suggested he live with us when he was looking for a research position at the University of Kentucky. His dog, ben, came with him. We soon discovered the truth of Ralph McGill's words: "The fleas come with the dog." We had to depend on our values when we decided that our son meant much more to us than fussing about fleas in our carpet.

Randy was a lot of company during the four years he lived with us. As soon as the school year was over each June, he flew to Canada to bring his daughters, Alethia and Kara, to live with us during the summer. He had to make two trips each time to take them back and forth until they were old enough to fly on their own. The same double trip had to be made ever other year at Christmas. He also tried to visit with them as often as he could to maintain a healthy relationship with them. It was expensive but well worth the cost. Judy helped by not asking him to pay alimony or child support. And we enjoyed having children in our home again. Phyllis and I had some wonderful years of being their grandparents.

Paul called to say he was getting married to Susan. She was from Virginia but was living in Athens when she and Paul met. A year earlier I had questioned Paul about when he planned to get married. He said, "Not until I can find as good a woman as you found." I was pleased that he admired his mother that much and wanted to make a wise choice for a wife. Susana came from Bloomington to Wilmore to join Randy, Phyllis, and me to travel to Virginia Beach for the wedding. Paul asked me to be his best man.

Before the wedding, Paul didn't tell me the surprise he had in store for us. He told his mother while dancing with her at the reception; she waited until the next morning to tell me. I went for a walk on the beach after she told me that Paul was going to change his last name to Sellew, Susan's last name. His was doing this because she was an only child and the last person to have the name in her family of origin. On the one hand, I was proud of him for caring that much for her. On the other hand, I was troubled. I finally came to the conclusion that I would have given him away during the wedding had I known he was planning to change his name. I had wanted to give him away during his teen years. It still feels strange to hear him called by a different last name, but I've accepted his decision.

In 1994 Phyllis and I decided to spend Thanksgiving week with Ruth and her growing family in Atlanta. We wanted to see two-year-old Kelly and six-month-old Elizabeth. Walter and Becky surprised us by flying in from Tulsa with Jared, their new biracial adoptive baby. The house was filled with six adults and three small children.

We smelled smoke on Tuesday morning while breakfast was being. Since I was a guest in Bob and Ruth's home, I waited for them and Walter, our electrical engineer son, to find the cause. I went upstairs to take a quick shower. While I was drying off, I thought the vapor from the shower was unusual thick. For some reason I opened the attic access in the bathroom and saw flames. I quickly put on my shorts and ran to the top of the stairs, yelling, "Fire! Fire in the attic! Call the Fire Department and get everyone out of the house." I slipped on a shirt and trousers as quickly as possible and grabbed the suitcase I thought had Phyllis's half-completed cathedral window quilt.

Bob and Walter tried to put out the flames with a small fire extinguisher, but that didn't work. The house was filled with smoke by the time the first of many fire trucks arrived. All nine of us got out safely and were across the street when the firemen got there.

Like a mother hen, Becky had the three children under her arms. A neighbor invited us into her home to get out of the chilly weather. We were amazed to see the firemen go through the house to make sure no one was inside and to fight the flames. The whole top floor burned off. Three layers of roofing tiles hindered the firefighting and instead helped feed the flames.

As I was standing outside, I felt an arm around my shoulder. I looked to see who was comforting me. It was Rev. Elaine Puckett, the pastor of a nearby UM church. A few years earlier I had been her counselor during a crisis at a church where she was the associate minister.

While the firemen were completing their task of extinguishing the flames, I remembered that I taught crisis counseling classes in the seminary. I said to myself, *Burrell, you and your families are in a crisis, what do you need to do?* I recalled we hadn't eaten breakfast; I needed to get us some food, because we were burning a lot of energy while the house burned. I also decided to get some safety equipment for going into the burned-out house to get what was not destroyed and make an inventory of the losses.

A major television station filmed the scene while the house was on fire and interviewed Bob and Ruth. Bob was an editor at this station. The crew came back on Thanksgiving to film us at the table and tell the story of the fire. Their closing words were, "By the way, they're eating smoked turkey for this Thanksgiving meal."

When the insurance company learned that Bob worked on the investigatory unit of a television station, they assigned their top adjuster to the case and paid top dollar to rebuild the house and replace the losses. The fire inspector reported the fire probably started at the master power-distributing switch in the attic. My suspicion was that squirrels in the attic caused the fire. After six months of rebuilding, they moved back into a much better house.

Some of the things I loved about teaching at ATS included half-year sabbaticals every three years and continuing education funds to attend professional conferences. I enjoyed traveling with department leader Fred VanTatenhove to many of these conferences. When my turn came to go on sabbatical in the fall of 1995, I followed the example of several colleagues by studying at St. John's University near St. Cloud, Minnesota. We stopped in Louisville on our way north in early September for me to help officiate at the wedding of a student. She was one of many students I had counseled at the seminary, and I had done their premarital counseling. It was a grand occasion with three bishops, several pastors, and numerous faculty members in attendance.

St. John's University is owned and operated by Benedictine monks. Hosting professors on sabbatical is just one of their many ministries. They provided comfortable apartments, offices in the library basement, seminars, and editing assistants. We were given all the privileges of visiting professors. I attended the 7 a.m. and 7 p.m. prayers in the large sanctuary and often went to mass in the late afternoon.

I wanted to take the sacrament but not without permission from the abbot. I accepted the monks' offer of spiritual direction. They do spiritual direction by walking the forest trails on four square miles of land that belongs to the monastery. Father Finning and I walked many miles as we talked. He helped me heal from the emotional and spiritual pain I experienced at Roswell. I asked him if I could take the sacrament at mass. He gave the usual response about the pope not allowing Protestants to do this, but he said that the abbot was in charge of the monastery, so I could take it by not saying anything about it. I responded that I would not take it without the abbot's permission and requested that he ask the abbot for me.

Phyllis flew to Pennsylvania to visit her sister while I went to Wilmore to teach a week in the Beeson Pastor Program. Upon my return to our St. Cloud apartment, I dressed with thermal underwear and warm clothes for the half-mile walk in freezing weather to attend evening prayers at the monastery. Once there I soon got overheated. The next thing I knew I was being rolled out in a wheelchair to the infirmary, where I was told I had fainted during prayers. They called a doctor who decided I needed to go to the hospital to be checked for a possible heart attack. The hospital kept me three days for a battery of tests. In the end, the doctor changed my heart medication.

Father Finning told me on our next walk that I really scared the monks. He said he had asked the abbot while he was visiting me in the infirmary about my wanting to take the sacrament at mass, and the abbot said that he had no problem with that. Father Finning was pleased with the answer and taught me the importance of choosing the proper time to ask for something important.

Randy took good care of the house while we were in Minnesota. I made good progress with my writing, but not enough to complete the manuscript I had proposed on bondage analysis. I had completely reversed my approach to counseling from trying to understand the causes of problems through analyzing past experiences to a solution that focused on the future. I was no longer looking in the rearview mirror but was more concerned with the windshield to help counselees create a vision for where they wanted to go with their lives. I was applying in my counseling and teaching what I was learning from attending the seminars on solution-focused counseling and narrative counseling at the annual meetings of the American Association of Marriage and Family Therapy.

I learned even more by traveling to Vancouver, Canada, two times to attend the international narrative therapy conferences led by Michael White from Australia and David Epstine from New Zealand. I overlooked their agnostic philosophy and translated their theories to create a Christian-oriented approach to pastoral counseling. Narrative counseling became a required class in the master's counseling program. Later I completed a manuscript titled "Narrative Pastoral Counseling."

Phyllis and I were invited to join the monthly Wilmore book club that had started over six decades earlier. We were also invited to join a small friendship group of ATS faculty and spouses that went out for dinner once a month. Phyllis attended the monthly faculty spouses meeting until it ran out of steam because too many spouses had full-time employment.

One of the problems with teaching at most seminaries is low salaries. I accepted a 30 percent pay cut from the counseling ministry at Roswell to go to a teaching ministry at ATS. Getting out of debt and paying for our children's college education kept us from building savings for retirement. Now that I was fifty-nine, we needed to make up for time lost. We had the maximum amount allowed deducted from my salary to be invested in TIAA funds and used extra income from teaching overload classes and counseling students to help pay household expenses.

Phyllis did not have a job outside the home, but she made up for that with frugality. She was a great help to me. We always invited my students to come to our home for a meal toward the end of each semester. She prepared sack lunches for me take to the office to eat with my faculty colleagues, and she often put flowers from the garden on the desk of the counseling department's administrative assistant and in my office. By doing all the housework, she made it easier for me to do my job, especially the long hours of grading. We grew a wonderful garden in the rich soil that had once been farmland. I did most of the garden work, and Phyllis did all the cooking as well as canning from the garden. We shared extra vegetables with neighbors and international students.

In my attempt to get over the grief of leaving Brazil, I had repressed and forgotten how to communicate in Portuguese before we moved to Wilmore. This was about to change. A Brazilian student in the master's in missions program asked for counseling from me. I knew his father when we lived in Paraná, and Phyllis had been his junior-age Sunday school teacher in Londrina. He was now a medical doctor and had come to Asbury to prepare for missionary service in Paraguay. Though he spoke very good English, he insisted on having counseling in Portuguese. My objections were overcome when he offered to help me counsel in Portuguese. At first I understood very little and was very awkward in my responses to him, but slowly the language came back to me. His therapy issues came from his childhood, so it made sense to have counseling in his native language.

Before long another Brazilian showed up at the admissions office to enroll at the seminary. I was asked to interview him and help evaluate his transcripts to make sure he was a qualified student. My visual impression brought back memories of poor farm workers in Brazil. Though Ivailton Soares did not look educated, he had a college degree and more.

He said that he had studied in Israel. And while he was on his way to Israel through New York, his wife had gone into labor and given birth to their son there. They lived and worked in a kibbutz in Israel while he earned a master's in Old Testament at the Hebrew University. He said God had told him not to return directly to Brazil but to go to England to learn English. He learned the language, but they almost starved trying to live in London. Upon his return to Brazil, his church appointed him to teach at the seminary. Then he said God had told him to go to the United States to study at ATS, though he knew very little about the institution.

I spite of my reservations about his ability, I helped him to enroll. His professors soon learned he was capable of doing a doctorate, but he insisted on pursuing the master of divinity program so he would have a broad range of courses to teach in Brazil. Five years later he was chosen to be the president of a new seminary at Anápolis, near the capital city of Brasília. He invited me to teach at the seminary three different times.

Louis Wesley de Souza, another Brazilian, studied at ATS. His father was a colleague and one of the leading pastors in the conference where I worked in Paraná. Phyllis and I invited him to stay with us several weeks until his wife and four children came to the States. He could read English but had to complete a year of academic English at the University of Kentucky before he was admitted to take seminary classes. He took my pastoral care class in his first semester at ATS, so he could write his papers in Portuguese. Phyllis corrected his papers for other classes until he was proficient in English. I helped him transfer to the PhD program in intercultural studies. He returned to Brazil to teach, but after the seminary in Londrina had trouble paying salaries, he applied for a teaching fellowship at Emory University and was subsequently invited to join the faculty of the Candler School of Theology.

Anselmo Amaral showed up with a transcript from a Brazilian seminary. I interviewed him in Portuguese because he couldn't understand English and soon discovered that he came only on the strength of his faith. I almost told the registrar to turn him down because he lacked English fluency and adequate financial resources, but then I decided to wait and pray. He gave me a twenty-page Portuguese document that described his work in Brazil, which was starting new churches and reviving stagnated churches with short-term lay missionaries. I was impressed with his creativity, organizational skills, and understanding of the mission of the church. Though he was a high risk as an international student, I knew I had to help him to enroll. I interpreted the Brazilian system of education to help the admissions office understand how his coursework was equivalent to ours. He was conditionally accepted into the doctor of missiology program, provided he successfully complete a year of study in academic English at the University of Kentucky. He was happy to go back to Brazil to finish his year of pastoral appointment and then move his wife and three children to Kentucky. But by the time he had completed his English studies, his money was running out.

When I learned that Bill and Phyllis Johnson from Roswell had merged their office park property into a REIT company, and he no longer had administrative responsibilities, I suggested that the seminary president invite them to join a small group of potential donors who would be visiting the seminary. This gave Phyllis and me a chance to show them around and renew our friendship.

I invited Anselmo to meet them and tell them his story. After I told them about his financial problems, they agreed to help him. With their support over a period of five years he completed his doctoral studies and his wife, Miriam, completed a master's degree in counseling and a doctor of ministry degree. They returned to Brazil and served a large church as co-pastors, teachers, counselors, and authors.

Bill and Phyllis Johnson continued to financially support ATS. Instead of giving direct support to students, as they did for Anselmo and Miriam, they gave several million dollars to fund scholarships for international students, new church planters, and other seminary projects.

The week after Christmas in 1996 we planned to travel to Atlanta to visit Ruth and her family, have dinner with our friends, Roy and Pat Chapman, and go on to Florida to visit with several of my siblings. The day before, while I was taking a shower, a very strange thing happened. I heard imperative words (not with my ears but in my spirit) as plainly as I have ever heard anything with my ears: *When you are having dinner with Roy and Pat Chapman, say to them, If ATS had the money, Phyllis and I would probably move to Florida to help start another campus for Asbury Seminary.*

I was startled by such a strange idea spoken so clearly and forcefully. Ever since working at Oral Robert's University I had been very cautious about claiming that I had heard something from the Holy Spirit. I told Phyllis I had had a "brainstorm."

She said, "Let me sit down before you tell me."

She was just as mystified as I was by these words, but she suggested I do exactly what I had been told to do.

I got increasingly nervous when we ate with the Chapmans. I finally got the courage to say what I had heard the "voice" tell me to say. The Chapmans showed no special interest, however, and I felt an immediate release of responsibility along with a sense of peace. The conversation soon moved on to other subjects.

Later, when Roy and I were sitting in their living room after dinner, he said, "Burrell, are you serious about moving to Florida to help start a seminary?"

Though I believed I was only bluffing, I said, "Yes. I'm sure we would."

He said he would ask his son, a wealthy businessman in Tampa, to give us some financial help to start the seminary. The conversation ended there.

On the way to Florida, I decided to consult with my sister Ruth and her husband, Jim, about the feasibility of ATS starting a campus in Florida. He had been a leading Methodist pastor and retired as senior pastor of the First UMC in Lakeland. He told me that the Methodist church had turned down Florida Southern University when they proposed starting a seminary on their campus. He thought an ATS campus was needed and would be a success.

Then we traveled to see Ed and Patsy. Ed had just retired as president of the Florida Methodist Children's Home. Before that he had been a district superintendent and knew Florida Methodism as well as anyone. He was very positive about the idea and thought it would be a great asset to the churches in Florida.

On the trip back to Wilmore, I grew apprehensive and told Phyllis that I didn't want to say any more about the subject, because I didn't want to move to Florida. I reminded her that I had heard her say several times that she enjoyed vacationing in Florida, but she did not want to live there.

Phyllis said, "Have I ever refused to go anywhere you felt like God was calling us to go?"

I then asked if she thought I should talk with Maxie Dunnam about what we had learned on our trip. She said I should tell him what I had learned. The next week, I called Sheila, Maxie's administrative assistant, to tell her I would like to talk with Maxie about a potential major donor.

When we met, he listened to my story and said, "Burrell, the seminary has no interest in starting another campus. That is not a part of our strategic planning, but I would like to talk with Mr. Chapman about becoming a donor to the seminary."

I felt somewhat foolish but relieved by thinking that we may not need to move. I told him that it wouldn't be productive to talk with Tom without a plan on how the money would be used, and the original idea for his giving was to help start an ATS campus.

Maxie asked what I thought he should do to develop a plan. I suggested he meet with the ATS graduates serving in Florida for an open discussion about the feasibility of an ATS campus in the state. The next thing I heard was that Maxie reported to the board of trustees that he had had such a meeting, and they wanted to ask the board to open a campus in Orlando. The board then asked Maxie to continue the study and present a strategic plan for the next board meeting.

The Wilmore seminary faculty was not excited about the idea of starting a seminary in Florida. Serious skepticism and vocal resistance quickly developed among some faculty members. I was thrust into the role of major supporter of the vision. Maxie wavered under the pressure of faculty resistance and the financial responsibilities of starting a new campus. That semester I was one of five faculty members invited to meet weekly in the president's home for prayer. These were the critical months of decision about starting the Orlando campus. As Maxie shared his struggles with the decision, I kept encouraging him to move forward. Fortunately, a bear stock market was adding to the seminary's endowment investments during that time.

Maxie shared with us one morning that the decision to move forward was final, and he had chosen Steve Harper to be the vice president for the new campus. I leaped out of my chair for joy. Phyllis and I had gotten to know Steve and Jeannie at the Brick-By-Brick UMC in Lexington, and I had done the premarital counseling for their daughter and son-in-law.

Six faculty members responded to Maxie's request for their interest in moving to Orlando, but five soon dropped out when they considered the implications of moving. This left only me, and I didn't want to move, but I was so much a part of the original vision for the Florida campus that I felt obligated to go if asked to do so.

I was seated next to Maxie at a faculty lunch when another professor asked if I was moving to teach in Orlando. I responded that I didn't know because I hadn't been asked to go. I was not about to say that I would be going until Maxie asked me and we could talk about salary, moving expenses, and benefits in Florida. My research on the cost of living showed that Florida would be at least five thousand dollars a year more expensive. I did not want to make the same financial mistake I made when we moved from Atlanta to Tulsa in 1977.

The day before the trustees met in the spring of 1999, Maxie called me in to ask if I would move to the new campus. I refused to answer until we discussed finances. I tried to convince him that the faculty in Florida needed to be paid five thousand dollars more than their colleagues in Wilmore. When I failed to convince him, I bargained for myself, saying I needed at least five thousand dollars more a year for five years. He agreed to that and said I would get fifteen the first year and ten thousand the second year.

Phyllis and I turned our attention to preparing for another move after a season of seven wonderful years in Wilmore.

At the start of my fourth year in Wilmore I was happy to invite my doctoral mentor at Emory, John Patton, to speak at chapel service for my installation in the E. A. Seamands Chair of Pastoral Leadership. The provost told me I had to give up that academic chair when we moved to Orlando. Maxie asked me for permission to ask Bill and Phyllis Johnson to endow a chair to pay my salary in Orlando. They did not endow a chair, but they did agree to pay the same salary and benefits for a chair in their name as long as I taught there.

Randy had been living in his own house in Lexington and working on soybean research at the University of Kentucky. We were concerned about his low salary and the fact that he had to raise his own salary by writing grants for his research. He also was looking for other job opportunities. We were not too concerned about moving away from him, because we thought he would soon be leaving Lexington. After several interviews he found a good-paying and stable position as a senior research scientist with the US Department of Agriculture Forage Research station at the University of Kentucky.

We did not want to sell the house in Wilmore. We considered teaching one semester in Florida and the other in Wilmore, but we realized we would have friends in neither place if we did this. We had to make a clean break and let it go as we had reluctantly done with our other homes. We decided to sell it ourselves as we had done before. I posted on the ATS intranet: REWARD: a free dinner for four persons in the restaurant of your choice in the Bluegrass area for the party that buys or refers the buyer for our house in Wilmore.

Without thirty minutes I had six telephone calls for more information. The person who called first visited that evening and agreed to pay our asking price and signed a contract.

We were sad when we left Wilmore but excited about the opportunity to turn the vision of a new ATS in Orlando into reality. Our seven-year season in Wilmore was as happy and fulfilling as anywhere we ever lived.

CHAPTER 18

Following a Vision

The future belongs to those who see possibilities
before they become obvious.

—John Scully

We started looking for a house in Orlando once we signed a sales contract on the Wilmore house. Our first stop was the home of Jeannie and Steve Harper. They had been our friends in Kentucky, and he would be my immediate supervisor in Florida. Though we had sent a wish list for a house to the real estate agent Steve and Jeannie recommended, we found her to be very frustrating. She showed us a number of pink houses, which I had specifically stated we did not want. She finally admitted she hadn't read my e-mail about our specifications.

So we found a new agent before our next trip to Florida during the 1999 spring break. She was very friendly and well prepared. We looked at a few houses with her, and then she drove us to the Remington Park subdivision, halfway between Oviedo and the University of Central Florida. After walking through the house, I was about to tell her that it was nice but above our price range. I looked at Phyllis to see if she was in agreement, and I saw her eyes glowing.

I said, "You like this house, don't you."

Her wide eyes and smile communicated as much as her head nodded a big yes.

We had found our new home.

After hours of negotiation, we signed a contract to buy the house. The owners accepted our offer because they were in a hurry to move to Texas.

We were concerned about owning an empty house in Orlando four months before we would be moving in. A former student in Wilmore, Anna Jackson, was now the Wesley Foundation director at the University of Central Florida. Her office was in the University Carillon UMC across the street from the university. When she learned we had bought a house close to the church, she called to ask that we allow the University Carillon UMC building superintendent, Joe Manuel, to live in our house until we moved.

At the time, Joe was sleeping at the church because he had no place to stay until his own house sold and his divorce was finalized. He demonstrated his gratitude for having a place to stay by volunteering to paint the house for us if we would buy the paint. After we moved in, we agreed to let him continue to stay in the back bedroom and bath for several months. Joe became a great friend and help for us. I was able to offer informal counseling to help him about parenting his son and dealing with his emotionally disturbed wife through a very troublesome divorce.

We planned to visit several United Methodist churches before making a decision about our choice for a church home, but once we visited University Carillon UMC, where Joe worked and only a mile from our house, we looked no farther. It was a ten-year-old church plant with both traditional and contemporary worship services. The pastor was a handsome former Coast Guard officer and Duke graduate with a winsome style of communication. We soon made friends in a Sunday school class and felt like we had found a church home.

The oppressive summer heat forced us to do our walking at daybreak. When we complained to a neighbor about the high humidity and heat, he told us it would take three summers to get accustomed to it. He was right. We loved walking in and out of the many cul-de-sacs in Remington Park. It had very little traffic in the one-entrance subdivision. I noticed there were five styles of houses in the 150-house development, but each one had unique tropical landscaping.

Steve and Jeannie did a great job of welcoming the new ATS faculty. They soon developed a sense of community with our families. We had no idea how many students would show up for our inaugural class, but we were excited about our future. I had learned from being a pioneer and church planter that it takes a unique kind of person to be willing to start something completely new, without knowing in advance the outcome. The capacity to embrace ambiguity (the willingness to act without knowing what will happen) is the first requirement for pioneers of faith.

Maxie had three false starts finding the location of the seminary before Joe McLaren, a local UMC pastor, told him about a recently closed medical clinic building that was for sale. Joe had taken my doctor of ministry class and chose me to be his dissertation mentor in the Beeson program at Wilmore. Though the building cost more than Maxie had planned to pay, it was well situated, well constructed, and had a large paved parking area. But everything had to be torn out and rebuilt inside the building before we could start classes. The construction was completed in time to put the books on the bookshelves just days before the students arrived for our first day of classes in 1999.

One of my primary reasons for starting a Florida campus was for the purpose of reaching the Hispanic community. From there we could reach out to all of Latin American. We had no idea how we would connect with the Latinos, but this question was answered in the strangest way.

On Thanksgiving morning I felt very weak. When I fainted and fell to the floor at home, my pulse and temperature increased. Phyllis took me to the emergency room of the Florida Hospital. The doctor ran several tests and told me I had diverticulitis and needed surgery. He said the surgeon would not operate until I had taken enough antibiotics to reduce the swelling of my colon. They kept me almost a week so a cardiologist could manage my atrial-fibrillation heart problem. Surgery was scheduled for early January.

When the chief chaplain of the hospital visited me, I told him about the new seminary and how much we wanted to provide theological education to the Hispanic community. He said he would send a Puerto Rican chaplain resident to talk with me about this. Soon after the intern came to my room and heard about our seminary, I knew he would become the point of contact with Spanish-speaking pastors in the area. He told me the senior pastor of the church where he worked on Sundays was president of the Central Florida Latin American Pastors Association.

A few weeks later a group of Latino pastors came to the seminary unannounced to check us out. As we communicated in English, Spanish, and Portuguese, we were told that other seminaries had said they would do what we were saying, but they had not kept their promises. So they were skeptical of us. We ended the meeting with a decision to have a more formal meeting to discuss how we could work together.

When we met again, we decided the language for the meeting would be in Spanish and we would not promise to do anything but be good listeners to them and their concerns. They told us about the difficulties of having good church leaders to develop multicultural churches. They needed help in training potential leaders. Only two of the pastors in their association had a seminary education. We ended the meeting with a decision to have the same Puerto Rican resident I met at the Florida Hospital to do his research project on the concerns and needs of the Spanish-speaking churches so that we could develop seminars and courses to target those needs.

From his research, he discovered the most pressing need was pastoral care of families in a multicultural immigrant population. Since pastoral care was my discipline, I volunteered to teach the first course. I soon found my Portuguese was not communicating with Spanish-speaking students. A recently arrived professor of social ethics, Hugo Magallanes, a native of

Mexico, was instrumental in gaining the confidence of the Latino pastors. He volunteered to translate from English to Spanish the first class taught in the Latino/Latina Studies program.

We were excited about starting theological education for Latin American immigrants, but we faced a major institutional problem with the seminary in Wilmore. They did not know what we were doing. Had the provost known, he would have ordered us to stop. These prospective students did not have a college education and could not meet the requirements for master's programs, the only degrees the seminary was accredited to offer. They lacked the financial resources to pay tuition. Nor had the idea of teaching them been approved by the faculty in Wilmore. If the provost had quashed us before we got started, we would be just like the other seminaries that had promised to teach Spanish-speaking pastors in Central Florida and failed to deliver.

We decided to call these courses certificates in theological education to get around the accreditation double bind. We did not know how to pay for this, because the nominal fee we planned to charge would not be the same as for a seminary education. We had the vision. We had the professors. We had the students. But we did not have institutional approval. Yet Steve courageously decided to go ahead with our plans without informing Wilmore. I told Steve to do what Admiral Farragut did when he was told there were mines in front of his ships at the battle of Mobile Bay: "Damn the torpedoes! Full speed ahead!"

We decided to follow through with our plans without risking academic disapproval until Maxie Dunnam visited the campus. I said that Maxie had specifically commissioned us to be innovative and creative in our approach to theological education in Florida and not be just a carbon copy of Wilmore. I knew his heart for evangelism enough to believe he would be inspired when he saw the enthusiasm of the students and the classes in action. He could then use his authority as president of the seminary to prevent the academics in Wilmore from stopping us.

I admired Steve and Maxie for having the courage to go against tradition in the seminary and for their willingness to face the backlash for their courageous administrative decisions. I had the authority to do no more than teach and encourage them. I used my experience in Brazil with the familiar sayings *dar um jeito* ("make a way") and *quebra galho* ("find someone to help").

We had over twenty-five students in our first Latino/Latina Studies class. I thought the young Puerto Rican female in the back of the room shedding tears most of the first class had serious emotional problems. I decided not to approach her while she was crying. When I read the reflection paper she wrote about the class, I learned that she had been crying tears of joy. She wrote that God had called her into ministry, and she had been praying for an opportunity to go to seminary, but she could not leave her family responsibilities in Florida. Now our seminary had come to her. She wrote that she helped develop several pioneer parachurch ministries as an administrative assistant, but she felted called to be a minister.

After reading her paper I immediately thought she could be the kind of person we needed to help us develop and administer the Latino/Latina Studies program. I asked her to see me and to bring her résumé with her. When I had read her résumé, I asked her how she knew how to do all the things she had done when she had no formal education to do it.

She said, "I'm anointed by God to do it."

Within five minutes of our first conversation, I asked Jo Ann Solis if she would like to work for us. I knew I was going out on a limb offering a job that had not yet been designated or had any funds to pay her salary. I believed by faith that, if what we were doing God's will, he would help others to see the same thing I saw, and he would provide the financial resources for her to work at the seminary to help us relate to the Latino/Latina community and provide classes in Spanish to meet their needs.

With tears in her eyes, she told me about walking down the hall to the classroom on the first day at the seminary and God telling her that her next job would be to work at the seminary. He even showed her the room that would become her office.

With the help of two trustees who were sufficiently inspired by what we were doing, they provided the funds to pay her salary. She did a wonderful job developing our Latino/Latina Studies program. She enrolled and completed the master of divinity program, married Dan, another MDiv student. She left to get her PhD and is now teaching at Indiana Wesleyan Seminary. She has been an inspiration to me. I'm so glad our paths crossed when they did.

Phyllis and I gradually adjusted to life in Central Florida. The year after we moved, Phyllis surprised me when we were talking about how we would use the twenty-five thousand dollars the seminary provided for extra expenses. She said, "If I'm going to live in Florida, I want a Florida swimming pool."

I couldn't believe what I was hearing. She's one of the most frugal persons I've ever known. Here was my frugal Phyl saying that she wanted to splurge on something completely unnecessary. Most other houses in the subdivision either had pools installed when the houses were constructed or, like our house, had space reserved for the option of putting in a pool at a later date. We could not have purchased the house had a pool been there when we were looking for a place to live. I was wishing we had a pool like some of our neighbors, but I didn't want to spend the money to install one. But if Phyllis wanted a pool, I wanted one too.

This turned out to be a good investment. It provided many hours of relaxation, exercise, and hospitality. It expanded the use of the back of the house. With the help of a rooftop solar heater, we swam in the pool eight months out of the year.

I enjoyed visiting my Florida siblings more often and fishing with my brothers, especially Horace. I bought a bass boat that he kept at his house in Winter Haven. He was a great fisherman. He never taught me how to use the boat, because he wanted to be in charge of it whenever we fished. We had many happy hours on the lakes. The boat was useful for the Brother's Seven semiannual fishing retreats with all six Dinkins brothers.

Phyllis and I no longer had to travel long distance to the semiannual family reunions at Daytona Beach. I was pleased to live much closer to my siblings and their families. Pauline and Aaron lived in Frostproof, ninety minutes away from us. I enjoyed fishing with him and was able to be with his family when he died at the Tampa Veterans Hospital. I had frequent visits with my sister Ruth after she and Jim moved to Carpenter Village in Lakeland, where Ed and Patsy also lived. Ruth's health declined until she died a few days before we left Florida.

In December 2000, Ivailton Soares, the Brazilian student I enroll at seminary in Wilmore, invited me to teach at a new seminary in Anápolis, Goias, Brazil. He was the founding president of the seminary for his Pentecostal Presbyterian denomination. He said he would translate for me because my Portuguese was not adequate to teach a class. He wanted me to be there in time to speak to about seventy-five pastors in his presbytery on the Sunday before classes started. Phyllis and I arrived two days early. The sights, smells, and taste of the food awakened my sensory system from our earlier years in Brazil. With this came the long neglected words and sounds of the Portuguese language. Before I spoke to the pastors on Sunday, I suggested to Ivailton that he let me try to communicate without him translating. He looked amazed and I was thrilled as the words flowed from my mouth as freely as they would have in English. I learned from this experience just how important culture and sensory systems are in learning another language.

We traveled from Anápolis to Londrina, where we had last lived in Brazil, for me to teach a week at an interdenominational seminary. Then we traveled to Rudge Ramos, São Paulo, where I had taught at the seminary before the bishops shut it down.

Joe Manuel, our friend and building superintendent at University Carillon UMC, picked us up at the Orlando airport when we returned. On the way home, he told us that he was very concerned about our two pastors joking so much about sex with two women who worked part time at the church. I told him I would make an appointment with the senior pastor to find out what was going on and to warn him about the danger.

I found out it was too late to intervene when the district superintendent called a few days later and asked to see me right away. He said he had enough information to place our senior pastor on administrative leave for sexual misconduct and wanted to know how best to approach the situation at the church. We worked out a plan to have the associate pastor preach the sermon, and he would make the announcement before communion was served. I told him I would be available to help people who wanted to talk and pray after the service. Before the district superintendent left my office, I suggested that he question the associate pastor to find out if he had crossed any ethical boundaries.

He called me the next morning to say that the associate pastor was involved with one of the women and the senior pastor with both of them.

Very few people were aware of what was going on Sunday morning, though people wondered why the bulletin indicated the senior pastor was going to preach the sermon. The district superintendent, instead, led the service and preached the sermon. I grew more and more apprehensive as he read the prepared statement that he was placing the senior pastor on administrative leave due to ethical concerns. Though the specific reasons were not given, most people had no problem guessing what they were. I heard gasping and crying. Just as reality and the shock from what they heard started to sink in, the district supervisor said he also had the sad responsibility of placing the associate pastor on administrative leave for the same reason. It was as if everyone had been hit in the stomach, and just as they began to get their breath back, they were struck another blow.

The district superintendent said he would be assuming pastoral leadership of the church until further notice and moved to the communion table to start the ritual for the first Sunday in December communion service. I got up to follow him. Three other ordained pastors who had been recruited to serve communion and be available for prayer at the end of the service joined us. A few people left the service before taking communion, but most came forward with tears in their eyes. I used the old communion words to offer the broken bread to them: "Take and eat this for your healing." It was the saddest Sunday anyone there could remember.

I invited all staff members and their spouses to meet at the church that night. My plan was to help them get through the early phase of the crisis as healthy as possible so they could help the general membership get through it. Before we met, I attended the youth meeting to help the youth pastor, who was a student at the seminary, talk with the youth. We had to be very careful about what we said, because the son of the senior pastor was in the youth group, though he was not there that night.

I also met with key lay leaders early the next week to help them face the reality of sexual immorality of the founding pastor—the only pastor some of the lay leaders had ever had—as well as the new associate pastor. I was very blunt with them about the possibility of lower worship attendance and a drop in financial resources that would require some tough decisions on their part. I placed the responsibility for mature lay leadership on their shoulders. They needed to step up to cushion the impact of the crisis on the church by assuming more responsibility for the future of the church. I volunteered to be present at the church as much as possible during the week to help the staff and members process their grief and their concerns.

By Monday morning the senior pastor had moved his personal items out of his office. I felt very sad sitting in his empty office to minister to the staff and church members who needed to talk to a pastor.

Attendance dropped off. Giving went down, but not as much as I feared. One reason is that some church members used their influence to keep the news media from reporting the ethical problems of the former pastors. The district superintendent assumed pastoral leadership of the worship services and recruited a retired pastor to be present to provide pastoral care during the week. I could not continue giving as much time as the church needed. The former pastors surrendered their ordination credentials, but they had to deal with a lawsuit that the conference lawyers settled out of court.

The marriages of the former pastors almost did not survive. A very good pastoral counselor helped the pastors terminate the emotional attachments to their lovers and recommit themselves to their marriages. The competition between the senior pastor and the associate pastor for the affection of one woman ended when the biology of sex made the final decision. The associate won by getting her pregnant. It was a costly victory. The judge ordered him to pay child support for a child he did not get to know while he and his wife reared their own four children.

The church struggled several months to heal from the crisis. Different pastors preached when the district superintendent could not be there on Sunday. He did not realize that he was not a very good preacher and that the people preferred to hear other pastors. When attendance dropped even lower, I decided to act. I told the district superintendent that the church could not continue without a serious loss of membership if he did not appoint a new pastor to lead us by Easter. He should not wait another two months to appointment a new pastor at the conference. Then I told him that Joe McLaren planned to ask to come off his leave of absence at the conference and take an appointment, but he was available to be appointed before then.

The district superintendent was getting weary from doing his district job and trying to pastor the church. He liked my idea and asked the bishop to appoint Joe as our new pastor, starting the Sunday after Easter.

I did not tell the district superintendent that I had been counseling with Joe and his wife, Pat, for some time about grief over the death of Joe's father and the decision to take a leave of absence. Joe soon discovered he didn't like the stress of raising money for his own salary and doing all the administrative work without having a staff to do it for him. And Pat wanted to be his wife, not his administrative assistant.

I was happy when Joe came to be our pastor. The first thing I told him was to be a future-oriented pastoral leader, not the healer of a traumatized church, otherwise he would be with us only a couple of years until most of the healing was completed.

Phyllis and I spent a month in 2001 with a family in San José, Costa Rica, while we took an intensive course in Spanish. We returned to the same language school in 2002 for five months during my sabbatical. This time we rented a house close to the school where two former students had been living for a year. We bought their refrigerator, automobile, and several household things they could not ship to Peru.

We were under the illusion that our Portuguese background would make Spanish easy to learn, but we quickly discovered it was as much a hindrance as a help. We got there too late for the first quarter and started with the second one. This meant our classmates were more advanced than we. Many vocabulary words were familiar, but the sounds taught in the first semester were very different from Portuguese. Phyllis's college English major helped her with the grammar, but mine was problematic. We went to classes on weekday mornings and spent the rest of the day studying. We hired a maid to do housecleaning and cook each Monday, Wednesday, and Friday so Phyllis would have time to study. The maid cooked enough food to have leftovers the next day. With her background of working for missionaries in the language, our maid was able to help us with our conversational Spanish.

Public transportation made it easy to get around in San José. We used the car for shopping and to make longer trips outside the city. We travel to a mountaintop resort overlooking the Pacific to celebrate our anniversary. Ray and Lidia Zirkel were a big help to us. We enjoyed visiting, going to church, and traveling with them. They had been my students and counselees in Wilmore and were now serving as missionaries here. Ray and I went deep-sea fishing. We caught several tuna, and I caught a large sailfish. The boat capital saw me getting worn out from reeling him in and helped me by reversing the engine.

I learned enough Spanish to teach in Costa Rica, Ecuador, Colombia, and Cuba, but soon found it was difficult to use in Orlando with the Puerto Rican and Mexican students who spoke different dialects. We should have gone to San Juan, Puerto Rico.

After another trip to teach in Brazil, Portuguese reasserted itself as the second language of choice. I was not able to teach in Spanish again. When

Phyllis and I returned from Brazil, I noticed the trees and shrubbery uprooted at the Orlando airport and on the way home. We did not know that a hurricane had blown through Central Florida until we got back. I told Phyllis to get emotionally prepared to see our house badly damaged.

When we got home, the house showed little damage, but we lost two trees in our front yard. Joe Manuel and some church members had cleared and stacked the remains of the trees on the street. Truckloads of debris from other houses almost filled the streets. Before the city workers could clear them, another hurricane headed our way. We hunkered down inside our boarded-up house on two different Sunday mornings as two more hurricanes came through our area.

The first Sunday I suggested to Phyllis that we watch a movie to distract us from the reporting on the storm. We chose *Gone with the Wind* while the wind and rain howled outside the house. Damage to our house did not look too serious. I observed that all the roofs in the neighborhood were being replaced. Our insurance company adjuster decided we didn't need a new one. I realized then that I had made a mistake by climbing on the roof to nail the shingles that had blown off back in place to keep the inside from being damaged. I should have placed a blue tarp over the roof as neighbors had done. Anger pushed me to visit to the office of our insurance agent to tell him about this unfair treatment. Fortunately, I kept my anger under control. The woman we talked with first said, as she was escorting us into the agent's office, that she enjoyed hearing my sermon when I preached at University Carillon. We requested a more thorough inspection of damages to the house by another adjuster. Over twenty-two thousand dollars in repairs were done to the roof and inside the house. Sometimes it's wiser not to be so quick to minimize damages.

School was going well. My class sizes were smaller in Orlando than most of the classes in Wilmore. This meant I had fewer papers to grade and found it was easier to learn the names of all the students at the seminary.

I have always had difficulty learning and remembering names. The right hemisphere of my brain must be much stronger than the left, because names and factual details are not easy for me to recall. My strength has been a strong intuitive sense about people, situations, and pastoral responsibilities. These helped when I was designing syllabi, teaching, and counseling. I was the first professor at ATS to use team assignments. I designed the narrative pastoral counseling class and redesigned several syllabi for required classes. They are still being used at the seminary.

The contemporary chapel format suited the students. I had the privilege of preaching several times, including a dialogical sermon with Phyllis. After Bill Johnson spoke in chapel, I invited him to join Paul Badour to speak to my class on the subject of ministering with people of wealth. Bill and Paul were trustees of the seminary as well as major donors. They had been instrumental in helping us start the Florida ATS campus and gave extra support for the LLSP program. I learned while visiting with a wealthy landowner near the Warsaw church I served when I was a seminary student that people of wealth have special pastoral care needs that pastors often don't consider. I wanted my students to learn what Bill and Paul had to teach them.

When the hours for our chapel services on Tuesday and Thursday were shifted from before lunch to after lunch, it interfered with my accustomed nap habits. After my morning classes, I would enjoy the wonderful lunches Phyllis prepared for me before I took a nap in my van. My colleagues named the van "Dinkins napmobile." A nap helped me stay awake during chapel. When I started to turn to look through the skylight in the back of the van after my naps and observe airplanes slowly descending on their approach to the Orlando airport, I started thinking about places I would go after retirement.

The seminary community and our children helped Phyllis and me celebrate our fiftieth wedding anniversary in August 2005. This milestone added to thoughts about retirement. I was now seventy-one and had been working since getting my social security card at age nine, the year my father died. I was feeling the double bind of a "Janus complex." Janus was the double-faced Roman god with one head looking to the past and the other looking to the future. On the one hand, I loved teaching students and wanted to continue doing what felt like my greatest joy and gave significance to my life. On the other hand, I was getting tired of grading papers and looking at a computer monitor so much of the day. I felt no pressure from the seminary administration to retire. My student class evaluations continued to be at the top in the counseling department; however, I realized I had lost interest in attending professional conferences and reading new material in my discipline. This was a sure indication I had the symptoms of professors who needed to retire for the sake of quality education for the students. I was negotiating in my own mind for more time to teach to keep from facing the unknown of retirement.

The decision came to a head in the sunroom of our daughter Ruth's home. Phyllis and my two daughters confronted me with the idea that I could continue teaching, but I should retire in order to do other things while I was still healthy enough to travel. Our daughters are the designated executrixes of our wills. Every year I prepare a statement and send a copy to them about our annual income and assets so they will be informed enough to make decisions when called upon to do so. They knew our financial resources were adequate for me to afford to retire. I bargained for more time by promising to retire a year after my upcoming sabbatical.

The sabbatical went by faster than anticipated. With the help of an editor, I completed my book, *Narrative Pastoral Counseling*. I had to self-publish it because several publishers responded that the potential readership for the subject was too small to risk the cost of publication. After the book was published, I made several trips to teach in Latin American and started research for a manuscript on the subject of eudemonism, the philosophical word for happiness.

Doubts about retirement were dispelled by a decision to start a master's program in counseling like the one at ATS in Wilmore. I worked hard to get us ready to do this, but I dreaded the additional administrative responsibilities that were inevitable for leading the program. I decided it would be best to start with a new professor who would have fresh ideas and enough energy to lead it over a number of years, not someone who was so close to retirement.

Tapiwa Mucharewa, originally from Zimbabwe, had taken my position when I left Wilmore. He and I were rooming together at Daytona Beach during a seminar for teaching sexual ethics when I asked him to consider moving to Florida to take my position and start the new counseling program. I wanted new blood for the seminary, and I wanted it to be someone with a cross-cultural background. After hearing that he was interested, I asked to meet with Steve Harper and Hugo Magellan, the vice provost and dean. I informed them that I would be retiring in June 2007.

A few days later I told the provost, Joel Green, when he visited the Florida campus about my intentions to retire. He quickly jumped at the idea and suggested I retire in June 2006. He said I could meet the requirement to teach at least one year after a sabbatical by teaching the same number of courses spread out over three years as an adjunct professor. I thought he was being generous, but later I realized he wanted to get me off the seminary medical insurance policy for full-time faculty. It turned out to be a good decision for each party. Teaching part time helped ease the transition from working full time to full retirement.

Phyllis and I talked many hours about where we would live. We seriously considered moving back to Atlanta and even looked at the house next door to Ruth as one option, but we decided it was too small for us. A visiting professor of missions told me about how much he enjoyed living in the Penney Farms retirement community near Jacksonville, Florida. He invited Phyllis and me to visit with him and his wife to learn more about it. After two visits, we liked Penney Farms so much that we decided this was where we wanted to live. We made a deposit to get in line for a house when one became available. We talked with our children about our decision at Christmas and showed them a film of the place so they would understand why we had chosen this place. But all our carefully made plans were changed a few months later.

Ruth called to tell us that the house next door had a for-sale sign in the front yard. She thought we might be interested. Ruth and Bob had befriended the elderly couple that lived there. Their daughter inherited the house when they died, but she couldn't bring herself to sell it. So she rented it for several years, but then she got tired of dealing with landlord problems from where she lived in North Carolina and decided to sell it. Ruth found out the asking price and was given a caveat: she would sell it to us at a considerably reduced price out of appreciation for the way Ruth and Bob had cared for her parents.

Phyllis and I changed our travel plans for a conference in North Carolina to come through Atlanta to look at the house again. We questioned Ruth and Bob about the wisdom of our living that close to them. They and their two daughters reassured us several times that they wanted us to live there.

I asked Phyllis where she really wanted to live. I told her that she had been willing to live any place God called me to work. Now it was time for her to decide where we lived. When she responded that she wanted to live close to one of her children, I knew what we needed to do.

Phyllis and I decided to buy the house and move to Atlanta.

I went into a depression from the loss of a path not taken while writing the letter to inform Penney Farms about our decision. I was grieving over giving up the opportunity to have close male friendships in the later years of my life. Phyllis had sacrificed so much for me in the fifty years of our marriage. Moving next door to our daughter and her family was something I could do for her happiness, and I had faith that I would like it too. I had several friends in Atlanta and could make more friends.

I also knew we would be living less than three miles from Emory with the advantages of the Emory healthcare system. Having access to the

Styles Bradley Fund for paying hospital expenses beyond Medicare and insurance policies of clergy of the North Georgia Annual Conference was another reason to move to Atlanta.

I started a new tradition at ATS when I retired. I requested a special worship service to recognize my retirement with the sermon to be preached by the pastor of my choice: Bishop Wayne Felton from Minneapolis–St. Paul. He was an African American student who lived in the same apartment building where we lived our first year in Wilmore. When he was a seminary student, I felt led to be very tough on him, because I saw so much potential for good or evil in his future ministry. He responded to my confrontations by choosing a mentor-mentee relationship with me and had kept in touch with me over the years since then. He grew up without a father in his home. He adopted Dr. Massey, a professor at Tuskegee University, as his substitute father and called me his "white father."

Bishop Felton preached a wonderfully appropriate sermon that affirmed my ministry of teaching and released my soul to face retirement. He and his beautiful wife stayed another day for my retirement dinner. No one but Phyllis knew how sick I was this week from a reaction to an antibiotic medication my doctor prescribed to fight a bladder infection.

The radical change involved in the process of retirement and moving to Atlanta was hard. We had learned how to get from one place to another. Each move was different and was done for different reasons. We learned the importance of saying good-bye to colleagues and friends. We learned how to express gratitude for the blessings received in each place we lived, including the houses in which we lived. We learned how to sell the houses we owned, to let go of things we no longer wanted, and to pack what we wanted to keep. We learned that we could move our belongings, but we couldn't move our support systems. We learned to make friends wherever we lived and to let go of them when we could no longer be physically present to nurture the relationships. We learned how to protect our hearts by focusing on the moving task when the pain of losses sought to overwhelm us. We learned to hate the tyranny of things as we packed the last things before the movers arrived.

The rapid rise in the price of houses in Orlando peaked by the time we put ours on the market in 2006. We were fortunate to sell it for almost twice the price we paid seven years earlier. Starting in 2007, prices dropped precipitously over the following six years, until they were back to where they had been when we moved to Orlando in 1999. We were happy that the remodeling work on the house in Atlanta was completed by the time we were able to move after our Orlando house sold.

We followed the vision of starting a seminary in Orlando when we left Wilmore to move there in 1999. At that time no one knew if the vision would become a reality. In seven short years we saw the birth, development, and establishment of what started as only a dream. It took the risk of faith, many hours of hard work, prayers, and generous givers to turn the dream into a reality. Phyllis and I left Orlando with the satisfaction of knowing our mission was accomplished.

CHAPTER 19

The Return of the Homing Pigeons

In my end is my beginning.

—T. S. Elliot, "East Coker"

With our many moves we are learning the importance of intentionally accepting the consequences of transitions. Moving can be both a blessing and a curse. The pain of giving up the presence of friends, colleagues, and a church community is our biggest curse. We have learned how to move our things, but we can never move our support systems. To give up the presence of people we have learned to love and depend on requires the pain of grief and rituals of saying good-bye. Though we may stay in touch with some of them through Christmas letters and occasional visits, it is never the same again.

Moving means giving up valuable social capital accumulated over time and with much effort. Something very precious is lost voluntarily or involuntarily, and it hurts. We take time to intentionally say good-bye to close friends. When we did not do this with past moves, we were cautious about making friends in a new place. The unexpected delay in completing the remodeling of our Atlanta house provided extra time to say our *despididas* ("good-byes") with our Florida friends before we moved from Oviedo.

On the other end, we felt like homing pigeons returning fifty-one years later to live only three miles from our first home after we married in 1955. This was our fifth time to live in the Atlanta area, and we were glad to be back in familiar territory, where the streets are etched in the crevices of my brain.

Traveling to Orlando twice a year to teach one-week intensive classes for the first three years after retirement helped me make the transition from full-time employment to full-time retirement. I missed having an office and the routine of daily work away from home. I felt relieved from the responsibilities of grading papers and administrative tasks.

I considered starting a counseling practice in Atlanta but decided not to when I realized I would have to go back to school to take the necessary courses for licensure as a counselor in Georgia. Neither did I want to pay the cost of maintaining a part-time counseling office. I had worked outside the home to some degree from age nine to seventy-two. It was time to stop. We felt confident that our retirement income, savings, and investments, if we carefully managed them, would support us in the years ahead. After considering the situation, I felt blessed not to need to be gainfully employed.

My mind had all this worked out, but my spirit took time to accept it all. Many nights during the first two years or retirement, my dreams were like dramas as I frantically looked for a job to make money to support us before we ran out of funds. The deeply ingrained provider syndrome fought to stay in control. My self-worth depended on a paycheck to pay the bills. When work for a living ceased, I had to search for a new identity as a man.

I began to gain weight. The availability of the refrigerator and pantry during the day soon helped me realize I had to take action against their temptations. I think I was eating between meals to fill the emptiness from no longer being gainfully (meaningful) employment.

We did what many recent retirees do. We traveled overseas. I made several solo trips to Brazil and Latin America to teach. When Phyllis accompanied, she had little to do besides read. We traveled to Scandinavia and St. Petersburg, Russia, with Frank Terry, our Asbury College classmate and his wife, Hazel. We also enjoyed traveling with them on a fifteen-day riverboat voyage from Amsterdam to Budapest on the Main, Rhine, and Danube Rivers. We parted ways in Budapest so Phyllis and I could spend a few days with David and Beth Greenawalt, two ORU students who were serving as missionaries with the Methodist Church of Hungary.

I needed a project to keep my mind focused on something besides reading and writing and eating. The addition of an organic garden in the open space in our backyard seemed a logical choice. I had had gardens in Tulsa, Roswell, and Wilmore to help save money and provide healthy vegetables. The sandy soil in Oviedo, which was contaminated with lawn chemicals, discouraged me from trying to grow a garden there. Having a swimming pool where I could have put a garden solved that issue.

A garden in Atlanta restored the joy of digging in the dirt for me again. It helped us to save money, added upper-body exercise to our daily walks, created healthy vegetables for our table, and provided a hobby that Phyllis and I could share. We invited our daughter Ruth's family to become our gardenees to receive surplus vegetables. Instead of planning classes, I focused my attention on the homiletical acrostic of five P's: planning, preparation, planting, picking, and problem solving.

The plants took the place of my students. I wanted both the students and the plants to thrive in an environment suitable for their growth. I cared for their well-being and enjoyed seeing them grow. This analogy needs to stop before it is pushed too far. I blessed the students, but I eat the vegetables.

Phyllis and I focus our attention on creating a happy home. When the house was remodeled, we chose bright colors for the rooms and hired an interior decorator to hang our paintings and help us create an attractive and peaceful *ambiente*. This Portuguese word can be translated as "environment," but it's much more than that. It means "the experience and feelings one gets from being in a place."

Most of the year, I grow seasonal flowers to put in vases throughout the house for additional beauty. Orchids and amaryllis blooms provide us with flowers in the winter months. The fire in the soapstone woodstove in the family room adds warmth, beauty, and comfort on winter days. Music and the smell of fresh vegetables mixed with herbs cooking in the kitchen nurture our bodies and our spirit. In warmer weather we often sit on our back screened porch where we enjoy our meals while looking at birds, flowers, and vegetables in the garden. We are learning to take responsibility for our happiness by intentionally creating a happy *ambiente*.

We also care for our souls by going to church and Sunday school every week, but we soon realized this was not sufficient spiritual nourishment. Many times in our family life we started but failed to maintain regular morning devotions before starting our day. With retirement there are no excuses. We take turns reading aloud to each other as distinctly as if we were reading to a large audience. We use a variety of resources for our devotions, such as the Bible, prayers, poetry, hymns, spiritual classics, and modern devotional writers. We borrowed from our daughter Susana's family the custom of keeping a journal of two things each day for which we are grateful. We end our devotional time by reading what we were grateful for on the same day the year before. Reading from the Message translation of the Bible has been a very rewarding experience.

We learned at ORU the science and practice of caring for the health aspect of our soul through regular exercises, especially the importance of jogging and walking. We now walk over two miles every other day for aerobic exercise. Housekeeping, gardening, and other household responsibilities also help keep our bodies in good shape.

We try to keep our marriage strong by practicing synchronicity. We eat our meals together. We go to bed and get up about the same time each day. We plan our meals together. Synchronicity has it limits, though. We have learned not to shop together, because each one has unique shopping habits. Neither do we cook together. We seem to have our separate responsibilities for getting the house ready to receive visitors. Phyllis does the bookkeeping and filing, but I do most of the financial planning and management of our money. We do what the poet Gibran suggested—"Let there be spaces in your togetherness"—by having our own space to be alone.

We practice good health habits in our retirement, but we have discovered how vulnerable we are to health issues that require medical attention. An MRI of my neck showed that I suffered no damage from a fall on ice, but it revealed that I have an advanced case of stenosis of the upper spine. This led to corrective surgery and further surgery to correct the damage caused by an over-aggressive physical therapist. Recuperation from surgery and the accompanying pain put a pause on some travel plans.

We had a health scare in 2009 when Phyllis's fifty-year benign breast tumor turned malignant (probably from over-radiation during an annual mammogram). This led to surgery, chemotherapy, radiation therapy, and five years of medication with annual checkups to make sure the problem was solved.

One reason we decided to move to Atlanta is the Emory healthcare system. Our house is less than three miles from the university. We have utilized their services in many ways. One of the best gerontologists in the country agreed to be our primary physician. We chose a gerontology dentist to care for our teeth, and we have needed him more than we have ever needed a dentist. Our teeth have become a major expense. They seem to be running out of warranty after seventy-five years.

Our Sunday school class at the Decatur First UMC has become a reliable support system. We had intended to visit several classes before choosing a regular one, but we never got beyond the Debtors, the first class we visited. They have invited me to teach the class on several Sundays. Since we returned to the States in 1971, I have made a special effort to befriend our pastors. It has not been easy or done quickly, but it has always been a blessing to be friends with my pastors. Decatur was no exception. After several lunches together, he started trusting me and invited me to preach once a year. For the first four years I attended a morning breakfast group of retired pastors, but that disbanded after several illnesses among the members. Phyllis and I attend the first Friday of the month John Boy's retired clergy couple's group.

I was welcomed back into the North Georgia UMC Conference by being appointed to the Board of Ordained Ministry of the conference. This requires attendance at several meetings a year and participating in interviews of candidates for commissioning and ordination. The colleagueship with other members of the board has been a blessing to me. I am able to use my experience in theological education to help the candidates and board members on a wide range of issues.

Moving back to Atlanta helped Phyllis and me to reconnect with a retired Brazilian missionary friend who lives in this area. We had been friends with Parke Renshaw ever since we arrived in Brazil in 1961. When we moved to Atlanta, we found him grieving over his health condition that limited his ability to drive across the city to attend the Monday morning meetings of the Concerned Black Clergy of Metropolitan Atlanta. He was instrumental in starting this organization twenty-five years ago. I volunteered to be his chauffer. A few years later he slide into dementia before his death. While helping his wife, Mary, manage his funeral I saw how much the black clergy of Atlanta appreciated his ministry. After going with him to the meetings for three years, I was faced with the decision. Would I continue attending the meetings or not? Often I was the only white person in attendance. When they saw my commitment to be with them, they asked me to be a board member and to serve on several committees. I have learned a great deal about the issues in the black community as well as their perspective on them. The forums permit a wide range of presentations and discussions on religion, politics, economics, health, public safety, and other issues I would not know about without being a member of this organization. It's a major commitment to give Monday morning to CBC, but it has been well worth the effort.

Moving to Atlanta made it more difficult to visit with my sister Pauline. She spent the last years of her beautiful life in a nursing home in Winter Heaven, Florida. I had the honor of preaching her funeral sermon in the Frostproof Methodist Church. I will always miss the warm greetings that made me feel as if I were the most important person in the world who had arrived just to see her. Two years later, Horace, the youngest member of my family of origin, died in Winter Haven. He was my fishing buddy. As I mentioned before, I had bought a bass boat and kept it at his home for him to use as he pleased. With his tragic death from lymphoma after over fifty years of smoking and spraying chemicals for a pest control company where he was chief entomologist, I lost my love for fishing. We spent many hours fishing on the beautiful Central Florida lakes. Fishing would never be the same again for me.

Moving to Atlanta shortened the distance between us and our children and their families. At the time of this writing in 2015, Randy is only six hours away in Lexington, Kentucky. He is a senior scientist in a forage research center at the University of Kentucky. Ruth is only a few feet away next door. Walter lived the farthest from us—Anchorage, Alaska—but he now lives in Tulsa, where he works as an engineer for Centralift, a company that supplies equipment for the oil industry. Susana lives in College Park, Maryland. She works as a grant specialist for the HUD homelessness division of the federal government. Paul is a middle-school language arts teacher in Athens, Georgia.

This last chapter is the shortest because the stories of our lives are unfinished. We are preparing to celebrate sixty years of marriage on August 5, 2015. There are more stories to come before our stories end. A postscript can be added when our account ends. For now we are happy with our lives. We hope to age in place. We believe that the best is yet to come and the most painful is yet to be faced, but our faith in God is secure. Our personal relationships are good. Our finances are sufficient. Our *ambiente* is beautiful. And our love is stronger than ever. What more could we want?

We have written these stories from memory. "Memory is identity," wrote Julian Barnes in *Nothing to Be Frightened Of.* He added, "You are what you have done; what you have done is your memory; what you remember defines who you are." Therefore, memories of our stories tell more about who we are than the actual events themselves. These stories are more than events in the flow of our lives. They tell of our past as it is remembered in the present. Changing synapses in the brain and conversations with persons present at the genesis of the stories could modify any of them. New stories will obscure the original stories, but the best of our stories will survive longer than we do if the reader remembers these and passes the best ones on to future generations.

Made in the USA
Charleston, SC
27 July 2015